WITH YOUR TONGUE
DOWN MY THROAT

A PAPERBACK MAGAZINE OF NEW WRITING

D0066768

22

Editor: Bill Buford
Assistant Editor: Richard Rayner
Managing Editor: Angus MacKinnon
Associate Publisher: Piers Spence
Advertising and Promotion: Monica McStay
Associate Editor: Carole Morin
Subscriptions: Gillian Kemp
Design: Chris Hyde
Editorial Assistants: Helen Casey, Alicja Kobiernicka
Contributing Editor: Todd McEwen
Photo Consultant: Alice Rose George
Executive Editor: Pete de Bolla
US Editor: Jonathan Levi, Granta, 250 West 57th Street, Suite 1203, New York, NY 10107, USA.

Editorial and Subscription Correspondence: Granta, 44a Hobson Street, Cambridge CB1 1NL. Telephone: (0223) 315290.
All manuscripts are welcome but must be accompanied by a stamped, self-addressed envelope or they cannot be returned.

Subscriptions: £15.00 for four issues. Overseas add £3 postage.

Granta is photoset by Hobson Street Studio Ltd, Cambridge, and is printed by Hazell Watson and Viney Ltd, Aylesbury, Bucks.

Granta is published by Granta Publications Ltd and distributed by Penguin Books Ltd, Harmondsworth, Middlesex, England; Viking Penguin Inc., 40 West 23rd St, New York, New York, USA; Penguin Books Australia Ltd, Ringwood, Victoria, Australia; Penguin Books Canada Ltd, 2801 John Street, Markham, Ontario, Canada L3R 1B4; Penguin Books (NZ) Ltd, 182–90 Wairau Road, Auckland 10, New Zealand. This selection copyright © 1987 by Granta Publications Ltd.

Cover by Chris Hyde

Granta 22, Autumn 1987

ISBN 014-00-8601-3

SUPPORTED BY THE
EASTERN
Arts

MICHAEL ONDAATJE

IN THE SKIN OF A LION

New Fiction from Faber

DENNIS POTTER
Blackeyes
£8.95

MANUEL PUIG
Pubis Angelical
£9.95

JAYNE ANNE PHILLIPS
Fast Lanes
£8.95

MURRAY BAIL
Holden's Performance
£10.95

PAUL AUSTER
The New York Trilogy
£10.95

RACHEL INGALLS
The End Of Tragedy
£10.95

LARRY HEINEMANN
Paco's Story
£10.95

LAUREL GOLDMAN
The Part of Fortune
£10.95

MAURICE GEE
Prowlers
£10.95

WILSON HARRIS
The Infinite Rehearsal
£8.95

faber and faber

CONTENTS

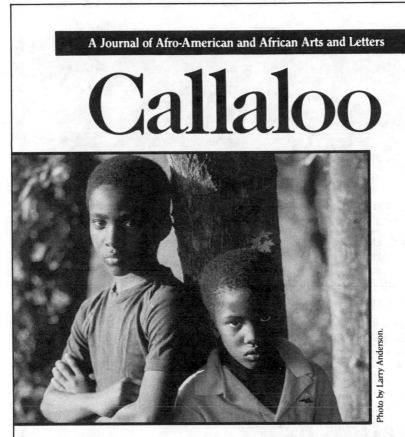

OBSERVATIONS

Events in the Skies
Doris Lessing

I once knew a man, a black man, who told me he had been brought up in a village so far from the nearest town he had to walk a day to reach it. Later he knew this 'town' was itself a village, having in it a post office, a shop and a butcher. He had still to experience the white men's towns, which he had heard about. This was in the southern part of Africa. They were subsistence farmers, and grew maize, millet, pumpkins, chickens. They lived as people have done for thousands of years except for one thing. Every few days a little glittering aeroplane appeared in the sky among the clouds and the circling hawks. He did not know what it was, where it came from or where it went. Remote, unreachable, a marvel, it appeared over the forest where the sun rose, and disappeared where it went down. He watched for it. He thought about it. His dreams filled with shining and fragile emanences that could sit on a branch and sing or that ran from his father and the other hunting men like a duiker or a hare, but that always escaped their spears. He told me that when he remembered his childhood that aeroplane was in the sky. It connected not with what he was now, a sober modern man living in a large town, but with the tales and songs of his people, for it was not real, not something to be brought down to earth and touched.

When he was about nine his family went to live with relatives near a village that was larger than either the handful of huts in the bush or the 'town' where they had sometimes bought a little sugar or tea or a piece of cloth. There the black people worked in a small gold mine. He learned that twice a week an aeroplane landed in the bush on a strip of cleared land, unloaded parcels, mail and sometimes a person, and then flew off. He was by now going to a mission school. He walked there with his elder brother and his younger sister every morning, leaving at six to get there at eight, then walked back in the afternoon. Later, when he measured distances not by the time it took to cover them, but by the miles, yards and feet he learned in school, he knew he walked eight miles to school and eight back.

This school was his gateway to the life of riches and plenty enjoyed by white people. This is how he saw it. Motor cars, bicycles, the goods in the shops, clothes—all these things would be his if he did well at school. School had to come first, but on Saturdays and Sundays and holidays he went stealthily to the edge of the airstrip, sometimes with his brother and sister, and crouched there waiting for the little plane. The first time he saw a man jump down out of its high uptilted front his heart stopped, then it thundered, and he raced shouting exuberantly into the bush. He had not before understood that this apparition of the skies, like a moth but made out of some substance unknown to him, had a person in it: a young white man, like the storemen or the foremen in the mines. In the village of his early childhood he had played with grasshoppers, pretending they were aeroplanes. Now he made little planes out of the silver paper that came in the packets of cigarettes that were too expensive for his people to smoke.

With these infant models in his hands the aeroplane seemed close to him, and he crept out of the bush to reach out and touch it, but the pilot saw him, shouted at him—and so he ran away. In his mind was a region of confusion, doubt and delight mixed, and this was the distance between himself and the plane. He never said to himself, 'I could become a pilot when I grow up.' On the practical level what he dreamed of was a bicycle, but they cost so much—five pounds—that his father, who had one, would need a year to get it paid off. (His father had become a storeman in a mine shop, and that job, and the move to this new place, was to enable his children to go to school and enter the new world.) No, what that aeroplane meant was wonder, a dazzlement of possibilities, but they were all unclear. When he saw that aeroplane on the landing strip or, later, that one or another in the skies, it made him dream of how he would get on his bicycle when he had one, and race along the paths of the bush so fast that . . .

When he had finished four years at school he could have left. He already had more schooling than most of the children of his country at that time. He could read a little, write a little and do sums rather well. With these skills he could get a job as a boss boy or perhaps working in a shop. But this is not what his father wanted. Because these children were clever, they had been invited to attend another mission school, and the fees meant the father had to work not only at the store job in the day time, but at night as a watchman. And they, the children, did odd jobs at weekends and through holidays, running errands, selling fruit at the back doors of white houses with their mother. They all worked and worked; and, again, walking to and from the new school took the children four hours of every day. (I once knew a man from Czechoslovakia who said he walked six miles to school and six miles back in snow or heat or rain, because he was a poor boy, one of eleven children, and this is what he had to do to get an education. He became a doctor.)

This man, the African, at last finished school. He had understood the nature of the cloudy region in his mind where the aeroplane still lived. He had seen much larger planes. He knew now the shining creature of his childhood was nothing compared to the monsters that went to the big airports in the cities. A war had come and gone, and he had read in the newspapers of great battles in Europe and the East, and he understood what aeroplanes could be used for. The war had not made much difference to him and his family. Then his country, which until then had been loosely ruled by Britain in a way that affected him personally very little (and he knew this was unlike some of the countries further south) became independent and had a black government. By now the family lived in the capital of the country. They had a two-roomed house in a township. This move, too, this bettering, was for the children. Now the brother took a job in a store as a clerk, and the sister was a nurse in the hospital, but he decided to go on learning. At last he became an accountant and understood the modern world and what had separated that poor black child he had been from the aeroplane. These days he might smile at his early imaginings, but he loved them. He still loved the little aeroplane. He said to himself: 'It was never possible for me to fly an aeroplane, it never occurred to me, because black men did not become pilots. But my son . . .'

His son, brought up in a town where aeroplanes came and went every day, said, 'Who wants to be a pilot? What a life!' He decided to be a lawyer, and that is what he is.

My friend, who told me all this, said, 'My son would never understand, never in his life, what that little plane meant to me and the kids in the bush.'

But I understood. On the farm where I grew up, once a week I watched a small aeroplane appear, coming from the direction of the city. It descended over the ridge into the bush on to the airstrip of the Mandora Mine, a Lonrho mine. I was transported with delight and longing. In those days ordinary people did not fly. A lucky child might get taken up for a 'flip' around the sky, price five pounds. It was a lot of money, and I did not fly for years.

L ast year I met a little Afghan girl, a refugee with her family in Pakistan. She had lived in a village that had water running through it from the mountains, and it had orchards and fields, and all her family and her relatives were there. Sometimes a plane crossed the sky from one of the larger cities of Afghanistan to another. She would run to the edge of the village to get nearer to that shining thing in the sky, and stand with her hands cradling her head as she stared up . . . up . . . up . . . Or she called to her mother, 'An aeroplane, look!'

And then the Russians invaded, and one day the visiting aeroplane was a gunship. It thundered over her village, dropped its bombs and flew off. The house she had lived in all her days was rubble, and her mother and her little brother were dead. So were several of her relatives. And as she walked across the mountains with her father, her uncle, her aunt and her three surviving cousins, they were bombed by the helicopters and the planes, so that more people died. Now, living in exile in the refugee camp, when she thinks of the skies of her country she knows they are full of aircraft, day and night, and the little plane that flew over her village with the sunlight shining on its wings seems like something she once imagined, a childish dream.

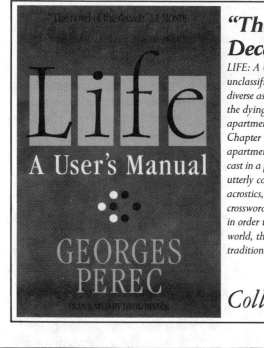

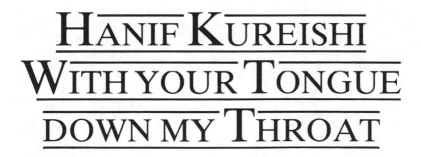

I tell you, I feel tired and dirty, but I was told no baths allowed for a few days, so I'll stay dirty. Yesterday morning I was crying a lot and the woman asked me to give an address in case of emergencies and I made one up. I had to undress and get in a white smock and they took my temperature and blood pressure five times. Then a nurse pushed me in a wheel-chair into a green room where I met the doctor. He called us all 'ladies' and told jokes. I could see some people getting annoyed. He was Indian, unfortunately, and he looked at me strangely as if to say, 'What are you doing here?' But maybe it was just my imagination.

I had to lie on a table and they put a needle or two into my left arm. Heat rushed over my face and I tried to speak. The next thing I know I'm in the recovery room with a nurse saying, 'Wake up, dear, it's all over.' The doctor poked me in the stomach and said, 'Fine.' I found myself feeling aggressive. 'Do you do this all the time?' I asked. He said he does nothing else.

They woke us at six and there were several awkward-looking, sleepy boyfriends outside. I got the bus and went back to the squat.

A few months later we got kicked out and I had to go back to Ma's place. So I'm back here now, writing this with my foot up on the table, reckoning I look like a painter. I sip water with a slice of lemon in it. I'm at Ma's kitchen table and there are herbs growing in pots around me. At least the place is clean, though it's shabby and all falling apart. There are photographs of Ma's women friends from the Labour Party and the Women's Support Group and there is Blake's picture of Newton next to drawings by her kids from school. There are books everywhere, on the Alexander Method and the Suzuki Method and all the other methods in the world. And then there's her boyfriend.

Yes, the radical (ha!) television writer and well-known toss-pot Howard Coleman sits opposite me as I record him with my biro. He's reading one of his scripts, smoking and slowly turning the pages, but the awful thing is, he keeps giggling at them. Thank Christ Ma should be back any minute now from the Catholic girls' school where she teaches.

It's Howard who asked me to write this diary, who said write down some of the things that happen. My half-sister Nadia is about

21

to come over from Pakistan to stay with us. Get it all down, he said.

If you could see Howard now like I can, you'd really laugh. I mean it. He's about forty-three and he's got on a squeaky leather jacket and jeans with the arse round his knees and these trainers with soles that look like mattresses. He looks like he's never bought anything new. Or if he has, when he gets it back from the shop, he throws it on the floor, empties the dust-bin over it and walks up and down on it in a pair of dirty Dr Martens. For him dirty clothes are a political act.

But this is the coup. Howard's smoking a roll-up. He's got this tin, his fag papers and the stubby yellow fingers with which he rolls, licks, fiddles, taps, lights, extinguishes and re-lights all day. This rigmarole goes on when he's in bed with Ma, presumably on her chest. I've gone in there in the morning for a snoop and found his ashtray by the bed, condom on top.

Christ, he's nodding at me as I write! It's because he's so keen on ordinary riff-raff expressing itself, especially no-hoper girls like me. One day we're writing, the next we're on the barricades.

Every Friday Howard comes over to see Ma.

To your credit, Howard the hero, you always take her somewhere a bit jazzy, maybe to the latest club (a big deal for a poverty-stricken teacher). When you get back you undo her bra and hoick your hands up her jumper and she warms hers down your trousers. I've walked in on this! Soon after this teenage game mother and lover go to bed and rattle the room for half an hour. I light a candle, turn off the radio and lie there, ears flapping. It's strange, hearing your Ma doing it. There are momentous cries and gasps and grunts, as if Howard's trying to bang a nail into a brick wall. Ma sounds like she's having an operation. Sometimes I feel like running in with the first-aid kit.

Does this Friday thing sound remarkable or not? It's only Fridays he will see Ma. If Howard has to collect an award for his writing or go to a smart dinner with a critic he won't come to see us until the next Friday. Saturdays are definitely out!

We're on the ninth floor. I say to Howard: 'Hey, clever boots. Tear your eyes away from yourself a minute. Look out the window.'

The estate looks like a building-site. There's planks and window frames everywhere—poles, cement mixers, sand, grit, men with mouths and disintegrating brick underfoot.

'So?' he says.

'It's rubbish, isn't it? Nadia will think we're right trash.'

'My little Nina,' he says. This is how he talks to me.

'Yes, my big Howard?'

'Why be ashamed of what you are?'

'Because compared with Nadia we're not much, are we?'

'I'm much. You're much. Now get on with your writing.'

He touches my face with his finger. 'You're excited, aren't you? This is a big thing for you.'

It is, I suppose.

All my life I've been this only child living here in a council place with Ma, the drama teacher. I was an only child, that is, until I was eleven, when Ma says she has a surprise for me, one of the nicest I've ever had. I have a half-sister the same age, living in another country.

'Your father had a wife in India,' Ma says, wincing every time she says *father*. 'They married when they were fifteen, which is the custom over there. When he decided to leave me because I was too strong a woman for him, he went right back to India and right back to Wifey. That's when I discovered I was pregnant with you. His other daughter Nadia was conceived a few days later but she was actually born the day after you. Imagine that, darling. Since then I've discovered that he's even got two other daughters as well!'

I don't give my same-age half-sister in another country another thought except to dislike her in general for suddenly deciding to exist. Until one night, suddenly, I write to Dad and ask if he'll send her to stay with us. I get up and go down the lift and out in the street and post the letter before I change my mind. That night was one of my worst and I wanted Nadia to save me.

On some Friday afternoons if I'm not busy writing ten-page hate letters to DJs, Howard does imagination exercises with me. I have to lie on my back on the floor, imagine things like mad and describe them. It's so sixties. But then I've heard him say of people: Oh, she had a wonderful sixties!

'Nina,' he says during one of these gigs, 'you've got to work out this relationship with your sister. I want you to describe Nadia.'

I zap through my head's TV channels—Howard squatting beside me, hand on my forehead, sending loving signals. A girl materializes sitting under a palm tree, reading a Brontë novel and drinking yogurt. I see a girl being cuddled by my father. He tells stories of tigers and elephants and rickshaw wallahs. I see . . .

'I can't see any more!'

Because I can't visualize Nadia, I have to see her.

So. This is how it all comes about. Ma and I are sitting at breakfast, Ma chewing her vegetarian cheese. She's dressed for work in a long, baggy, purple pinafore dress with black stockings and a black band in her hair, and she looks like a 1950s teenager. Recently Ma's gone blonde and she keeps looking in the mirror. Me still in my T-shirt and pants. Ma tense about work as usual, talking about school for hours on the phone last night to friends. She tries to interest me in child-abuse, general incest and its relation to the GCSE. I say how much I hate eating, how boring it is and how I'd like to do it once a week and forget about it.

'But the palate is a sensitive organ,' Ma says. 'You should cultivate yours instead of—'

'Just stop talking if you've got to fucking lecture.'

The mail arrives. Ma cuts open an airmail letter. She reads it twice. I know it's from Dad. I snatch it out of her hand and walk round the room taking it in.

> Dear You Both,
> It's a good idea. Nadia will be arriving on the 5th. Please meet her at the airport. So generous of you to offer. Look after her, she is the most precious thing in the entire world to me.
> Much love.

At the bottom Nadia has written: 'Looking forward to seeing you both soon.'

Hummmm . . .

Ma pours herself more coffee and considers everything. She has these terrible coffee jags. Her stomach must be like distressed leather. She is determined to be business-like: not emotional. She says I have to cancel the visit.

'It's simple. Just write a little note and say there's been a misunderstanding.'

And this is how I react: 'I don't believe it! Why? No way! But why?' Christ, don't I deserve to die, though God knows I've tried to die enough times.

'Because, Nina, I'm not at all prepared for this. I really don't know that I want to see this sister of yours. She symbolizes my betrayal by your father.'

I clear the table of our sugar-free jam (no additives).

'Symbolizes?' I say. 'But she's a person.'

Ma gets on her raincoat and collects last night's marking. You look very plain, I'm about to say. She kisses me on the head. The girls at school adore her. There, she's a star.

But I'm very severe. Get this: 'Ma. Nadia's coming. Or I'm going. I'm walking right out that door and it'll be junk and prostitution just like the old days.'

She drops her bag. She sits down. She slams her car keys on the table. 'Nina, I beg you.'

2

Heathrow. Three hours we've been here, Ma and I, burying our faces in doughnuts. People pour from the exit like released prisoners to walk the gauntlet of jumping relatives and chauffeurs holding cards: Welcome Ngogi of Nigeria.

But no Nadia. 'My day off,' Ma says, 'and I spend it in an airport.'

But then. It's her. Here she comes now. It is her! I know it is! I jump up and down waving like mad! Yes, yes, no, yes! At last! My mirror. My sister!

We both hug Nadia, and Ma suddenly cries and her nose runs and she can't control her mouth. I cry too and I don't even know who the hell I'm squashing so close to me. Until I sneak a good look at the girl.

You. Every day I've woken up trying to see your face, and now you're here, your head jerking nervously, saying little, with us drenching you. I can see you're someone I know nothing about. You make me very nervous.

You're smaller than me. Less pretty, if I can say that. Bigger nose. Darker, of course, with a glorious slab of hair like a piece of chocolate attached to your back. I imagined, I don't know why (pure prejudice, I suppose), that you'd be wearing the national dress, the baggy pants, the long top and light scarf flung all over. But you have on F.U. jeans and a faded blue sweatshirt—you look as if you live in Enfield. We'll fix that.

Nadia sits in the front of the car. Ma glances at her whenever she can. She has to ask how Nadia's father is.

'Oh yes,' Nadia replies. 'Dad. The same as usual, thank you. No change really, Debbie.'

'But we rarely see him,' Ma says.

'I see,' Nadia says at last.

'So we don't,' Ma says, her voice rising, 'actually know what "same as usual" means.'

Nadia looks out the window at green and grey old England. I don't want Ma getting in one of her resentful states.

After this not another peep for about a decade and then road euphoria just bursts from Nadia.

'What good roads you have here! So smooth, so wide, so long!'

'Yes, they go all over,' I say.

'Wow. All over.'

Christ, don't they even have fucking roads over there?

Nadia whispers. We lean towards her to hear about her dear father's health. How often the old man pisses now, running for the pot clutching his crotch. The sad state of his old gums and his obnoxious breath. Ma and I watch this sweetie compulsively, wondering who she is: so close to us and made from my substance, and yet so other, telling us about Dad with an outrageous intimacy we can never share. We arrive home, and she says in an accent as thick as treacle (which makes me hoot to myself when I first hear it): 'I'm so tired now. If I could rest for a little while.'

'Sleep in my bed!' I cry.

Earlier I'd said to Ma I'd never give it up. But the moment my sister walks across the estate with us and finally stands there in our flat above the building site, drinking in all the oddness, picking up Ma's method books and her opera programmes, I melt, I melt. I'll have to kip in the living room from now on. But I'd kip in the toilet for her.

'In return for your bed,' she says, 'let me, I must, yes, give you something.'

She pulls a rug from her suitcase and presents it to Ma. 'This is from Dad.' Ma puts it on the floor, studies it and then treads on it.

And to me? I've always been a fan of crêpe paper and wrapped in it is the Pakistani dress I'm wearing now (with open-toed sandals—handmade). It's gorgeous: yellow and green, threaded with gold, thin summer material.

I'm due a trip to the dole any minute now and I'm bracing myself for the looks I'll get in this gear. I'll keep you informed.

I write this outside my room waiting for Nadia to wake. Every fifteen minutes I tap lightly on the door like a worried nurse.

'Are you awake?' I whisper. And: 'Sister, sister.' I adore these new words. 'Do you want anything?'

I think I'm in love. At last.

Ma's gone out to take back her library books, leaving me to it. Ma's all heart, I expect you can see that. She's good and gentle and can't understand unkindness and violence. She thinks everyone's just waiting to be brought round to decency. 'This way we'll change the world a little bit,' she'd say, holding my hand and knocking on doors at elections. But she's lived on the edge of a nervous breakdown for as long as I can remember. She's had boyfriends before Howard but none of them lasted. Most of them were married because she was on this liberated kick of using men. There was one middle-class Labour Party smoothie I called Chubbie.

'Are you married?' I'd hiss when Ma went out of the room, sitting next to him and fingering his nylon tie.

'Yes.'

'You have to admit it, don't you? Where's your wife, then? She knows you're here? Get what you want this afternoon?'

You could see the men fleeing when they saw the deep needy

well that Ma is, crying out to be filled with their love. And this monster kid with green hair glaring at them. Howard's too selfish and arrogant to be frightened of my Ma's demands. He just ignores them.

Whith a job it is, walking round in this Paki gear!
I stop off at the chemist's to grab my drugs, my trancs. Jeanette, my friend on the estate, used to my eccentricities—the coonskin hat with the long rabbit tail, for example—comes along with me. The chemist woman in the white coat says to Jeanette, nodding at me when I hand over my script: 'Does she speak English?'

Becoming enthralled by this new me now, exotic and interior. With the scarf over my head I step into the Community Centre and look like a lost woman with village ways and chickens in the garden.

In a second, the communists and worthies are all over me. I mumble into my scarf. They give me leaflets and phone numbers. I'm oppressed, you see, beaten up, pig-ignorant with an arranged marriage and certain suttee ahead. But I get fed up and have a game of darts, a game of snooker and a couple of beers with a nice lesbian.

Home again I make my Nadia some pasta with red pepper, grated carrot, cheese and parsley. I run out to buy a bottle of white wine. Chasing along I see some kids on a passing bus. They eyeball me from the top deck, one of them black. They make a special journey down to the platform where the little monkeys swing on the pole and throw racial abuse from their gobs.

'Curry breath, curry breath, curry breath!'

The bus rushes on. I'm flummoxed.

She emerges at last, my Nadia, sleepy, creased around the eyes and dark. She sits at the table, eyelashes barely apart, not ready for small talk. I bring her the food and a glass of wine which she refuses with an upraised hand. I press my eyes into hers, but she doesn't look at me. To puncture the silence I play her a jazz record—Wynton Marsalis's first. I ask her how she likes the record and she says nothing. Probably doesn't do much for her on first hearing. I watch her eating. She will not be interfered with.

She leaves most of the food and sits. I hand her a pair of black
Levi 501s with the button fly. Plus a large cashmere polo-neck
(stolen) and a black leather jacket.

'Try them on.'

She looks puzzled. 'It's the look I want you to have. You can
wear any of my clothes.'

Still she doesn't move. I give her a little shove into the bedroom
and shut the door. She should be so lucky. That's my best damn
jacket. I wait. She comes out not wearing the clothes.

'Nina, I don't think so.'

I know how to get things done. I push her back in. She comes
out, backwards, hands over her face.

'Show me, please.'

She spins round, arms out, hair jumping.

'Well?'

'The black suits your hair,' I manage to say. What a vast
improvement on me, is all I can think. Stunning she is, dangerous,
vulnerable, superior, with a jewel in her nose.

'But doesn't it . . . doesn't it make me look a little rough?'

'Oh yes! Now we're all ready to go. For a walk, yes? To see the
sights and everything.'

'Is it safe?'

'Of course not. But I've got this.'

I show her.

'Oh, God, Nina. You would.'

Oh, this worries and ruins me. Already she has made up her
mind about me and I haven't started on my excuses.

'Have you used it?'

'Only twice. Once on a racist in a pub. Once on some mugger
who asked if I could spare him some jewellery.'

Her face becomes determined. She looks away. 'I'm training to
be a doctor, you see. My life is set against human harm.'

She walks towards the door. I pack the switch-blade.

Daddy, these are the sights I show my sister. I tow her out of
the flat and along the walkway. She sees the wind blaring
through the busted windows. She catches her breath at the
humming bad smells. Trapped dogs bark. She sees that one idiot's
got on his door: *Dont burglar me theres nothin to steel ive got rid of*

it all. She sees that some pig's sprayed on the wall: *Nina's a slag dog.* I push the lift button.

I've just about got her out of the building when the worst thing happens. There's three boys, ten or eleven years old, climbing out through a door they've kicked in. Neighbours stand and grumble. The kids've got a fat TV, a microwave oven and someone's favourite trainers under a little arm. The kid drops the trainers.

'Hey,' he says to Nadia (it's her first day here). Nadia stiffens. 'Hey, won't yer pick them up for me?'

She looks at me. I'm humming a tune. The tune is 'Just My Imagination'. I'm not scared of the little jerks. It's the bad impression that breaks my heart. Nadia picks up the trainers.

'Just tuck them right in there,' the little kid says, exposing his armpit.

'Won't they be a little large for you?' Nadia says.

'Eat shit.'

Soon we're out of there and into the air. We make for South Africa Road and the General Smuts pub. Kids play football behind wire. The old women in thick overcoats look like lagged boilers on little feet. They huff and shove carts full of chocolate and cat food.

I'm all tense now and ready to say anything. I feel such a need to say everything in the hope of explaining all that I give a guided tour of my heart and days.

I explain (I can't help myself): this happened here, that happened there. I got pregnant in that squat. I bought bad smack from that geezer in the yellow T-shirt and straw hat. I got attacked there and legged it through that park. I stole pens from that shop, dropping them into my motorcycle helmet. (A motorcycle helmet is very good for shop-lifting, if you're interested.) Standing on that corner I cared for nothing and no one and couldn't walk on or stay where I was or go back. My gears had stopped engaging with my motor. Then I had a nervous breakdown.

Without comment she listens and nods and shakes her head sometimes. Is anyone in? I take her arm and move my cheek close to hers.

'I tell you this stuff which I haven't told anyone before. I want us to know each other inside out.'

She stops there in the street and covers her face with her hands.

'But my father told me of such gorgeous places!'

'Nadia, what d'you mean?'

'And you show me filth!' she cries. She touches my arm. 'Oh Nina, it would be so lovely if you could make the effort to show me something attractive.'

Something attractive. We'll have to get the bus and go east, to Holland Park and round Ladbroke Grove. This is now honeyed London for the rich who have preservatives in their conservatories. Here there are *La* restaurants, wine bars, bookshops, estate agents more prolific than doctors, and attractive people in black, few of them aging. Here there are health food shops where you buy tofu, nuts, live-culture yogurt and organic toothpaste. Here the sweet little black kids practise on steel drums under the motorway for the Carnival and old blacks sit out in the open on orange boxes shouting. Here the dope dealers in Versace suits travel in from the suburbs on commuter trains, carrying briefcases, trying to sell slummers bits of old car tyre to smoke.

And there are more stars than beggars. For example? Van Morrison in a big overcoat is hurrying towards somewhere in a nervous mood.

'Hiya, Van! Van? Won't ya even say hello!' I scream across the street. At my words Van the Man accelerates like a dog with a winklepicker up its anus.

She looks tired so I take her into Julie's Bar where they have the newspapers and we sit on well-woven cushions on long benches. Christ only knows how much they have the cheek to charge for a cup of tea. Nadia looks better now. We sit there all friendly and she starts off.

'How often have you met our father?'

'I see him every two or three years. When he comes on business, he makes it his business to see me.'

'That's nice of him.'

'Yes, that's what he thinks. Can you tell me something, Nadia?' I move closer to her. 'When he'd get home, our father, what would he tell you about me?'

If only I wouldn't tempt everything so. But you know me: can't live no life with slack in it.

'Oh, he was worried, worried, worried.'

'Christ. Worried three times.'

'He said you . . . no.'

He said what?'

'No, no, he didn't say it.'

'Yes, he did, Nadia.'

She sits there looking at badly-dressed television producers in linen suits with her gob firmly closed.

'Tell me what my father said or I'll pour this pot of tea over my head.'

I pick up the teapot and open the lid for pouring-over-the-head convenience. Nadia says nothing; in fact she looks away. So what choice do I have but to let go a stream of tea over the top of my noddle? It drips down my face and off my chin. It's pretty scalding, I can tell you.

'He said, all right, he said you were like a wild animal!'

'Like a wild animal?' I say.

'Yes. And sometimes he wished he could shoot you to put you out of your misery.' She looks straight ahead of her. 'You asked for it. You made me say it.'

'The bastard. His own daughter.'

She holds my hand. For the first time, she looks at me, with wide-open eyes and urgent mouth. 'It's terrible, just terrible there in the house. Nina, I had to get away! And I'm in love with someone! Someone who's indifferent to me!'

'And?'

And nothing. She says no more except: 'It's too cruel, too cruel.'

I glance around. Now this is exactly the kind of place suitable for doing a runner from. You could be out the door, half-way up the street and on the tube before they'd blink. I'm about to suggest it to Nadia, but, as I've already told her about my smack addiction, my two abortions and poured a pot of tea over my head, I wouldn't want her to get a bad impression of me.

'I hope,' I say to her, 'I hope to God we can be friends as well as relations.'

Well, what a bastard my Dad turned out to be! Wild animal! He's no angel himself. How could he say that? I was always on my best behaviour and always covered my wrists and arms. Now I can't stop thinking about him. It makes me cry.

This is how he used to arrive at our place, my daddy, in the days when he used to visit us.

First there's a whole day's terror and anticipation and getting ready. When Ma and I are exhausted, having practically cleaned the flat with our tongues, a black taxi slides over the horizon of the estate, rarer than an ambulance, with presents cheering on the back seat: champagne, bicycles, dresses that don't fit, books, dreams in boxes. Dad glows in a £3,000 suit and silk tie. Neighbours lean over the balconies to pleasure their eyeballs on the prince. It takes two or three of them working in shifts to hump the loot upstairs.

Then we're off in the taxi, speeding to restaurants with menus in French where Dad knows the manager. Dad tells us stories of extreme religion and hilarious corruption and when Ma catches herself laughing she bites her lip hard—why? I suppose she finds herself flying to the magnet of his charm once more.

After the grub we go to see a big show and Mum and Dad hold hands. All of these shows are written, on the later occasions, by Andrew Lloyd Webber.

This is all the best of life, except that, when Dad has gone and we have to slot back into our lives, we don't always feel like it. We're pretty uncomfortable, looking at each other and shuffling our ordinary feet once more in the mundane. Why does he always have to be leaving us?

After one of these occasions I go out, missing him. When alone, I talk to him. At five in the morning I get back. At eight Ma comes into my room and stands there, a woman alone and everything like that, in fury and despair.

'Are you involved in drugs and prostitution?'

I'd been going with guys for money. At the massage parlour you do as little as you can. None of them has disgusted me, and we have a laugh with them. Ma finds out because I've always got so much money. She knows the state of things. She stands over me.

'Yes.' No escape. I just say it. Yes, yes, yes.

'That's what I thought.'

'Yes, that is my life at the moment. Can I go back to sleep now? I'm expected at work at twelve.'

'Don't call it work, Nina. There are other words.'

She goes. Before her car has failed to start in the courtyard, I've run to the bathroom, filled the sink, taken Ma's lousy leg razor and jabbed into my wrists, first one, then the other, under water, digging for veins. (You should try it sometime; it's more difficult than you think: skin tough, throat contracting with vomit acid sour disgust.) The nerves in my hands went and they had to operate and everyone was annoyed that I'd caused such trouble.

Weeks later I vary the trick and swallow thirty pills and fly myself to a Surrey mental hospital where I do puzzles, make baskets and am fucked regularly for medicinal reasons by the art therapist who has a long nail on his little finger.

Suicide is one way of saying you're sorry.

With Nadia to the Tower of London, the Monument, Hyde Park, Buckingham Palace and something cultural with a lot of wigs at the National Theatre. Nadia keeps me from confession by small talk which wears into my shell like sugar into a tooth.

Ma sullen but doing a workmanlike hospitality job. Difficult to get Nadia out of her room most of the time. Hours she spends in the bathroom every day experimenting with make-up. And then Howard the hero decides to show up.

Ma not home yet. Early evening. Guess what? Nadia is sitting across the room on the sofa with Howard. This is their first meeting and they're practically on each other's laps. (I almost wrote lips.) All afternoon I've had to witness this meeting of minds. They're on politics. The words that ping off the walls are: pluralism, democracy, theocracy and Benazir! Howard's senses are on their toes! The little turd can't believe the same body (in a black cashmere sweater and black leather jacket) can contain such intelligence, such beauty, and yet jingle so brightly with facts about the Third World! There in her bangles and perfume I see her speak to him as she hasn't spoken to me once—gesticulating!

'Howard, I say this to you from my heart, it is a corrupt country! Even the revolutionaries are corrupt! No one has any hope!'

In return he asks, surfacing through the Niagara of her

conversation: 'Nadia, can I show you something? Videos of the TV stuff I've written?'

She can't wait.

None of us has seen her come in. Ma is here now, coat on, bags in her hands, looking at Nadia and Howard sitting so close their elbows keep knocking together.

'Hello,' she says to Howard, eventually. 'Hiya,' to Nadia. Ma has bought herself some flowers, which she has under her arm— carnations. Howard doesn't get up to kiss her. He's touching no one but Nadia and he's very pleased with himself. Nadia nods at Ma but her eyes rush back to Howard the hero.

Nadia says to Howard: 'The West doesn't care if we're an undemocratic country.'

'I'm exhausted,' Ma says.

'Well,' I say to her. 'Hello, anyway.'

Ma and I unpack the shopping in the kitchen. Howard calls through to Ma, asking her school questions which she ignores. The damage has been done. Oh yes. Nadia has virtually ignored Ma in her own house. Howard, I can see, is pretty uncomfortable at this. He is about to lift himself out of the seat when Nadia puts her hand on his arm and asks him: 'How do you create?'

'How do I create?'

How does Howard create? With four word-kisses she has induced in Howard a Nelson's Column of excitement. How do you create, is the last thing you should ever ask one of these guys.

'They get along well, don't they?' Ma says, watching them through the crack of the door. I lean against the fridge.

'Why shouldn't they?'

'No reason,' she says. 'Except that this is my home. Everything I do outside here is a waste of time and no one thanks me for it and no one cares for me, and now I'm excluded from my own flat!'

'Hey Ma, don't get—'

'Pour me a bloody whisky, will you?'

I pour her one right away. 'Your supper's in the oven, Ma.' I give her the whisky. My Ma cups her hands round the glass. Always been a struggle for her. Her dad in the army; white trash. She had to fight to learn. 'It's fish pie. And I did the washing and ironing.'

'You've always been good in that way, I'll give you that. Even when you were sick you'd do the cooking. I'd come home and there it would be. I'd eat it alone and leave the rest outside your door. It was like feeding a hamster. You can be nice.'

'Are you sure?'

'Only your niceness has to live among so many other wild elements. Women that I know. Their children are the same. A tragedy or a disappointment. Their passions are too strong. It is our era in England. I only wish. I only wish you could have some kind of career or something.'

I watch her and she turns away to look at Howard all snug with the sister I brought here. Sad Ma is, and gentle. I could take her in my arms to console her now for what I am, but I don't want to indulge her. A strange question occurs to me. 'Ma, why do you keep Howard on?'

She sits on the kitchen stool and sips her drink. She looks at the lino for about three minutes, without saying anything, gathering herself up, punching her fist against her leg, like someone who's just swallowed a depth-charge. Howard's explaining voice drifts through to us.

Ma gets up and kick-slams the door.

'Because I love him even if he doesn't love me!'

Her tumbler smashes on the floor and glass skids around our feet.

'Because I need sex and why shouldn't I! Because I'm lonely, I'm lonely OK and I need someone bright to talk to! D'you think I can talk to you? D'you think you'd ever be interested in me for one minute?'

'Ma—'

'You've never cared for me! And then you brought Nadia here against my wishes to be all sweet and hypercritical and remind me of all the terrible past and the struggle of being alone for so long!'

Ma sobbing in her room. Howard in with her. Nadia and me sit together at the two ends of the sofa. My ears are scarlet with the hearing of Ma's plain sorrow through the walls.

'Yes, I care for you,' Howard's voice rises. 'I love you, baby. And I love Nina, too. Both of you.'

'I don't know, Howard. You don't ever show it.'

'But I'm blocked as a human being!'

I say to Nadia: 'Men are pretty selfish bastards who don't understand us. That's all I know.'

'Howard's an interesting type,' she says coolly. 'Very open-minded in an artistic way.'

I'm getting protective in my old age and very pissed off.

'He's my mother's boyfriend and long-standing lover.'

'Yes, I know that.'

'So lay off him. Please, Nadia. Please understand.'

'What are you, of all people, accusing me of?'

I'm not too keen on this 'of all people' business. But get this.

'I thought you advanced Western people believed in the free intermingling of the sexes?'

'Yes, we do. We intermingle all the time.'

'What then, Nina, is your point?'

'It's him,' I explain, moving in. 'He has all the weaknesses. One kind word from a woman and he thinks they want to sleep with him. Two kind words and he thinks he's the only man in the world. It's a form of mental illness, of delusion. I wouldn't tangle with that deluded man if I were you!'

All right!

A few days later.

Here I am slouching at Howard's place. Howard's hole, or 'sock' as he calls it, is a red brick mansion block with public school, stately dark oak corridors, off Kensington High Street. Things have been getting grimmer and grimmer. Nadia stays in her room or else goes out and pops her little camera at 'history'. Ma goes to every meeting she hears of. I'm just about ready for artery road.

I've just done you a favour. I could have described every moment of us sitting through Howard's television *œuvre* (which I always thought meant *egg*). But no—on to the juicy bits!

There they are in front of me, Howard and Nadia cheek to cheek, within breath-inhaling distance of each other, going through the script.

Earlier this morning we went shopping in Covent Garden. Nadia wanted my advice on what clothes to buy. So we went for a couple of sharp dogtooth jackets, distinctly city, fine brown and white wool, the jacket caught in at the waist with a black leather belt; short panelled skirt; white silk polo-neck shirt; plus black pillbox, suede gloves, high heels. If she likes something, if she wants it, she buys it. The rich. Nadia bought me a linen jacket.

Maybe I'm sighing too much. They glance at me with un-delight.

'I can take Nadia home if you like,' Howard says.

'I'll take care of my sister,' I say. 'But I'm out for a stroll now. I'll be back at any time.'

I stroll towards a café in Rotting Hill. I head up through Holland Park, past the blue sloping roof of the Commonwealth Institute (or Nigger's Corner as we used to call it) in which on a school trip I pissed into a waste-paper basket. Past modern nannies—young women like me with dyed black hair—walking dogs and kids.

The park's full of hip kids from Holland Park School, smoking on the grass; black guys with flat-tops and muscles; yuppies skimming frisbees and stuff; white boys playing Madonna and Prince. There are cruising turd-burglars with active eyes, and the usual London liggers, hang-gliders and no-goodies waiting to sign-on. I feel outside everything, so up I go, through the flower-verged alley at the end of the park, where the fudge-packers used to line up at night for fucking. On the wall it says: *Gay solidarity is class solidarity.*

Outside the café is a police van with grills over the windows full of little piggies giggling with their helmets off. It's a common sight around here, but the streets are a little quieter than usual. I walk past an Asian policewoman standing in the street who says hello to me. 'Auntie Tom,' I whisper and go into the café.

In this place they play the latest calypso and soca and the new Eric Satie recording. A white Rasta sits at the table with me. He pays for my tea. I have chili with a baked potato and grated cheese, with tomato salad on the side, followed by Polish cheesecake. People in the café are more subdued than normal; all the pigs making everyone nervous. But what a nice guy the Rasta is. Even nicer, he takes my hand under the table and drops something in my palm. A chunky chocolate lozenge of dope.

'Hey. I'd like to buy some of this,' I say, wrapping my swooning nostrils round it.

'Sweetheart, it's all I've got,' he says. 'You take it. My last lump of blow.'

He leaves. I watch him go. As he walks across the street in his jumble-sale clothes, his hair jabbing out from his head like tiny bedsprings, the police get out of their van and stop him. He waves his arms at them. The van unpacks. There's about six of them surrounding him. There's an argument. He's giving them some heavy lip. They search him. One of them is pulling his hair. Everyone in the café is watching. I pop the dope into my mouth and swallow it. Yum-yum.

I go out into the street now. I don't care. My friend shouts across to me: 'They're planting me. I've got nothing.'

I tell the bastard pigs to leave him alone. 'It's true! The man's got nothing!' I give them a good shouting at. One of them comes at me.

'You wanna be arrested too!' he says, shoving me in the chest.

'I don't mind,' I say. And I don't, really. Ma would visit me.

Some kids gather round, watching the rumpus. They look really straggly and pathetic and dignified and individual and defiant at the same time. I feel sorry for us all. The pigs pull my friend into the van. It's the last I ever see of him. He's got two years of trouble ahead of him, I know.

When I get back from my walk they're sitting on Howard's Habitat sofa. Something is definitely going on, and it ain't cultural. They're too far apart for comfort. Beadily I shove my aerial into the air and take the temperature. Yeah, can't I just smell humming dodginess in the atmosphere?

'Come on,' I say to Nadia. 'Ma will be waiting.'

'Yes, that's true,' Howard says, getting up. 'Give her my love.'

I give him one of my looks. 'All of it or just a touch?'

We're on the bus, sitting there nice and quiet, the bus going along past the shops and people and the dole office when these bad things start to happen that I can't explain. The seats in front of me, the entire top deck of the bus in fact, keeps rising up. I turn my head to the window expecting that the street at least will be anchored to the earth, but it's not. The whole street is throwing itself up at my head and heaving about and bending like a high-rise in a tornado. The shops are dashing at me, at an angle. The world has turned into a monster. For God's sake, nothing will keep still, but I've made up my mind to have it out. So I tie myself to the seat by my fists and say to Nadia, at least I think I say, 'You kiss him?'

She looks straight ahead as if she's been importuned by a beggar. I'm about to be hurled out of the bus, I know. But I go right ahead.

'Nadia. You did, right? You did.'

'But it's not important.'

Wasn't I right? Can't I sniff a kiss in the air at a hundred yards?

'Kissing's not important?'

'No,' she says. 'It's not, Nina. It's just affection. That's normal. But Howard and I have much to say to each other.' She seems depressed suddenly. 'He knows I'm in love with somebody.'

'I'm not against talking. But it's possible to talk without r-r-rubbing your tongues against each other's tonsils.'

'You have a crude way of putting things,' she replies, turning sharply to me and rising up to the roof of the bus. 'It's a shame you'll never understand passion.'

I am crude, yeah. And I'm about to be crushed into the corner of the bus by two hundred brown balloons. Oh sister.

'Are you feeling sick?' she says, getting up.

The next thing I know we're stumbling off the moving bus and I lie down on an unused piece of damp pavement outside the Albert Hall. The sky swings above me. Nadia's face hovers over mine like ectoplasm. Then she has her hand flat on my forehead in a doctory way. I give it a good hard slap.

'Why are you crying?'

If our father could see us now.

'Your bad behaviour with Howard makes me cry for my Ma.'

'Bad behaviour? Wait till I tell my father—'

'Our father—'

'About you.'

'What will you say?'

'I'll tell him you've been a prostitute and a drug-addict.'

'Would you say that, Nadia?'
'No,' she says, eventually. 'I suppose not.'
She offers me her hand and I take it.
'It's time I went home,' she says.
'Me, too,' I say.

3

It's not Friday, but Howard comes with us to Heathrow. Nadia flicks through fashion magazines, looking at clothes she won't be able to buy now. Her pride and dignity today is monstrous. Howard hands me a pile of books and writing pads and about twelve pens.

'Don't they have pens over there?' I say.

'It's a Third World country,' he says. 'They lack the basic necessities.'

Nadia slaps his arm. 'Howard, of course we have pens, you stupid idiot!'

'I was joking,' he says. 'They're for me.' He tries to stuff them all into the top pocket of his jacket. They spill on the floor. 'I'm writing something that might interest you all.'

'Everything you write interests us,' Nadia says.

'Not necessarily,' Ma says.

'But this is especially . . . relevant,' he says.

Ma takes me aside: 'If you must go, do write, Nina. And don't tell your father one thing about me!'

Nadia distracts everyone by raising her arms and putting her head back and shouting out in the middle of the airport: 'No, no, no, I don't want to go!'

My room, this cell, this safe, bare box stuck on the side of my father's house, has a stone floor and whitewashed walls. It has a single bed, my open suitcase, no wardrobe, no music. Not a frill in the grill. On everything there's a veil of khaki dust waiting to irritate my nostrils. The window is tiny, just twice the size of my head. So it's pretty gloomy here. Next door there's a smaller room with an amateur shower, a sink and a hole in the ground over which you have to get used to squatting if you want to piss and shit.

Despite my moans, all this suits me fine. In fact, I requested this room. At first Dad wanted Nadia and me to share. But here I'm out of everyone's way, especially my two other half-sisters: Gloomie and Moonie I call them.

I wake up and the air is hot, hot, hot, and the noise and petrol fumes rise around me. I kick into my jeans and pull my Keith Haring T-shirt on. Once, on the King's Road, two separate people came up to me and said: Is that a Keith Haring T-shirt?

Outside, the sun wants to burn you up. The light is different too: you can really see things. I put my shades on. These are cool shades. There aren't many women you see in shades here.

The driver is revving up one of Dad's three cars outside my room. I open the door of a car and jump in, except that it's like throwing your arse into a fire, and I jiggle around, the driver laughing his red jutting teeth as if he never saw anything funny before.

'Drive me,' I say. 'Drive me somewhere in all this sunlight. Please. Please.' I touch him and he pulls away from me. Well, he is rather handsome. 'These cars don't need to be revved. Drive!'

He turns the wheel back and forth, pretending to drive and hit the horn. He's youngish and thin—they all look undernourished here—and he always teases me.

'You stupid bugger.'

See, ain't I just getting the knack of speaking to servants? It's taken me at least a week to erase my natural politeness to the poor.

'Get going! Get us out of this drive!'

'No shoes, no shoes, Nina!' He's pointing at my feet.

'No bananas, no pineapples,' I say. 'No job for you either, Lulu. You'll be down the Job Centre if you don't shift it.'

Off we go then, the few yards to the end of the drive. The guard at the gate waves. I turn to look back and there you are standing on the porch of your house in your pyjamas, face covered with shaving cream, a piece of white sheet wrapped around your head because you've just oiled your hair. Your arms are waving not goodbye. Gloomie, my suddenly-acquired sister, runs out behind you and shakes her fists, the dogs barking in their cage, the chickens screaming in theirs. Ha, ha.

We drive slowly through the estate on which Dad lives with all
the other army and navy and air force people: big houses and big
bungalows set back from the road, with sprinklers on the lawn,
some with swimming pools, all with guards.

We move out on to the Superhighway, among the painted
trucks, gaudier than Chinese dolls, a sparrow among peacocks.
What a crappy road and no fun, like driving on the moon. Dad says
the builders steal the materials, flog them and then there's not
enough left to finish the road. So they just stop and leave whole
stretches incomplete.

The thing about this place is that there's always something
happening. Good or bad it's a happening place. And I'm thinking
this, how cheerful I am and everything, when bouncing along in the
opposite direction is a taxi, an old yellow and black Morris Minor
stuck together with Sellotape. It's swerving in and out of the traffic
very fast until the driver loses it, and the taxi bangs the back of the
car in front, glances off another and shoots off across the
Superhighway and is coming straight for us. I can see the driver's
face when Lulu finally brakes. Three feet from us the taxi flies into
a wall that runs alongside the road. The two men keep travelling,
and their heads crushed into their chests pull their bodies through
the windscreen and out into the morning air. They look like
Christmas puddings.

Lulu accelerates. I grab him and scream at him to stop but we
go faster and faster.

'Damn dead,' he says, when I've finished clawing him. 'A wild
country. This kind of thing happen in England, yes?'

'Yes, I suppose so.'

Eventually I persuade him to stop and I get out of the car.

I'm alone in the bazaar, handling jewellery and carpets and pots
and I'm confused. I know I have to get people presents.
Especially Howard the hero who's paying for this. Ah, there's
just the thing: a cage the size of a big paint tin, with three chickens
inside. The owner sees me looking. He jerks a chicken out,
decapitates it on a block and holds it up to my face, feathers flying
into my hair.

I walk away and dodge a legless brat on a four-wheeled trolley
made out of a door, who hurls herself at me and then disappears

through an alley and across the sewers. Everywhere the sick and the uncured, and I'm just about ready for lunch when everyone starts running. They're jumping out of the road and pulling their kids away. There is a tidal wave of activity, generated by three big covered trucks full of soldiers crashing through the bazaar, the men standing still and nonchalant with rifles in the back. I'm half knocked to hell by some prick tossed off a bike. I am tip-toeing my way out along the edge of a fucking sewer, shit lapping against my shoes. I've just about had enough of this country, I'm just about to call for South Africa Road, when—

'Lulu,' I shout. 'Lulu.'

'I take care of you,' he says. 'Sorry for touching.'

He takes me back to the car. Fat, black buffalo snort and shift in the mud. I don't like these animals being everywhere, chickens and dogs and stuff, with sores and bleeding and threats and fear.

'You know?' I say. 'I'm lonely. There's no one I can talk to. No one to laugh with here, Lulu. And I think they hate me, my family. Does your family hate you?'

I stretch and bend and twist in the front garden in T-shirt and shorts. I pull sheets of air into my lungs. I open my eyes a moment and the world amazes me, its brightness. A servant is watching me, peeping round a tree.

'Hey, peeper!' I call, and carry on. When I look again, I notice the cook and the sweeper have joined him and they shake and trill.

'What am I doing?' I say. 'Giving a concert?'

In the morning papers I notice that potential wives are advertised as being 'virtuous and fair-skinned'. Why would I want to be unvirtuous and brown? But I do, I do!

I take a shower in my room and stroll across to the house. I stand outside your room, Dad, where the men always meet in the early evenings. I look through the wire mesh of the screen door and there you are, my father for all these years. And this is what you were doing while I sat in the back of the class at my school in Shepherd's Bush, pregnant, wondering why you didn't love me.

In the morning when I'm having my breakfast we meet in the living room by the bar and you ride on your exercise bicycle. You pant and look at me now and again, your stringy body sways and tightens, but you say fuck-all. If I speak, you don't hear. You're one of those old-fashioned romantic men for whom women aren't really there unless you decide we are.

Now you lie on your bed and pluck up food with one hand and read an American comic with the other. A servant, a young boy, presses one of those fat vibrating electric instruments you see advertised in the *Observer Magazine* on to your short legs. You look up and see me. The sight of me angers you. You wave furiously for me to come in. No. Not yet. I walk on.

In the woman's area of the house, where visitors rarely visit, Dad's wife sits sewing.

'Hello,' I say. 'I think I'll have a piece of sugar cane.'

I want to ask the names of the other pieces of fruit on the table, but Wifey is crabby inside and out, doesn't speak English and disapproves of me in all languages. She has two servants with her, squatting there watching Indian movies on the video. An old woman who was once, I can see, a screen goddess, now sweeps the floor on her knees with a handful of twigs. Accidentally, sitting there swinging my leg, I touch her back with my foot, leaving a dusty mark on her clothes.

'Imagine,' I say to Wifey.

I slip the sugar cane into my mouth. The squirting juice bounces off my taste buds. I gob out the sucked detritus and chuck it in front of the screen goddess's twigs. You can really enjoy talking to someone who doesn't understand you.

'Imagine my Dad leaving my Ma for you! And you don't ever leave that seat there. Except once a month you go to the bank to check up on your jewellery.'

Wifey keeps all her possessions on the floor around her. She is definitely mad. But I like the mad here: they just wander around the place with everyone else and no one bothers you and people give you food.

'You look like a bag lady. D'you know what a bag lady is?'

Moonie comes into the room. She's obviously heard every word I've said. She starts to yell at me. Wifey's beaky nozzle turns to me with interest now. Something's happening that's even more interesting than TV. They want to crush me. I think they like me here for that reason. If you could see, Ma, what they're doing to me just because you met a man at a dance in the Old Kent Road and his French letter burst as you lay in front of a gas fire with your legs up!

'You took the car when we had to go out to work!' yells Moonie. 'You forced the driver to take you! We had to sack him!'

'Why sack him?'

'He's naughty! Naughty! You said he drives you badly! Nearly killed! You're always causing trouble, Nina, doing some stupid thing, some very stupid thing!'

Gloomie and Moonie are older than Nadia and I. Both have been married, kicked around by husbands arranged by Dad, and separated. That was their small chance in life. Now they've come back to daddy. Now they're secretaries. Now they're blaming me for everything.

'By the way. Here.' I reach into my pocket. 'Take this.'

Moonie's eyes bulge at my open palm. Her eyes quieten her mouth. She starts fatly towards me. She sways. She comes on. Her hand snatches at the lipstick.

'Now you'll be able to come out with me. We'll go to the Holiday Inn.'

'Yes, but you've been naughty.' She is distracted by the lipstick. 'What colour is it?'

'Can't you leave her alone for God's sake? Always picking on her!' This is Nadia coming into the room after work. She throws herself into a chair. 'I'm so tired.' To the servant she says: 'Bring me some tea.' At me she smiles. 'Hello, Nina. Good day? You were doing some exercises, I hear. They rang me at work to tell me.'

'Yes, Nadia.'

'Oh sister, they have such priorities.'

For the others I am 'cousin'. From the start there's been embarrassment about how I am to be described. Usually, if it's Moonie or Gloomie they say: This is our distant cousin from England. It amuses me to see my father deal with this. He can't bring himself to say either 'cousin' or 'daughter' so he just says Nina and leaves it. But of course everyone knows I am his illegitimate daughter. But Nadia is the real 'daughter' here. 'Nadia is an impressive person,' my father says, on my first day here, making it clear that I am diminished, the sort with dirt under her nails. Yes, she is clever, soon to be doctor, life-saver. Looking at her now she seems less small than she did in London. I'd say she has enough dignity for the entire government.

'They tear-gassed the hospital.'

'Who?'

'The clever police. Some people were demonstrating outside. The police broke it up. When they chased the demonstrators inside they tear-gassed them! What a day! What a country! I must wash my face.' She goes out.

'See, see!' Moonie trills. 'She is better than you! Yes, yes, yes!'

'I expect so. It's not difficult.'

'We know she is better than you for certain!'

I walk out of all this and into my father's room. It's like moving from one play to another. What is happening on this set? The room is perfumed with incense from a green coiled creation which burns outside the doors, causing mosquitoes to drop dead. Advanced telephones connect him to Paris, Dubai, London. On the video is an American movie. Five youths rape a woman. Father— what do I call him, Dad?—sits on the edge of the bed with his little legs sticking out. The servant teases father's feet into his socks.

'You'll get sunstroke,' he says, as if he's known me all my life and has the right to be high-handed. 'Cavorting naked in the garden.'

'Naked is it now?'

'We had to sack the driver, too. Sit down.'

I sit in the row of chairs beside him. It's like visiting someone in hospital. He lies on his side in his favourite mocking-me-for-sport position.

'Now—'

The lights go out. The TV goes off. I shut my eyes and laugh. Power-cut. Father bounces up and down on the bed. 'Fuck this motherfucking country!' The servant rushes for candles and lights them. As it's Friday I sit here and think of Ma and Howard meeting today for food, talk and sex. I think Howard's not so bad after all, and even slightly good-looking. He's never deliberately hurt Ma. He has other women—but that's only vanity, a weakness, not a crime—and he sees her only on Friday, but he hasn't undermined her. What more can you expect from men? Ma loves him a lot—from the first moment, she says; she couldn't help herself. She's still trusting and open, despite everything.

Never happen to me.

Dad turns to me: 'What do you do in England for God's sake?'

'Nadia has already given you a full report, hasn't she?'

A full report? For two days I gaped through the window lip-reading desperately as nose to nose, whispering and giggling, eyebrows shooting up, jaws dropping like guillotines, hands rubbing, Father and Nadia conducted my prosecution. The two rotund salt and pepper pots, Moonie and Gloomie, guarded the separate entrances to this room.

'Yes, but I want the full confession from your mouth.'

He loves to tease. But he is a dangerous person. Tell him something and soon everyone knows about it.

'Confess to what?'

'That you just roam around here and there. You do fuck-all full-time, in other words.'

'Everyone in England does fuck-all except for the yuppies.'

'And do you go with one boy or with many?' I say nothing. 'But your mother has a boy, yes? Some dud writer, complete failure and playboy with unnatural eyebrows that cross in the middle?'

'Is that how Nadia described the man she tried to—'

'What?'

'Be rather close friends with?'

The servant has a pair of scissors. He trims Father's hair, he snips in Father's ear, he investigates Father's nostrils with the clipping steel shafts. He attaches a tea-cloth to Father's collar, lathers Father's face, sharpens the razor on the strop and shaves Father clean and reddish.

'Not necessarily,' says Father, spitting foam. 'I use my imagination. Nadia says eyebrows and I see bushes.'

He says to his servant and indicates me: 'An Englisher born and bred, eh?'

The servant falls about with the open razor.

'But you belong with us,' Dad says. 'Don't worry, I'll put you on the right track. But first there must be a strict course of discipline.'

The room is full of dressed-up people sitting around Dad's bed looking at him lying there in his best clothes. Dad yells out cheerful slanders about the tax-evaders, bribe-takers and general scumbags who can't make it this evening. Father obviously a most popular man here. It's better to be entertaining than good. Ma would be drinking bleach by now.

At last Dad gives the order they've been waiting for.

'Bring the booze.'

The servant unlocks the cabinet and brings out the whisky.

'Give everyone a drink except Nina. She has to get used to the pure way of life!' he says, and everyone laughs at me.

The people here are tractor-dealers (my first tractor-dealer!), journalists, landowners and a newspaper tycoon aged thirty-one who inherited a bunch of papers. He's immensely cultured and massively fat. I suggest you look at him from the front and tell me if he doesn't look like a flounder. I look up to see my sister standing at the window of Dad's room, straining her heart's wet eyes at the Flounder who doesn't want to marry her because he already has the most pleasant life there is in the world.

Now here's a message for you fuckers back home. The men here invite Nadia and me to their houses, take us to their club, play tennis with us. They're chauvinistic as hell, but they put on a great show. They're funny and spend money and take you to their farms and show you their guns and kill a snake in front of your eyes. They flirt and want to poke their things in you, but they don't expect it.

Billy slides into the room in his puffy baseball jacket and pink Plimsolls and patched jeans. He stands there and puts his hands in his pockets and takes them out again.

'Hey, Billy, have a drink.'

'OK. Thanks . . . Yeah. OK.'

'Don't be shy,' Dad says. 'Nina's not shy.'

So the entire room looks at shy Billy and Billy looks at the ground.

'No, well, I could do with a drink. Just one. Thanks.'

The servant gets Billy a drink. Someone says to someone else: 'He looks better since he had that break in Lahore.'

'It did him the whole world of damn good.'

'Terrible what happened to the boy.'

'Yes. Yes. Ghastly rotten.'

Billy comes and sits next to me. Their loud talking goes on.

'I've heard about you,' he says under the talking. 'They talk about you non-stop.'

'Goody.'

'Yeah. Juicy Fruit?' he says.

He sits down on the bed and I open my case and give him all my tapes.

'Latest stuff from England.'

He goes through them eagerly. 'You can't get any of this stuff here. This is the best thing that has ever happened to me.' He looks at me. 'Can I? Can I borrow them? Would you mind, you know?' I nod. 'My room is on top of the house. I'll never be far away.'

Oh, kiss me now! Though I can see that's a little premature, especially in a country where they cut off your arms or something for adultery. I like your black jeans.

'What's your accent?' I say.

'Canadian.' He gets up. No, don't leave now. Not yet. 'Wanna ride?' he says.

In the drive the chauffeurs smoke and talk. They stop talking. They watch us. Billy puts his baseball cap on my head and touches my hair.

'Billy, push the bike out into the street so no one hears us leave.'

I ask him about himself. His mother was Canadian. She died. His father was Pakistani, though Billy was brought up in Vancouver. I turn and Moonie is yelling at me. 'Nina, Nina, it's late. Your father must see you now about a strict discipline business he has to discuss!'

'Billy, keep going.'

He just keeps pushing the bike, oblivious of Moonie. He glances at me now and again, as if he can't believe his luck. I can't believe mine, baby!

'So Pop and I came home to live. Home. This place isn't my home. But he always wanted to come home.'

We push the bike up the street till we get to the main road.

'This country was a shock after Vancouver,' he says.

'Same for me.'

'Yeah?' He gets sharp. 'But I'd been brought here to live. How can you ever understand what that's like?'

'I can't. All right, I fucking can't.'

He goes on. 'We were converting a house in 'Pindi, Pop and me. Digging the foundations, plastering the walls, doing the plumbing . . .'

We get on the bike and I hold him.

'Out by the beach, Billy.'

'Yeah. But it's not simple. You know the cops stop couples and ask to see their wedding certificates.'

It's true but fuck it. Slowly, stately, the two beige outlaws ride through the city of open fires. I shout an Aretha Franklin song into the night. Men squat by busted cars. Wild maimed pye-dogs run in our path. Traffic careers through dust, past hotels and airline buildings, past students squatting beside traffic lights to read, near where there are terrorist explosions and roads melt like plastic.

To the beach without showing our wedding certificate. It's more a desert than a beach. There's just sand: no shops, no hotels, no ice-creamers, no tattooists. Utterly dark. Your eyes search for a light in panic, for safety. But the curtains of the world are well and truly pulled here.

I guide Billy to the Flounder's beach hut. Hut—this place is bigger than Ma's flat. We push against the back door and we're in the large living room. Billy and I dance about and chuck open the shutters. Enter moonlight and the beach as Billy continues his Dad rap.

'Pop asked me to drill some holes in the kitchen. But I had to empty the wheel barrow. So he did the drilling. He hit a cable or something. Anyway, he's dead, isn't he?'

We kiss for a long time, about forty minutes. There's not a lot you can do in kissing; half an hour of someone's tongue in your mouth could seem an eternity, but what there is to do, we do. I take off all my clothes and listen to the sea and almost cry for missing South Africa Road so. But at least there is the light friction of our lips together, barely touching. Harder. I pull the strong bulk of his head towards mine, pressing my tongue to the corner of his mouth.

Soon I pass through the mouth's parting to trace the inside curve of his lips. Suddenly his tongue fills my mouth, invading me, and I clench it with my teeth. Oh, oh, oh. As he withdraws I follow him, sliding my tongue into the oven of his gob and lie there on the bench by the open shutters overlooking the Arabian Sea, connected by tongue and saliva, my fingers in his ears and hair, his finger inside my body, our bodies dissolving until we forget ourselves and think of nothing, thank fuck.

It's still dark and no more than ninety minutes have passed, when I hear a car pulling up outside the hut. I shake Billy awake, push him off me and pull him across the hut and into the kitchen. The fucking door's warped and won't shut so we just lie down on the floor next to each other. I clam Billy up with my hand over his gob. There's a shit smell right next to my nose. I start to giggle. I stuff Billy's fingers into my mouth. He's laughing all over the place too. But we shut up sharpish when a couple come into the hut and start to move around. For some reason I imagine we're going to be shot.

The man says: 'Curious, indeed. My sister must have left the shutters open last time she came here.'

The other person says it's lovely, the moonlight and so on. Then there's no talking. I can't see a sausage but my ears are at full stretch. Yes, kissing noises.

Nadia says: 'Here's the condoms, Bubble!'

My sister and the Flounder! Well. The Flounder lights a lantern. Yes, there they are now, I can see them: she's trying to pull his long shirt over his head, and he's resisting.

'Just my bottoms!' he squeals. 'My stomach! Oh, my God!'

I'm not surprised he's ashamed, looking in this low-light at the size of the balcony over his toy-shop.

I hear my name. Nadia starts to tell the Flounder—or 'Bubble' as she keeps calling him—how the Family Planning in London gave me condoms. The Flounder's clucking with disapproval and lying on the bench by the window looking like a hippo, with my sister squatting over his guts, rising and sitting, sighing and exclaiming sometimes, almost in surprise. They chat away quite naturally, fucking and gossiping and the Flounder talks about me. Am I promiscuous, he wants to know. Do I do it with just anyone? How is my father going to discipline me now he's got his hands on me? Billy shifts about. He could easily be believing this shit. I wish I had some paper and a pen to write him a note. I kiss him gently instead. When I kiss him I get a renewal of this strange sensation that I've never felt before today: I feel it's Billy I'm kissing, not just his lips or body, but some inside thing, as if his skin is just a representative of all of him, his past and his blood. Amour has never been this personal for me before!

Nadia and the Flounder are getting hotter. She keeps asking Bubble why they can't do this everyday. He says, yes, yes, yes, and won't you tickle my balls? I wonder how she'll find them. Then the Flounder shudders and Nadia, moving in rhythm like someone doing a slow dance, has to stop. 'Bubble!' she says and slaps him, as if he's a naughty child that's just thrown up. A long fart escapes Bubble's behind. 'Oh Bubble,' she says, and falls on to him, holding him closer.

Soon he is asleep. Nadia unstraddles him and moves to a chair and has a little cry as she sits looking at him. She only wants to be held and kissed and touched. I feel like going to her myself.

When I wake up it's daylight and they're sitting there together, talking about their favourite subject. The Flounder is smoking and she is trying to masturbate him.

'So why did she come here with you?' he is asking. Billy opens his eyes and doesn't know where he is. Then he sighs. I agree with him. What a place to be, what a thing to be doing! (But then, come to think of it, you always find me in the kitchen at parties.)

'Nina just asked me one day at breakfast. I had no choice and this man, Howard—'

'Yes, yes,' the Flounder laughs. 'You said he was handsome.'

'I only said he had nice hair,' she says.

But I'm in sympathy with the Flounder here, finding this compliment a little gratuitous. The Flounder gets up. He's ready to go.

And so is Billy. 'I can't stand much more of this,' he says. Nadia suddenly jerks her head towards us. For a moment I think she's seen us. But the Flounder distracts her.

I hear the tinkle of the car keys and the Flounder says: 'Here, put your panties on. Wouldn't want to leave your panties here on the floor. But let me kiss them first! I kiss them!'

There are sucky kissing noises. Billy is twitching badly and drumming his heels on the floor. Nadia looks at the Flounder with his face buried in a handful of white cotton.

'And,' he says with a muffled voice, 'I'm getting lead in my pencil again, Nadia. Let us lie down, my pretty one.'

The Flounder takes her hand enthusiastically and jerks it towards his ding-dong. She smacks him away. She's not looking too pleased.

'I've got my pants on, you bloody fool!' Nadia says harshly. 'That pair of knickers you've sunk your nose in must belong to another woman you've had here!'

'What! But I've had no other woman here!' The Flounder glares at her furiously. He examines the panties, as if hoping to find a name inside. 'Marks & Spencers. How strange. I feel sick now.'

'Marks & Spencers! Fuck this!' says Billy, forcing my hands off his face. 'My arms and legs are going to fucking drop off in a minute!'

So up gets Billy. He combs his hair and turns up the collar of his shirt and then strolls into the living room singing a couple of choruses from The The. I get up and follow him, just in time to see Nadia open her mouth and let off a huge scream at the sight of us. The Flounder, who has no bottoms on, gives a frightened yelp and drops my pants which I pick up and, quite naturally, put on. I'm calm and completely resigned to the worst. Anyway, I've got my arm round Billy.

'Hi, everyone,' Billy says. 'We were just asleep in the other room. Don't worry, we didn't hear anything, not about the condoms or Nina's character or the panties or anything. Not a thing. How about a cup of tea or something?'

I get off Billy's bike midday. 'Baby,' he says.

'Happy,' I say, wearing his checked shirt, tail out. Across the lawn with its sprinkler I set off for Dad's club, a sun-loved white palace set in flowers.

White-uniformed bearers humble as undertakers set down trays of foaming yogurt. I could do with a proper drink myself.

Colonels with Generals and ladies with perms, fans and crossed legs sit in cane chairs. I wish I'd slept more.

The old man. There you are, blazer and slacks, turning the pages of *The Times* on an oak lectern overlooking the gardens. You look up. Well, well, well, say your eyes, not a dull day now. Her to play with.

You take me into the dining room. It's chill and smart and the tables have thick white cloths on them and silver cutlery. The men move chairs for the elegant thin women, and the waiters take the jackets of the plump men. I notice there are no young people here.

'Fill your plate,' you say, kindly, 'And come and sit with me. Bring me something too. A little meat and some dhal.'

I cover the plate with food from the copper pots at the buffet in the centre of the room and take it to you. And here we sit, father and daughter, all friendly and everything.

'How are you today, Daddy?' I say, touching your cheek.

Around us the sedate upper-class fill their guts. You haven't heard me. I say once more, gently: 'How are you today?'

'You fucking bitch,' you say. You push away your food and light a cigarette.

'Goody,' I say, going a little cold. 'Now we know where we are with each other.'

'Where the fuck were you last night?' you inquire of me. You go on: 'You just fucked off and told no one. I was demented with worry. My blood pressure was through the roof. Anything could have happened to you.'

'It did.'

'That bloody boy's insane.'

'But Billy's pretty.'

'No, he's ugly like you. And a big pain in the arse.'

'Dad.'

'No, don't interrupt! A half-caste wastrel, a belong-nowhere, a problem to everyone, wandering around the face of the earth with no home like a stupid-mistake-mongrel dog that no one wants and everyone kicks in the backside.'

For those of you curious about the menu, I am drinking tear soup.

'You left us,' I say. I am shaking. You are shaking. 'Years ago, just look at it, you fucked us and left us and fucked off and never came back and never sent us money and instead made us sit through fucking Jesus Christ Superstar and Evita.'

Someone comes over, a smart judge who helped hang the Prime Minister. We all shake hands. Christ, I can't stop crying all over the place.

It's dusk and I'm sitting upstairs in a deckchair outside Billy's room on the roof. Billy's sitting on a pillow. We're wearing cut-off jeans and drinking iced water and reading old English newspapers that we pass between us. Our washing is hanging up on a piece of string we've tied between the corner of the room and the television aerial. The door to the room is open and we're listening again and again to 'Who's Loving You'—very loud—because it's our favourite record. Billy keeps saying: Let's hear it again, one mo' time, you know. We're like an old couple sitting on a concrete patio in Shepherd's Bush, until we get up and dance with no shoes on and laugh and gasp because the roof burns our feet so we have to go inside to make love again.

Billy goes in to take a shower and I watch him go. I don't like being separated from him. I hear the shower start and I sit down and throw the papers aside. I go downstairs to Nadia's room and knock on her door. Wifey is sitting there and Moonie is behind her.

'She's not in,' Moonie says.

'Come in,' Nadia says, opening her door. I go in and sit on the stool by the dressing table. It's a pretty room. There is pink everywhere and her things are all laid out neatly and she sits on the bed brushing her hair until it shines. I tell her we should have a bit of a talk. She smiles at me. She's prepared to make an effort, I can see that, though it surprises me. She did go pretty berserk the other day, when we came out of the kitchen, trying to punch me and everything.

'It was an accident,' I tell her now.

'Well,' she says. 'But what impression d'you think it made on the man I want to marry?'

'Blame me. Say I'm just a sicko Westerner. Say I'm mad.'

'It's the whole family it reflects on,' she says.

She goes to a drawer and opens it. She takes out an envelope and gives it to me.

'It's a present for you,' she says kindly. When I slip my finger into the flap of the envelope she puts her hand over mine. 'Please. It's a surprise for later.'

Billy is standing on the roof in his underpants. I fetch a towel and dry his hair and legs and he holds me and we move a little together to imaginary music. When I remember the envelope Nadia gave me, I open it and find a shiny folder inside. It's a ticket to London.

I'd given my ticket home to my father for safe-keeping, an open ticket I can use any time. I can see that Nadia's been to the airline and specified the date and booked the flight. I'm to leave tomorrow morning. I go to my Dad and ask him what it's all about. He just looks at me and I realize I'm to go.

4

Hello reader. As I'm sure you've noticed by now, I, Howard, have written this Nina and Nadia stuff in my sock, without leaving the country, sitting right here on my spreading arse and listening to John Coltrane. (And rolling cigarettes.) Do you think Nina could have managed phrases like 'an accent as thick as treacle' and 'But the curtains are well and truly pulled here' and especially 'Oh, oh, oh'? With her education? So all along, it's been me, pulling faces, speaking in tongues, posing and making an attempt on the truth through lies. And also, I just wanted to be Nina. The days Deborah and I have spent beating on her head, trying to twist her the right way round, read this, study dancing, here's a book about Balanchine and the rest of it. What does she make of all this force-feeding? So I became her, entered her. Sorry.

Nina in fact has been back a week, though it wasn't until yesterday that I heard from her when she phoned to tell me that I am a bastard and that she had to see me. I leave straightaway.

At Nina's place. There she is, sitting at the kitchen table with her foot up on the table by her ashtray in the posture of a painter. Deborah not back from school.

'You look superb,' I tell her. She doesn't recoil in repulsion when I kiss her.

'Do I look superb?' She is interested.

'Yeah. Tanned. Fit. Rested.'

'Oh, is that all?' She looks hard at me. 'I thought for a moment you were going to say something interesting. Like I'd changed or something. Like something had happened.'

We walk through the estate, Friday afternoon. How she walks above it all now, as if she's already left! She tells me everything in a soft voice: her father, the servants, the boy Billy, the kiss, the panties. She says: I was devastated to leave Billy in that country on his own. What will he do? What will happen to that boy? I sent him a pack of tapes. I sent him some videos. But he'll be so lonely. She is upset.

The three of us have supper and Deborah tries to talk about school while Nina ignores her. It's just like the old days. But Nina ignores Deborah not out of cruelty but because she is elsewhere. Deborah is thinking that probably Nina has left her for good. I am worried that Debbie will expect more from me.

The next day I fly to my desk, put on an early Miles Davis tape and let it all go, tip it out, what Nina said, how she looked, what we did, and I write (and later cross out) how I like to put my little finger up Deborah's arse when we're fucking and how she does the same to me, when she can comfortably reach. I shove it all down shamelessly (and add bits) because it's my job to write down the things that happen round here and because I have a rule about no material being sacred.

What does that make me?

I once was in a cinema when the recently uncovered spy Anthony Blunt came in with a friend. The entire cinema (but not me) stood up and chanted 'Out, out, out' until the old queen got up and left. I feel like that old spy, a dirty betrayer with a loudspeaker, doing what I have to.

I offer this story to you, Deborah and Nina, to make of it what you will, before I send it to the publisher.

Dear Howard,

How very kind of you to leave your story on my kitchen table casually saying, 'I think you should read this before I publish it.' I was pleased: I gave you an extra kiss, thinking that at last you wanted me to share your work (I almost wrote world).

I could not believe you opened the story with an account of an abortion. As you know I know, it's lifted in its entirety from a letter written to you by your last girlfriend, Julie. You were conveniently away in New York when she was having the abortion so that she had to spit out all the bits of her broken heart in a letter, and you put it into the story pretending it was written by my daughter.

The story does also concern me, our 'relationship' and even where we put our fingers. Your portrait of me as a miserable whiner let down by men would have desperately depressed me, but I've learned that unfeeling, blood-sucking men like you need to reduce women to manageable clichés, even to destroy them, for the sake of control.

I am only sorry it's taken me this long to realize what a low, corrupt and exploitative individual you are, who never deserved the love we both offered you. You have torn me apart. I hope the same thing happens to you one day. Please never attempt to get in touch again.

Deborah

Someone bangs on the door of the flat. I've been alone all day. I'm not expecting anyone, and how did whoever it is get into the building in the first place?

'Let me in, let me in!' Nina calls out. I open up and she's standing there soaked through with a sports bag full of things and a couple of plastic bags under her arm.

'Moving in?' I say.

'You should be so lucky,' she says, barging past me. 'I'm on me way somewhere and I thought I'd pop by to borrow some money.'

She comes into the kitchen. It's gloomy and the rain hammers into the courtyard outside. But Nina's cheerful, happy to be back in England and she has no illusions about her father now. Apparently he was rough with her, called her a half-caste and so on.

'Well, Howard, you're in the shit, aren't you?' Nina says. 'Ma's pissed off no end with you, man. She's crying all over the shop. I couldn't stand it. I've moved out. You can die of a broken heart, you know. And you can kill someone that way too.'

'Don't talk about it,' I say, breaking up the ice with a hammer and dropping it into the glasses. 'She wrote me a pissed-off letter.

Wanna read it?'

'It's private, Howard.'

'Read it, for Christ's sake, Nina,' I say, shoving it at her. She reads it and I walk round the kitchen looking at her. I stand behind her a long time. I can't stop looking at her today.

She puts it down without emotion. She's not sentimental; she's always practical about things, because she knows what cunts people are.

'You've ripped Ma off before. She'll get over it, and no one reads the shit you write anyway except a lot of middle-class wankers. As long as you get paid and as long as you give me some of it you're all right with me.'

I was right. I knew she'd be flattered. I give her some money and she gathers up her things. I don't want her to go.

'Where are you off to?'

'Oh, a friend's place in Hackney. Someone I was in the loony bin with. I'll be living there. Oh, and Billy will be joining me.' She smiles broadly. 'I'm happy.'

'Wow. That's good. You and Billy.'

'Yeah, ain't it just!' She gets up and throws back the rest of the whisky. 'Be seeing ya!'

'Don't go yet.'

'Got to.'

At the door she says: 'Good luck with the writing and everything.'

I walk to the lift with her. We go down together. I go out to the front door of the building. As she goes out into the street running with sheets of rain, I say: 'I'll come with you to the corner,' and walk with her, even though I'm not dressed for it.

At the corner I can't let her go and I accompany her to the bus stop. I wait with her for fifteen minutes in my shirt and slippers. I'm soaked through holding all her bags but I think you can make too much of these things. 'Don't go,' I keep saying inside my head. Then the bus arrives and she takes her bags from me and gets on and I stand there watching her but she won't look at me because she is thinking of Billy. The bus moves off and I watch until it disappears and then I go inside the flat and take off my clothes and have a bath. Later, I write down the things she said but the place still smells of her.

HANIF KUREISHI
FILM DIARY

2 JUNE 1986: 'I shove the script of *Sammy and Rosie Get Laid* through Stephen Frears's letter box and run. He rings a few hours later: 'This isn't an innocent act!' He refuses to read it, but he's going to Seattle for the weekend to attend a film festival and promises to look at it on the plane.

I have many doubts about the script, but I can't get any further with it at the moment. I can't even bear to look at it.

12 JUNE: Frears rings. He likes the script but is not going to be around for a while, being busy with *Prick up Your Ears*. I wonder if this is a subtle way of saying he doesn't want to direct the film.

13 JUNE: Stephen Frears always looks as if he's slept in his clothes, whatever he is wearing, and his hair stands straight up on the top of his head, shooting out at the sides as if he's been electrocuted. His idea of dressing up is to put on a clean pair of Plimsolls. The sartorial message is: I can't think about all that stuff. When we were shooting *My Beautiful Laundrette* someone approached Stephen, pressed twenty pence in his hand, and said: 'Buy yourself a cup of tea!'

I met Stephen three years ago when I sent him the first draft of *My Beautiful Laundrette*, which was then made six months later. Frears is in his mid-forties and has made three other feature films— *Gumshoe, The Hit* and *Prick up Your Ears*. I was drawn to him because of his irreverence and seriousness, his directness and kindness. While he hates words like 'artist' and 'integrity', he is immensely skilled and talented and, while he talks a lot about how much money certain directors earn, he never makes a film entirely for the money.

I ring Frears and give him an earful about why I think he should direct *Sammy and Rosie Get Laid*. He listens patiently. Then he suddenly says we should make the film for television, on 16mm. I'm not convinced. He argues that the equipment is much lighter; you can make films faster. He suggests we give it to the BBC. But they've become so reactionary, I say. They're terrified of ripe language and screwing, cowed by censors. If you want to show an arse on the BBC they behave as if their entire licence fee were at stake.

All the same, he says finally, he sees it as a TV thing.

63

I receive a letter from an aunt who lives in the north of England. After seeing *Laundrette*, she frequently rings my father. 'Can't you control the little bastard?' she asks him. 'Humiliating us in public! Suppose people find out I'm related to him!'

Her letter:

> I tried to phone you, but I believe you were in the USA boring the pants off the Americans with your pornography . . . Worst of all the film was offensive to your father's distinguished family. Uncle was portrayed in a very bad light, drunk in bed with his bottle of vodka and uncut toenails. . . This was totally uncalled for and mischievous. It only brings to light your complete lack of loyalty, integrity and compassion . . . We didn't know you were a 'poofter'. We do hope you're aware of AIDS and its dangers; if not, then a medical leaflet can be sent to you. Why oh why do you have to promote the widely held view of the British that all evil stems from Pakistani immigrants? Thank goodness for top-quality films like *Gandhi*.

Like *Laundrette*, *Sammy and Rosie* is quite personal, autobiographical not in its details, but in its emotions. The part of Rosie is based loosely on a friend (I'll call her Sarah) who asked to read the script. I wouldn't let her because the character will change as the film goes through several drafts; the actress playing the part will also change it, as will Frears when he starts to work on it. All the same, I'm nervous about what Sarah will think of it. I know that in certain passages I've been spiteful.

On the phone Frears talks about Art Malik for the part of Sammy. He's an attractive actor but we both wonder if he's fly enough for the role.

6 JULY: My agent rings me to suggest we form a company to make the film: Frears, Tim Bevan and Sarah Radclyffe, and I. This way we'll have control.

Sarah Radclyffe was one of the people who commissioned *My Beautiful Laundrette*. She and Bevan have been involved in several recent British successes: *Caravaggio, Personal Services, Wish You Were Here* and *A World Apart*, with more in the pipeline.

9 AUGUST: Lunch in Notting Hill with Bevan, Radclyffe and Frears. Shashi Kapoor, the great Indian actor, arrives with his secretary, after everyone else. He has on a loose brown costume, with a dark red and chocolate scarf flung over his shoulder. He is so regal and dignified, stylish and exotic that a shiver goes through the restaurant.

It's a sunny day and when Shashi leaves we stroll back to Frears's house, pleased about Shashi's enthusiasm. We talk a bit about the other parts: Claire Bloom as Alice, with Miranda Richardson or Judy Davis as Rosie perhaps. Frears talks about the part of Anna, the American photographer, saying she isn't sympathetic enough: I've parodied her. He's right; I lack grip on the character. I realize that the entire script will be subjected to this kind of scrutiny.

14 AUGUST: At last I give the script to Sarah to read. Sarah and I met at university and lived together for six years. Since she moved out we continue to see a lot of each other. When Sarah reads it, she is angry and upset. I've said things that are true, but which I've never said to her. The worry is, she adds, that people will think she is Rosie and she will be Rosie forever. She'll no longer be in reasonable control of the way people think of her. Won't they have this crude cinema idea?

All this makes me feel guilty and sneaky; it makes me think that writers are like spies, poking into failures and weaknesses for good stories.

1 SEPTEMBER: Frears has thought a great deal about *Sammy and Rosie* and has decided that the best thing is to make it on 35mm for theatrical release, keeping the budget as low as possible. Bevan thinks we can raise most of the money for the film in America. Frears thinks this is a good idea since it'll save Channel 4 money: they'll be able to give the money to film-makers who can't get money elsewhere.

18 DECEMBER: Suddenly we're going into production at the beginning of January, shooting in early March. So the script has to start looking ready. Try to get the story going earlier, Frears says. And the riots: we're too familiar with them from television.

Something more has to be going on than people throwing bottles at policemen.

Later Frears rings, delighted to be in the middle of an interview with a young Pakistani actor, Ayub Khan Din, who is upstairs having a pee and is being considered for the part of Sammy. Art Malik, whom we discussed first, has complained about being in bed with Anna and about the scene where he is meant to wank, snort coke and suck on a milkshake at the same time. The script, Malik says in the end, isn't good enough. I think he prefers more glamorous roles.

21 DECEMBER: Michael Barker from Orion Classics rings to say Orion is going to push for an Oscar nomination for me for *Laundrette*. He doesn't think I'll win—it will be Woody Allen for *Hannah and Her Sisters*—but he thinks he can swing the nomination.

5 JANUARY 1987: I get up at six in the morning unable to sleep: I'm paranoid about this thing ever getting re-written. I start to fiddle with the script, until I realize the futility of this fiddling and put a fresh sheet in the typewriter and start at page one. I do no planning, give it no thought and just go at it.

Today is the first day of pre-production and everyone officially starts work: the director, the casting director, the production manager, designer and so on. What a shame the script is disintegrating in my hands. Little of what I've written seems secure now, except the characters; certainly not the story.

8 JANUARY: I spend most of the day trying to write a final scene for the film, which at the moment has Rafi staggering around on the waste ground during the eviction, and Sammy standing on the motorway shouting down at Rosie without being heard. This isn't satisfactory. So I put the last few pages in the typewriter and re-write them, trying to quieten my mind and allow fresh ideas to pop up as they will. Then it occurs to me, or rather it writes itself, that Rafi should hang himself. As the words go down I know I'm on to something dramatic and powerful. I'm also doing something which will be depressing. I've no idea how this suicide will affect the rest

of the film and no idea what it means or says. I can work that out later. It's a relief to have had a new idea.

10 JANUARY: I accompany the location and production managers to North Kensington to look at locations for the scenes at the beginning of the film. To the thirtieth floor of a tower block that won design awards in the sixties, with several young kids in the lift. We walk around other blocks in the area. They are filthy, derelict places, falling down, graffiti-sprayed, wind-blown, grim and humming with the smell of shit, implacable in the hatred of humanity they embody. The surrounding shops are barricaded with bars and wire mesh. I was brought up in London. It's my city. I'm no Brit, but a Londoner. And it's more filthy and run-down than it's ever been.

13 JANUARY: Seven in the morning and freezing cold. Streets covered with snow. Behind me I can hear the tubes rattling along at the back of the house. I'm not in the mood for re-writing this thing.

These West London streets by the railway line have gone wrong. In 1978 most of the five-storey houses near the railway line here had crumbling pillars, peeling façades and broken windows. They were derelict, inhabited by itinerants, immigrants and drug-heads. On the balcony opposite a man regularly practised the bag-pipes at midnight. Now the street is crammed with people who work for a living. Young men wear striped shirts and ties; the women wear blue jumpers with white shirts, turned-up collars and noses, and pearls. They drive Renault 5s and late at night, as you walk along the street, you can see them in their clean, shameless basements, having dinner parties and playing Trivial Pursuits on white tablecloths. The centre of the city is now inhabited by the young rich and serviced by everyone else.

25 JANUARY: New York. The city is snowbound, and every time you look round, someone has skidded on to their back in the street.

Frears is a prisoner in his hotel room, doing publicity for *Prick Up Your Ears*. Food and drink are brought up. Between interviews he looks out of the window at Central Park. His schedule is exhausting. There was a time when I thought that talking about yourself to someone who said little, listened intently and recorded what you said, was the ideal relationship. But after the first three hours your tongue is dry, your mouth will not work, your jaws ache as after hours of fellatio.

26 JANUARY: We troop off to an award dinner. Like executioners, photographers in black balaclavas crowd the entrance. Going in, I realize we've arrived too early. We sit down and they bring us our food while others continue to arrive. Sissy Spacek and Lynne Redgrave, obviously experienced at the awards game, time it just right, so that when they appear the whole room is in place and is forced to turn and look at them. Photographers shove through the crowd and climb across tables to get to them.

I spot Norman Mailer. He is stocky, his face red and healthy, though he looks frail when he walks. I'm thrilled at having the great man in the audience when I receive my award for the *Laundrette* screenplay. When the playwright Beth Henley announces my name, I eagerly look out from the podium for Mailer. I start into my speech but I stutter and almost stop: Mailer's place is vacant and across the restaurant I see him rapidly mounting the stairs to watch the final of the Super Bowl on TV.

27 JANUARY: In the evening to the Café Luxembourg with Leon from Cinecom, the company that, along with Channel 4, is financing our film. Frears and I refer to Leon as 'the man who owns us', which he doesn't seem to mind. He's thirty-four, friendly and intelligent, with long hair in a pigtail. Bevan, Frears and I are apprehensive about pressure his company might put on us to massage or roll our film in a certain direction.

29 JANUARY: I ride the subway across New York to have lunch with Leon at the Russian Tea Room. In the subway car a couple with a kid kiss shamelessly. A legless black man in a wheelchair propels himself through the car, carrying a paper cup. Everyone gives him something. The streets here are full of beggars now; every block someone asks you for money. Before going out I ensure I have some loose change to give away, just as I would in Pakistan.

The young people on the street in New York are far less original than kids in Britain. Despite unemployment and poverty, the kids in London, have taste: they're adventurous and self-conscious. They're walking exhibitions: billboards of style, wearing jumble sale and designer clothes together. In Britain fashion starts on the street. Here the kids are sartorial corpses. They all wear sports clothes. There are even women wearing business suits and running shoes.

The Russian Tea Room has a festive atmosphere. There are shining samovars, red and gold pom poms on the lampshades, and the staff wear red tunics. It's Santa's grotto with waitresses. Powerful New York agents reserve several booths for their clients and associates and then move from booth to booth like door-to-door salesmen, dealing and negotiating.

Leon has brought some serious reinforcements to deal with the script 'difficulties', a beautiful and smart woman called Shelby.

Shelby leans forward and tells me she has just read all five drafts of the script. I am flattered. But more, she has compared and contrasted them all. More wine? She talks knowledgeably about each draft. She seems to know them better than I do. Scene eighty-one in draft two, she says, is sharper than scene seventy-nine in draft four. Perhaps I could go back to that? Well. I look at her. She is telling me all this in a kindly tone. In the end, she implies, it is all up to me. But . . . She expresses her reservations, which are quite substantial, and argued at length.

I nod to everything, not wanting to induce indigestion. I am also experimenting with the Zen method of bending with the wind, so that when the storm stops, the tree of my spirit will gaily snap back to its usual upright position. But will this helpful puffing ever stop?

We talk about the end of the film and the hanging of Rafi. They suggest Rafi be murdered by the Ghost. I manage to say that this would be predictable. Leon says: How can a ghost murdering a politician in an anarchist commune be predictable?

By now I am sucking and licking on light ice-cream with whipped cream and grenadine: Shelby is into her stride. Perhaps my lack of response means I am thinking about what she is saying? The script hasn't necessarily improved at all; it's become cruder, more obvious. Why have you developed the black women, Vivia and Rani? Well . . . I almost begin to fight back when she starts to fumble in her bag. She brings out a letter. There, read this please, she says. It's from someone who cares.

The letter, from a reader in the company, is addressed to me. Its tone implores me to see sense: 'The version I read in October was just about perfect and the fifth draft seems a little preachy and one-dimensional. It's lost so much for the sake of clarity and it's not nearly as successful . . . I hope you'll consider going back to the terrific screenplay you wrote in October.'

I leave the restaurant burping on caviar and heavy with ice-cream. All afternoon I wander round the city. Two dozen wasps are free within my cranium. Perhaps all those people are right. I don't know. Can't tell. God knows. My judgement has gone, swept away by the wind of all this advice. Eventually I settle down in an Irish bar—a grimy piece of Dublin—and have a few beers.

5 FEBRUARY: London. Good to talk to Frears again. We both see that some of the people around us have made us gloomy by expressing doubts. Frears is an extraordinarily cheerful man who takes great pleasure in his work and in the company of others. There's nothing poisonous or negative in him. He says this is the hardest film he's made. He said the same about *Laundrette*, and I remember feeling glad that we're doing something risky and dangerous.

12 FEBRUARY: I go into the production offices off Ladbroke Grove to talk about casting. There are a row of offices with glass partitions. About twenty yards away I can see Bevan waving his arms. He dashes up the corridor to tell me there's been a call from the States to say I've been nominated for an Oscar. I call my agent and she says: Goody, that'll put a couple of noughts on your fee.

17 FEBRUARY: To see Claire Bloom. Chat for a while to Philip Roth, who lives with Claire. Roth fizzes and whirls with mischief and vibrant interest in the world. I mention that I've written a story but it may not be accepted in the United States because of the sex and four-letter words in it. He says he's had similar trouble: imagine

the nuisance, he tells me, of having to find a suitable synonym for the perfectly adequate 'dogshit' just so your story can be published in the prissy *New Yorker*. He also tells us with great glee that he'd written a story called 'The Tormented Cunt' but had to change the title.

6 MARCH: Night shoot. A row of derelict houses and shops with asbestos over their windows with gas-fired jets in little boxes in front of them to give the impression of the neighbourhood in flames. There are exploding cars, fire-engines, ambulances and a mob of 200 extras, plus police with riot shields. There are four cameras. It's massive, for a British film, and brilliantly organized. I think of the script; it just says something like: *In the background the riot continues*!

The rioting itself is frightening and cathartic. It's not difficult to see how compelling taking part in a riot can be and how far out of yourself such compulsion can take you. On some takes, the kids playing rioters continue to attack the extras in uniform after we've cut. Some of the extras playing police threaten to go home.

13 MARCH: Today Frears rails at the actors for lacking flair, for thinking too much about their costumes, for being too passive and not helping him enough. He's been cheerful all through it, but now the strain is starting to tell. It's partly because the scene we're shooting is very complicated. The cold—working fifteen hours a day in snow flurries—is getting people down. Frears also blames me for this scene going badly: 'You should never set a scene as complicated as this outside,' he says. 'Haven't you learned that yet? I can't control it out here!'

20 MARCH: There is much in the newspapers today about the verdict of the Blakelock trial, where a policeman was hacked to death during an uprising on the Broadwater Farm Estate in North London. A man was sentenced to life imprisonment for the killing. The uprising followed the death of a respected middle-aged black woman, Cynthia Jarrett, who died of a heart attack during a police raid on her home on the estate. It's all depressing, as was the incident I based the opening of the film around: the shooting of a

71

black woman, Cherry Groce, who was permanently paralysed after being shot accidentally during another police raid.

But what are we doing using this material in the film? Today, when confronted once more by the racism and violence and waste of the Broadwater Farm Estate uprising, our little film has to be justified over again.

28 MARCH: Los Angeles. I wind down the window of the cab as we hit the freeway and accelerate. Air rushes in, gloriously warm to me after an English winter of freezing balls. I pull three layers of clothes over my head. LA is blazingly green and bright: everything is as resplendent as if I'd taken LSD. Walking into the hotel, the Château Marmont, I am convinced that the grass has been sprayed with gloss and the air pumped full of perfume. It is eucalyptus.

The phone calls begin as soon as I open the windows of my room: from agents, press people, producers, all recommending the numerous totally beautiful human beings I should impress in the next few days. I say to my agent: But most of these people do not interest me. She says: Dear, all that is important is that you interest them. As long as they're saying your name as they eat all round this city you've got nothing to worry about.

To bed to read Robert Stone's *Children of Light* about a burned-out screenwriter living at the Château Marmont, drinking and drugging himself while a screenplay he wrote is being shot in another country.

31 MARCH: The day of the Oscars. People leave work after lunch to get home in time to watch it on TV. All over the city, there are Oscar parties in lounges and beside pools. Turn on the TV and grave pundits are weighing the merits of Bob Hoskins and Paul Newman; open a paper and predictions are being made. The Oscars are unavoidable.

A last swim on my back in the hotel pool, watching the sky through the trees, followed by the extensive pleasures of the bathroom where I sip champagne and receive phone calls and gifts. Outside the limo is already waiting. By now I have definitely had enough of people saying: It's enough to be nominated, it's an honour in itself. By now that isn't enough; by now I want to win; by now, I know I will win!

When your black stretched limo pulls up outside the venue all you see are other limos, a shimmering sea of shining metal. When you slide out, you see the high grandstands lining the long walk to the entrance. In these packed grandstands screaming people wave placards with the names of their favourite films. '*Platoon, Platoon, Platoon!*' someone is yelling. Another person bellows: '*Room With A View, Room With A View!*' One man holds a placard which says: 'Read The Bible.'

Inside there are women in long dresses and men in tuxedos, with small signs around their necks saying, 'The 59th Academy Awards'. They are the seat-fillers. Their role is essential, so that when the cameras sweep across the auditorium there isn't an empty seat in the place, whereas in fact the sensible people are in the bar watching it all, like everyone else, on TV. In the bar with friends we look out for stars and discuss them: Didn't Elizabeth Taylor look tiny and didn't her head look big? Perhaps she's had all the fat in her body sucked out by the modish vacuum method. Doesn't Bette Davis look shrivelled and fragile? Doesn't Sigourney Weaver look terrific, and what was wrong with Jane Fonda and doesn't Dustin Hoffman always look the same?

When your award comes up and Shirley MacLaine starts to read out the names of the nominees, you silently run over your speech, remove a speck of dried semen from your collar and squeeze the arms of your seat, ready to propel yourself into the sight of a billion people. You wonder where in the sitting room you'll put it, or maybe you should hide it somewhere in case it's stolen. What does it weigh anyway? You'll soon find out.

When they make a mistake and don't read your name you vow never to attend any such ridiculous ceremony of self-congratulation, exhibitionism and vulgarity again.

1 APRIL: I spend the next day by the pool drinking iced tea; several young producers come by. My impression is that they have come to have a look at you, check you out, see if there's anything in you for them. One drives me around the city in his Jag. He asks me if I want to fly to San Francisco for lunch. I ask if there isn't

anywhere a little nearer we can go. He swears eternal love and a contract.

2 APRIL: I return to find Frears in heaven on the set, sitting with his Plimsolls up and gossiping, waiting for a shot to be set up. To ruin his day I tell him about the directors I've met in Hollywood and how much they earn and the kind of luxury in which they live. Frears goes into agonies of frustration and jealousy. He keeps saying: 'What am I doing here? Fuck all this art, just give me the money!' This makes Shashi laugh and laugh.

11 APRIL: In a tiny studio off the Harrow Road we film the interior scenes set in a caravan. As Frances and Roland roll around naked, Frears sinks down in a chair next to me.

'I've become completely paranoid,' he says. 'I've had it. Is this any good or not?'

'I don't know,' I say.

'What's it about anyway?' he says.

'Fuck knows,' I reply. He needs support. Anything above a whisper is interpreted as hatred.

'We should have had more time,' he says after a while. 'About two more weeks would have done it. But it would have cost 300,000 pounds and we didn't have it.'

I leave early and go to a book publishing party. On the way I see the police have stopped a black man and woman, and are questioning them.

It's odd going to the party: the world going on as normal. Later, I see someone I recognize coming towards me, black hair sticking up, face white, a week's growth on his face. I try to work out who it is. At last I know: Stephen Frears.

30 APRIL: Mick Audsley, the editor, has been furiously cutting the film for the last two weeks. When we all walk into the preview theatre, Mick's as nervous as a playwright on a first night. I reassure him. But it's his film now; this is his draft. 'I've taken some stuff out,' he says nervously. 'And moved other things around.'

For the first forty minutes I can't understand what's happened to the film. It's more shaped now, but less bizarre somehow, less unpredictable. I suppress my own laughter in order to register every gurgle and snort of pleasure around me. But there is nothing: complete silence. At the end I feel drained and disappointed. I feel like putting a jacket over my head.

21 MAY: Frears and I moan to each other about the Tory election broadcast which went out yesterday: its hideous nationalism, verging on neo-fascism; its talk of 'imported foreign ideologies like socialism' and its base xenophobic appeals.

An election has been called. I do some leafleting for the Labour Party. I cover estates that I walk past every day but haven't been inside since the last election. I wonder if they have really changed since the last time around. My trips to New York and Los Angeles now seem utterly unimportant when there are parts of my own city, streets but five minutes away, that are unknown to me.

I walk off the main road and across the grass to the entrance of the first block. The door is open; the glass in the door is smashed. A woman in filthy clothes stands in the entrance waving her arms around. She is stoned. I go on through and into the silver steel-cage of the lift. At the top of the block the windows are smashed and the wind blows sharply across the landing, shifting broken bottles, cans and general detritus.

Someone has a sign on their door: 'Don't burgle me I have nothin.' Many of the doors have been smashed in and are held together with old bits of wood. The stench of piss and shit fills the place.

An old distressed woman in a nightdress comes out of her flat and complains that a party has been going on downstairs for two days. One man comes to the door with a barely controlled Alsatian: 'Come and take back this fucking leaflet,' he screams at me, 'come and get it, mate!'

It is difficult to explain to the people who live here why they should vote Labour; it is difficult to explain to them why they should vote at all.

23 MAY: Last day of shooting. Bits and pieces. Sarah has yet to see the film. She rang me last night, angry at being excluded, thinking this was deliberate, or just more evidence of my general

indifference. Whatever it is, she has started to call the film *Hanif Gets Paid, Sarah Gets Exploited*.

8 JULY: To see the almost finished *Sammy and Rosie*.

I sit through the film in a kind of haze, unable to enjoy or understand it. I can see how complete it is now, but I have no idea of what it will mean for other people, what an audience seeing it fresh will make of it.

After the screening someone says how surprised he is that the film got made at all, that somehow the police didn't come round to the house and say: 'This kind of thing isn't allowed!' It won't be when the new Obscenity Bill goes through.

Later that night I go out for a drink with a friend in Notting Hill. We go to a pub. It's a dingy place, with a dwarf barmaid. It's mostly black men there, playing pool. And some white girls, not talking much, looking tired and unhealthy. On the walls are warnings against the selling of drugs on the premises. Loud music, a DJ, a little dancing. A fight breaks out in the next bar. Immediately the pub is invaded by police. They drag the fighters outside and throw them into a van. People gather round. It's a hot night. And soon the air is full of police sirens. Six police vans show up. The cops jump out and grab anyone standing nearby. They are very truculent and jumpy, though no one has been especially aggressive. We leave and drive along the All Saints Road, an area known for its drug dealers. Twice we're stopped and questioned: Where are we going? Why are we in the area? What are our names? Black people in cars are pulled out and searched. Eventually we park and walk around. The area is swamped with police. They're in pairs, stationed every twenty-five yards from each other. There's barely anyone else in the street.

WYCLIFFE KATO
AN ESCAPE FROM
KAMPALA

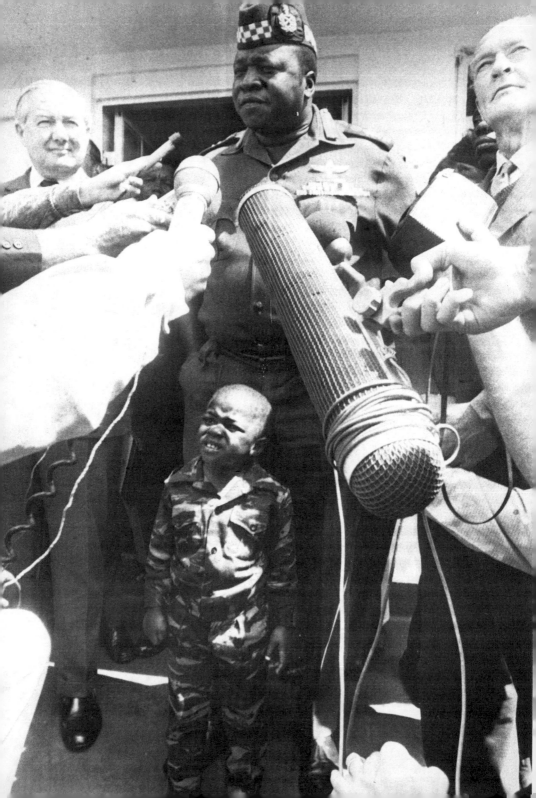

The Arrest

I have a story. It's an escape story, and one I have been wanting to tell for ten years. The story is set in Uganda: the Uganda of President Idi Amin Dada.

I was a professional man, with years of experience in civil aviation. And I was, I suppose, quite successful. I had a farm in the country, a wife and eight children. I had a place to stay when I worked in the city, a car, even a driver. I was not the kind of man who should figure in the story I am about to tell. Except that I was living then in the Uganda of President Idi Amin Dada, where coming from the wrong tribe, or having a beautiful girlfriend, or driving a shiny car, or being too strict at the office, or asking a messenger boy to make you a cup of tea, was a potential death sentence. And I had been an unwitting character in something much worse: President Idi Amin Dada's greatest humiliation.

My story begins on Friday, 9 September 1977, when I was arrested.

But it really begins in the early morning hours of 4 July 1976, when Israeli commandos flew 2,000 miles from Tel Aviv to release the hostages held at Entebbe Airport in Uganda. I was at the time Assistant Director General of Civil Aviation for the East African Community, and was responsible for air traffic in Kenya, Tanzania and Uganda. Although I was working in Nairobi when the Air France jet was hijacked to Entebbe, I was in touch with the Ugandan authorities on an hourly basis. At the outset, I informed the Ugandan Air Force that it must not rule out the possibility of a rescue attempt. I was told not to worry: everything was under control; Amin was negotiating with the hijackers; the Big Man himself was at the steering wheel. A few nights later the Israelis arrived, and killed the Ugandan soldiers guarding Entebbe, killed the terrorists and rescued the hijackers. Amin was furious. He took his hands off the steering wheel and sent his thugs from the State Research Bureau to look for scapegoats. They found many. They also found my friends Rweigembe and Muhindo. Why, the State Research Bureau demanded, hadn't this pair of unarmed air traffic controllers been able to stop the Israeli attack? Muhindo's body was discovered the following week in Namanve Forest. There were nails driven through his forehead. Rweigembe was also found. There was of course no autopsy and therefore no death certificate; I had to inspect the body myself to confirm his death for the Nairobi company that had insured his life.

Shortly thereafter I was arrested as well, but I was cleared of all suspicion, and several months later I was promoted to Director of Civil Aviation. I suppose I was able to understand Amin's fury—the Israeli raid was a national humiliation—but I was also made uneasy by it. For even though I had already been arrested once, I often feared that the events at Entebbe would catch up with me. On Friday, 9 September 1977, I found out how.

I remember the morning as fine and sunny. I had spent the night in Kampala and was driven that morning to Entebbe, about twenty-five miles from the city, for a flight to Montreal. I was going there along with several others for an international meeting on civil aviation, and had secured a travel clearance through one of the ministers. It was a new procedure, getting clearance through a minister, and it had only been introduced because the old system, under which all foreign travel had to be authorized by Amin's Vice-President, proved unworkable: the Vice-President couldn't read.

At the airport, all tickets had to be endorsed again, this time by a State Research official, who sat at a counter some twenty yards from the check-in. I was joined by Louis Kerujik, an under-secretary at the Aviation Ministry, who would be travelling with me. The State Research official was a woman. She looked as though she might be Rwandese. Or perhaps she came from the western part of the country. She was tall, with wide hips and shapely, attractive legs. She was cheerful and had an engaging smile. I could not understand how she could let herself work as an agent for Amin.

There was something that distressed her, however: our clearance to leave Uganda, she said, did not seem to be entirely in order. She asked us to step behind the counter, into the airport's State Research office.

Inside was another woman, sitting behind a desk, operating a radio. She was serious and fierce and said little. A young man came in and asked my friend to follow him. That was the last time I ever saw Mr Kerujik. I learned later that he was permitted to leave. He made it to Montreal. I suspect he had been set free because he came from Amin's home area of Arua. People from Amin's tribe rarely got into trouble.

I was alone, facing the State Research woman. I was in that office for over thirty minutes. State Research boys came in and out, laughing and joking. They were polite. But I was in a panic: I began to fear that I was about to be arrested, and, although I had survived arrest before, I also knew that an arrest usually ended in death. I thought of running away and stood up. The woman reached for a pistol. I sat down again. My panic increased. I had forgotten by then about my flight or reaching Montreal. I thought of my family. There was no phone on the farm; there was no way to reach my wife. There was no one here waiting with me at the airport, except for Louis Kerujik, and he had simply disappeared. Nobody would expect to hear from me for six weeks. If I was arrested, I would not be missed for perhaps two months. A lot can happen in two months.

The boys who worked for the State Research Bureau had quite a reputation. They were usually fairly young—between the the ages of eighteen and twenty-five—and were accomplished kidnappers. Their victims would be abducted, killed, the body disposed of, and only then would ransom be demanded from the relatives. It was the boys from the State Research Bureau who finally escorted me from the airport to the parking lot: 'There is something we would like to discuss with you.' There were six of them with me in the car. They were cheerful and talked constantly. '*Mzee*,' one asked, 'why are you so quiet? Are you scared?' They had pistols in their socks.

A few months before my brother-in-law had been taken by the State Research boys. I had searched through the corpses dumped in Namanve Forest for his body. A few of the corpses were fresh but most had rotted beyond recognition. Some had their wrists cut off. One had not, and my guide grabbed the arm and chopped off the hand: there was a watch on the wrist. He was pleased: it was rare to find a corpse with anything valuable. I had failed to find the body of my brother-in-law.

The State Research boys drove me towards the State House but went past the turn-off and on towards Kampala. We turned left up the Speke Road, past the Imperial Hotel and on to the junction at All Saints Cathedral. This is where Amin claimed that Archbishop Luwum had died in a car accident, together with Ministers Olyema and Oboth-Ofumbi. Whose hands had been on the steering wheel that time? We drove on and turned into an enclosure just past the cathedral, on the right-hand side. I tried to pray but I could not get past the first line of the Lord's Prayer: 'Our Father, who art in Heaven . . . Our Father, who art in Heaven.' I couldn't remember anything else. We had arrived at Nakasero. Nakasero was the headquarters of the State Research Bureau. It was notorious. It was Amin's slaughterhouse.

I was searched, and taken to a room on the ground floor. I told myself that there had been some kind of mistake: my documents were, after all, in order, and it was only a few months since I had been promoted—by Amin himself. But then the guards reappeared and emptied my briefcase. I was then kneed in the stomach, and kicked in the ribs and the side of the head.

When they left I noticed that there was one other person in the room, an old woman, sitting on the floor in the corner. She had swollen eyes and a terrible face. We sat together for several hours. The day before, she said, she shared this room with a married couple. During the night soldiers appeared, one after another, and raped the wife. The husband sat where I was sitting now, on an empty Pepsi-Cola crate. When the soldiers had finished with the wife, they removed the couple. She went on to tell me how people were tortured here and how they were killed. 'Be brave,' she said, 'pull yourself together. What you are about to see is worse than you ever imagined.'

She asked if I knew what Winston Churchill had called Uganda. He had called it the pearl of Africa. The next day, I was moved downstairs.

In the Cell

This is what the cell was like. It lay in a basement, at the bottom of two flights of concrete stairs. It was built from brick and painted white, but the paint was chipped and discoloured. The first thing I heard was a man screaming to Jesus to save him. The first thing I saw was a soldier kicking the same man in the head, and beating him with a rifle butt. But my first impression was the air: it was thick and hot, and there was an overpowering stench of stale sweat and human excrement.

At the bottom of the stairs was an open area. On the right was a long corridor closed off by an iron gate. This was called Cell One. There were about thirty prisoners in Cell One. There was no room to sit down and no ventilation. There was also no water. Some of the people in Cell One were handcuffed, some not; they were constantly begging cigarettes from guards, complaining of thirst. The men in this cell, I later learned, were coffee smugglers, pickpockets, thieves, rapists and murderers.

On the left was another cell, much less crowded, where all the prisoners were handcuffed. It was about forty or fifty feet wide and around thirty feet deep, with a pillar in the centre. There were three ventilators at the back, nine feet above the ground and about two feet across. The cell had once been used as a storage area, and in one corner there was a large pile of rubbish. There were crates and clothing and shoes. There were even two big film projectors, mounted on iron stands. The walls were chipped and stained. There was some graffiti, and, in the corners, mildew and moss. Near the gate, there was a steel dustbin, with excrement spilling down the side. The night before it had rained heavily and the rain had poured through the three ventilators, flooding the room. Everywhere in the water there was movement, and I realized that it was from rats. There were rats everywhere; I have no idea how many: maybe a hundred, maybe two hundred.

This was Cell Two. The guard handcuffed me and then removed my shoes. I was put inside.

There were only seven men in Cell Two, and they were waiting to die. They were uneasy at first, suspecting that I might be a spy. But it did not take them long to overcome their suspicions: they were desperate for news from outside the cell.

Fifteen others had been in the cell the day before, but they had been removed during the night. I was asked whether it was true that they had been executed. The guards had said so, but the soldiers were unreliable and liked to play tricks. I told them that I didn't know. But when I was driven through Kampala, I told them, I had seen a gathering for a public firing squad. And, while sitting in the room with the old woman, I had overheard the sentries outside talk of an execution. They had mentioned a man by the name of Nsereko. He was meant to have been a magician, for he refused to die. In the end, thirty-six shots had been fired into his chest.

For some time, no one said anything. Nsereko, it appears, was not a man, but a boy. He had been with them in the cell the day before.

Cell Two was for political prisoners. Only those arrested on orders from Amin himself were locked up in Cell Two, and only three people could authorize a prisoner's release or his death. These were Amin and his henchmen Adrisi and the hated Englishman Bob Astles. If anyone from Cell Two was killed without Amin's orders, Amin was notified directly and a report prepared. There was some consolation in this: it protected the prisoners from any unforeseen accidents and some of the guards' more uncontrolled excesses.

Most of the prisoners in Cell Two were from the Ugandan Air Force, and had been involved in the recent attempt to assassinate Amin. They had planned to ambush his car near the cemetery on the road from Entebbe. Amin was hoping that they would confess under torture, so that he could try them publicly before executing them.

I learned all this from Pilot Officer Cadet Nicodemus Kasujja Majwala, from Bukolwa, Bulemezi County in Buganda. Kasujja was twenty-seven and a chatterbox. He spent facts like small change. He was a helicopter pilot, trained in the USSR. He was very boastful. He was, for instance, the best pilot in the Ugandan Air Force, even though he was merely a cadet. He was also the best fighter. He was also the strongest. He was also the most handsome. In fact there were few accomplishments at which he did not excel. After a bout of food-poisoning, everyone in the cell suffered diarrhoea; Kasujja, true to form, claimed the greatest volume, the least noise, the most inoffensive smell . . . But Kasujja was also clever. He had found a piece of metal in the rubbish heap and honed it to a sharp point on the concrete floor. With this he was able to release the locks of our handcuffs. He said this was a triumph for Soviet training, which, of course, was the best there is.

There was something else about Kasujja: his right leg was amputated at the knee. He told me what had happened. After the coup failed, he was shot in the leg while trying to escape. He was dragged before Amin. Kasujja agreed to betray his fellow-conspirators and proceeded to take Amin's men on a wild goose chase all over Kampala, pretending disbelief and consternation when no one was found. Meanwhile, many of his friends escaped.

'Go and cut off his leg,' Amin had ordered.

Kasujja introduced me to the others in the cell.

First, Major Patrick Kimumwe: he was slender, disciplined, and somehow succeeded in wearing a tweed jacket, despite the heat and the damp of the prison. He had been in the army twelve years and was only thirty-one, although he looked like an older man. He had an officer's habit of behaving with great seriousness, so that he would be feared and, being feared, respected.

There was Lieutenant Nambale: small, about twenty-four, with a very dark skin. He had trained as a jet pilot, as had his friend Lieutenant Silvester Mutumba, also in his early twenties.

The other three from the Air Force were not pilots but technicians. Warrant Officer II Christopher Ssekalo had a broad chest and a bad temper. Kasujja said he usually lost it when playing draughts. 'It's because I beat him,' said Kasujja. Warrant Officer I Eddie Ssendawula was short and light-skinned, about thirty-three.

Which left Warrant Officer II John Okech. He was the most impressive of the lot. He was tall and extremely fat, a barrel of a man. He wore a black shirt—although most of the buttons had popped off—and a pair of trousers that were too long and kept getting tangled in his feet. Kasujja described Okech as a gentle man, unless you got to the food before him. 'Then he is no longer so gentle. Okech likes to share everything out himself, to make sure he gets the biggest portions.' Okech roared with laughter: a happy fat man.

It seems strange to say it, but I felt encouraged by the men around me, hopeful. My arrest was most certainly a mistake. After all, these men had actually tried to kill President Idi Amin Dada. I had committed no such offence. I had been associated with the Entebbe disaster, that was all. Or else someone in my office had informed on me, wanting to get back at me for being the boss. Assassination? I wasn't in the same division as these men.

Major Kimumwe asked me why I had been imprisoned.

I told him that I wasn't sure. I wasn't a political prisoner. I wasn't even opposed to the government. I believed in justice and the rule of law, and I had no reason to doubt that I would be treated fairly. On the whole, I had been treated fairly by the country, and had, in turn, obeyed its rules. My being here was an error. I would soon be released.

Kasujja whistled in disbelief.

Major Kimumwe pointed to the watch on his wrist. He said it had belonged to the boy who died the day before. He pointed to the chipped brick in the walls: they were from bullets. And after showing me the dried blood, he asked if I was, perhaps, out of my mind. Or just being naïve. 'Once you're in here, you don't get out alive,' he said.

I didn't entirely believe him.

Conversation at Nakasero Prison was always conducted in a whisper.

They spoke of women. What was the most important feature in a woman? Was it the breasts or the buttocks? Was it the legs? The lips?

They spoke of torture. They had suffered many different kinds. Whippings, electric shocks, dunkings, canes across the face. It was astonishing how much pain, for instance, could be administered by a simple cigarette lighter. They described what the pain was like when you were grabbed by the testicles and the testicles were twisted until you passed out.

They spoke of death. There were also many different ways to die at Nakasero. You could be strangled—that was quite common. You could be tortured or simply beaten until your brain bled. You could have your chest opened with a knife. Or you could be shot by firing squad. Everyone agreed that being shot by a firing squad was the best way to die.

> Germany is the right place where, when Hitler was the Prime Minister and supreme commander, he burnt over six million Jews. This is because Hitler and all German people knew that Israelis are not people who are working in the interest of the people of the world and that is why they burnt the Israelis alive with gas in the soil of Germany.
>
> Telegram from Idi Amin Dada to Dr Kurt Waldheim, Secretary General of the United Nations, 11 September 1972.

But mainly they spoke about escaping. How was it possible? How could they manage it? Could they overwhelm a guard and shoot their way out using his gun? Too risky. Could they somehow make a key? Or a hack-saw? Too difficult. It sounded as though they'd had this conversation a hundred times. Escape was an obsession.

In the afternoon a guard brought food: one banana between eight and a repulsive-smelling stew which Okech said was made from the head of a cow. 'No meat at all,' he said, serving the stew round the cell. Ssekalo and Kasujja played draughts. Kasujja won, and boasted of his superior brain, his success at draughts being the obvious proof. Ssekalo was furious, and swept the board aside, sending pieces skittering around the cell. He said that Kasujja was an idiot. Kasujja hopped up and down.

That evening Ssendawula advanced an idea that I was surprised had not occurred to the others long before.

'Gentlemen, behold our saviour,' Ssendawula said and made a melodramatic gesture towards the ventilator. There was a metal screen in front of it. He said, 'We have been stupid not to think of this before. We take away the screen, then up through the ventilation shaft and into the yard.' The suggestion resulted in a tremendous excitement. It was a new idea. It was also an idea that everyone thought would work. There was no debate: they decided to escape that night. I was asked to come along: I declined.

'Why should I risk my life in an escape attempt? And what will you do once you get out? Borrow a car from one of the soldiers? Wait for a bus? I have been arrested before, and I was cleared of all charges. I will be cleared again. There is still a system of justice.'

Major Kimumwe looked at me and said nothing.

At nine o'clock the fluorescent light above our heads was turned off. That night, before we fell asleep, the guards removed three prisoners from Cell One.

I slept through the escape attempt, and in the morning when I woke my seven companions were already up. Major Kimumwe began by saying prayers. Nambale was in a tetchy mood. He said there had bloody well better be an afterlife. The attempt had been a failure.

They explained what happened. At around two in the morning, Kasujja had unlocked the handcuffs, and Ssekalo, the tallest, climbed on top of two wooden crates to attack the ventilator. He had worked on it for several minutes before reporting that the grille of gauze wire could not be moved: it would have to be cut. There were glass slats which would have to be broken. And all this was going to make a lot of noise. Okech then tried to remove the grille, but he also failed. Their escape was obviously going to require more preparation.

Even though they had failed, the mood the next morning was one of optimism: at least there was the possibility of an escape; there was a strategy. They asked me again if I would join them, and again I declined.

Major Kimumwe reminded me of the three men who had been removed the night before. 'Where are they now?' he asked. 'What do you think has happened to them?' Major Kimumwe was right: they were still missing. 'How can we make you understand?' he said. 'No one has left this room alive. *No one.* Look at the blood. Look at the shoes. Where do you think they come from. Whose trousers do you think those are? You must think of escaping.'

I said nothing. My case was surely different from theirs. I said little all morning. I was thinking about my chances. I was praying.

Just before lunch, two State Research boys appeared at our cell gate. One was the leader of the group which had arrested me at the airport. He shouted, 'Where is the director of Civil Aviation?' Nobody said anything. 'Are you deaf, you fools?'

In 1952, I was told when I was going to die. I was told this in a dream. I was told also I will be the highest rank in the army in Uganda, I will be head of State and also when I have a lot of people criticizing me it's very good for me. I was also told that an attempt might be made on my life, and the people who made that attempt would be crushed completely. And it is true.

Idi Amin Dada, interviewed by David Frost,
1 April 1973.

I thought of two possibilities: freedom and death. I said, 'Here I am, sir.'

A sheaf of papers was thrust through the bars: the travellers' cheques I had bought for my trip, more than 3,500 American dollars.

'Sign all of them,' he said. 'Make sure you use your usual signature.'

I signed the cheques. They left, but returned within minutes. 'Look!' said the State Research boy, screaming with fury. 'Your signature on the cheques is different from that in your passport. Sign again. And this time sign on the back of each cheque as well.'

I did as instructed and they went, this time for good.

'Don't worry,' said Kasujja. 'Now they've taken all that money, you might be released. You probably will be released. They've no serious case against you. I wish I were you.'

There was a silence. Then Nambale spoke, quietly. He said Kasujja was being extremely stupid, as usual. He said he was sorry, but the taking of the money could only hasten my death. 'Don't you see? They will feel too guilty to release you. In fact, now, having got your signature, there is no reason to keep you alive. It confirms what we've been saying all along. They don't expect any of us to come out of here alive.'

That night two things happened.

There was a commotion in Cell One. An old Kenyan had asked for a razor blade to commit suicide. The guard agreed, but said the old man was not to slit his wrists; if he wanted to kill himself, he must chew the blade and swallow. The old man did this. His moaning was long and terrible. When he was dead, an hour later, the guard came over to our cell and picked Ssendawula and Okech and me to carry away the body. We took the old Kenyan up the steps and were instructed to throw the corpse on the back of a truck. His face had no lips. His mouth was a mess of blood and shredded flesh.

Later that night, there was a terrible thumping. There was an insistent rasping sound, and more thumping. It seemed to come from the top of the stairs.

'Strangulation,' Major Kimumwe whispered in the dark, 'is probably the most popular method here for killing the prisoners.'

'Major Kimumwe,' I said, 'I am with you. We must escape.'

The Escape Dream

Tuesday. Early in the morning the sentries came to check on us. They relieved their boredom by shouting abuse. They let us know we were at their mercy. They could make us eat our own shit, or theirs. They could torture us at will.

This no longer concerned us. We had our dream of escape: we would go out through the ventilator; we would cross the courtyard; and then, having crossed the courtyard, we would walk to safety. It would be simple, we said. We had searched through the rubbish and found a variety of nails, rusted spoons and other pieces of metal which could be used as tools. Ssekalo started in on the gauze. Progress was slow, terribly slow. It became obvious that we had underestimated the difficulty of the task. Ssekalo worked the entire morning to create a tiny hole in the gauze through which the glass could be seen. Then he widened the hole some more, and broke the glass.

The noise was a terrifying crack. We froze. Detection seemed certain. We awaited the arrival of the guards. And sure enough we heard boots coming down the concrete stairs. 'Let us pray,' said Major Kimumwe and Okech at once, as though they'd rehearsed it. We bowed our heads while Major Kimumwe said the Lord's Prayer and waited for the guard to unlock the gate and come in. He didn't. He turned round and went away.

Kasujja chose this moment to announce that Russian guns were remarkably, *unbelievably*, silent, and had in fact been used by the Israeli commandos in the raid at Entebbe. Everyone burst out laughing. 'You, Kasujja, are far too stupid to have been a pilot,' said Nambale.

Wednesday. Ssekalo reported that there were steel bars behind the glass.

'Bars?' said Major Kimumwe.

'Bars?' said Kasujja. 'We'll never be able to move them.'

Major Kimumwe said we shouldn't give up. If we could cut the rest of the gauze, if we could get rid of the glass and make space to lever at the bars, if we could do all this without being detected, and if we could do it before we were hauled before a firing squad, then there was a chance.

'Some chance,' said Kasujja.

Ssekalo pressed on. He cut through the gauze and now wrapped each of the glass slats in a shirt he had found in the rubbish heap before breaking it. The effect was like using a gun with a silencer. With extreme care the fragments of glass were removed.

The process was agonizingly slow. But at last he was face to face with the iron bars. He could not contain his excitement. So much energy had gone into removing the gauze and the glass slats that it seemed our problems were over. They weren't. Ssekalo leaped up and found the bars quite immovable. They were so close together that he could not even squeeze his head through.

'It's hopeless,' he said.

Each of us wanted to see for himself. One by one we climbed up. Kasujja boasted that he would pull the bars apart with his hands. He failed. Even Soviet training could not help here.

Thursday. We were despondent. That morning, instead of his usual prayers, Major Kimumwe said: 'I pray for the dead. I pray for the dead because we are as good as dead. May our souls rest in peace. God has given up on Uganda.'

Kasujja said, 'If only I had been trained in China. I would be a magician. Then I would get our heads through those bars, no problem.' Even Nambale could not be bothered to tease him.

Okech started talking about food. When things weren't going well he always liked to talk about food. He said, 'I imagine such a feast. Goats will be slaughtered and roasted. There will be three goats. No, I think there will be *four* goats. And I will roast them myself. And eat them myself. There will also be beer, lots of beer.'

'Champagne,' said Nambale. 'What about champagne?'

'I think not,' said Okech. 'Beers all around.'

The escape dream was over.

It was Ssendawula who got it going again. He dragged the two film projectors from the rubbish heap. 'Look,' he said, pointing to the stand on which each projector was mounted. The stand was made of two diagonal metal pieces attached to metal struts. It looked heavy and strong. 'We can take this thing to pieces. Use the stand to bend the bars. What do you think?'

'And what do we use for tools?'

'There must be something,' Ssendawula said. 'We can think of something.'

We inspected the projectors. Ssendawula had a point. It might work. Kasujja giggled, saying: 'These projectors. Weren't they made in Russia?'

'I think so,' Ssendawula said.

Kasujja said, 'In that case, the Lord really has delivered us.'

We tightened our own security. We hung a shirt to hide the hole in the ventilator. We posted watch. Our code words for the guards were *masse* (Luganda for 'rat') and *panya* (Kiswahili for 'rat'), because there were so many rats in the cell. Kasujja stood at the gate. He was good at chasing people off. He would demand cigarettes or spout information about Soviet technology. Guards stalked off, hurling insults.

Using his fingers Ssendawula removed piece after piece of the projector, fashioning them together so he could dismantle the rest. It took him almost the entire day. Then we inserted the stand between the bars, deadening the noise by wrapping old shirts around the base.

'*Panya!*' Kasujja shouted, '*Panya!*' A guard was coming down the stairs. We pulled the stand away, hid it in the rubbish, and took up our positions, trying to be casual, playing draughts or leaning against the pillar.

'What are you saying?' said the guard.

Kasujja hopped up and down. 'My Lord,' he said, 'My Lord, there are so many rats here.'

'Good,' said the guard. 'I hope they will nibble your toes in your sleep.'

Friday; Saturday morning. For the next two days, the escape dream was definitely on again. We pushed the stand against the bars. And pushed again. Guards came. And went. And we pushed. We were tortured on several occasions. We were weak from hunger. For two days we were brought no food or water. The thirst made Kasujja and Nambale quarrel even more than usual. But one of the bars was beginning to bend, very slightly.

Saturday afternoon. The projector stand disintegrated. It fell to pieces in Okech's hands. Major Kimumwe cursed the day he had been born. God had forsaken us, he said. Was there any reason why we should continue praying to Him?

S aturday night. Several prisoners were taken from Cell One and shot. We were taken for torture. Ssekalo and Kasujja returned with swollen eyes and cheeks, and bruises all over. I was next up. The torture room was at the top of the building. It was about fourteen feet square and dimly lit. Three soldiers held whips. The interrogator sat at a small table. I was asked about the flight I was going to take abroad.

'Where were you going that day at the airport?'

'Montreal.'

'You were running away?'

'It was business.'

'Why were you running away?'

'I wasn't . . .'

It went on like this for thirty minutes or so. And then I was beaten.

Back in the cell we talked again about what it would be like to die, the various ways we might be killed. By now, we had heard someone being strangled at the top of stairs on five different occasions. The sound of someone being strangled is very disturbing. We all agreed that it was the worst possible death.

Except Okech. He said, 'I'd hate to starve.'

Kasujja said, 'None of you feels the same sorrow as me.'

'You are so stupid,' said Nambale.

'You don't understand,' said Kasujja. 'You have a child. The only child I'll ever have is unborn. My girlfriend is pregnant. Can you imagine leaving a pregnant girlfriend behind?'

S unday. Kasujja said he wanted to make a saw. Nambale asked him if he was, really, normal. I helped Kasujja grind the saw from a piece of metal. Anything to keep the dream going. The saw took us two hours to make, and was useless. 'Another triumph for the Soviets,' said Nambale.

I suggested that we take the motor from the projector, rig it to the light socket with a piece of cable, and press the motor against the bars. It took us another two hours to get the motor out. We took the strip light out and hooked up the cable. The motor worked, and made a noise like the end of the world. That was the end of that plan.

Two more prisoners were taken from Cell One.

I suggested we dismantle the other projector and try to use that stand to lever the bars. Nobody liked the idea. I said we must do something. I said that this time we should proceed with caution, to make sure the stand did not break. Ssendawula went to work.

To keep up spirits I made everyone talk about the possible escape routes. What would we do once we were out of the cell? There were three possibilities. The shortest route was to turn right after coming out of the ventilator, then duck into the concrete drains which led towards the prison entrance and came out on the other side of the road. That sounded simple. It wasn't. There would certainly be poisonous snakes. The second possibility was to crawl around the back of the building, climb the fence and go out through the grounds of the French Embassy which lay next to the prison. But the problem was that the area was so well lit, detection was certain. Which left route number three: out across the fences that were immediately opposite our building and then through the neighbouring compound.

Kasujja thought the fences were electrified. He said, 'One of us will have to sacrifice himself. Whoever touches the fence first will be electrocuted. But at the same time the fuses will blow. This will let the rest of us out.'

Nambale said, 'Don't you know that you're at the mercy of the rest of us?'

And the rest of us joined in. We teased Kasujja. We said it would be impossible to take him with us. After all, he had only one leg. He'd delay us, he could be seen easily at a distance, we'd all be captured. Kasujja dropped to the floor. He proved his skill at disguise. He imitated a dog. He imitated a cat. He scampered around the cell to prove his agility. He leaped high to prove he could scale the fences.

'All right,' said Nambale. 'You can come along. So long as you don't mention the Soviet Union.'

That night we heard the shots of a firing squad. The two prisoners removed that morning had been killed.

Monday morning. We pushed at the bars.

Monday afternoon. We pushed at the bars. We also tried to dig them out with spoons and nails.

Tuesday morning. We pushed at the bars. We tried making another hack-saw. Like the first, it fell apart.

Tuesday afternoon. This afternoon it was Okech who pushed at the bars. And, finally, the incredible happened. They suddenly gave way.

'Do the rest of you see what I see?' said Okech.

He punched the air. At the gate Kasujja hopped up and down. And Major Kimumwe prayed. He thanked God for showing his power. He begged forgiveness for his lack of faith.

We worked the bars further and further apart until all our heads would go through. A memory from childhood told me that where the head would go the rest of the body could follow. We would leave that night. It would be Ssekalo first, then Nambale, Mutumba, Ssendawula, Okech, Kasujja, Major Kimumwe and myself.

Tuesday night. At one a.m. we were ready. We had taken off our handcuffs and opened up the hole. Ssekalo climbed on to the boxes and Okech lifted him up and pushed him into the ventilator. He moved his shoulders to and fro, working himself down the ventilator. He pushed his head through the bars. He wriggled and then cried out in pain. His shoulders were too wide. Major Kimumwe also tried, but without success. I'd been wrong about the idea of the shoulders always following the head through a hole.

'*Panya!*' screamed Kasujja. '*PANYA!*'

A soldier with a machine-gun was coming down the steps. We took down the projector stand and pushed it into the rubbish. We didn't have time to cover the hole in the ventilator. The soldier was at the gate, holding a ring of keys. He was coming in. Kasujja hopped like a frantic monkey. He pleaded for cigarettes. He roared facts about the firepower of Soviet helicopter gunships. The soldier had his key in the lock. If he came in, he was certain to discover the wrecked ventilator. There was a strong chance that we would be killed there and then: 'Shot trying to escape'—a report that Amin would certainly accept.

Kasujja rolled on the floor, crying in sudden and terrible agony, demanding medicine and a fresh bandage. He said he was dying. He ripped off the filthy rag wrapped round his leg, exposing the stump, and flexed his muscles, causing the wound to open and close like a fish sucking water. It was a repulsive sight.

'I'm not a doctor,' said the soldier, 'and if I were I wouldn't waste medicine on scum like you.' He locked the gate and removed the key.

'Yes, my Lord,' said Kasujja, beaming.

Wednesday. We spent the day widening the gap between the bars. We organized ourselves for the escape. That night we lifted Ssekalo once more. This time he was able to force himself through the bars, but only just. Which meant that Kasujja and Okech had no chance. We conferred—Ssekalo's legs still poking out of the wall—and agreed to delay the escape until we were sure that even Okech, the biggest, could get through. In the meanwhile Ssekalo had inched his way further along and was almost through, disappearing from our view. Okech grabbed his feet. Ssekalo kicked his hands away. Okech took one leg, Kasujja the other, and they tugged the wriggling Ssekalo back into the cell.

'Why shouldn't I go?' said Ssekalo.

'What about us, you selfish bugger?' said Kasujja.

There was a fierce argument. The thin ones didn't want to wait; they said we could be executed at any time. The fatties wanted to wait; they said no further attempt should be made until, as agreed, Okech could get out. The mediums (myself included) didn't know; we felt confused, wanting to be fair to everyone. We took a vote. The vote was five to three. We were to stay.

That night another prisoner from Cell One was strangled at the top of the stairs.

Thursday. It is difficult to describe the state we were in. It was almost hysterical. For some, an escape was not just a dream, but a real possibility, one that could be realized merely by slipping through a hole in the wall. But for all of us, death was an even greater possibility. We felt our time was running out. We believed that at any moment Amin would order us to be killed.

It was then that Major Kimumwe suggested an idea that I thought was preposterous. He wanted to confess. He wanted to be taken to Amin.

'If we confess now to the assassination attempt,' he said, 'it will buy us some safe time. Amin will not want to kill us straight away. The opportunity is too rich: he'll want a show trial. He'll want publicity. And only then will he want us executed.'

I am not superstitious. In my culture, however, there is a form of witchcraft: certain people are sometimes able to get what they want just by saying it. Moments after this idea had occurred to Major Kimumwe he was summoned, along with Ssekalo, Kasujja and Mutumba, to attend an interrogation by Major Faruk Minawa of the State Research Bureau.

Everything was happening far too quickly. I told Major Kimumwe to abandon his idea: he would be killed and then they would return to kill those of us remaining behind. But Major Kimumwe's idea had excited the others. As the four of them climbed the stairs out of the basement, I was convinced I would never see them again. I was convinced I was dead.

They were gone for the entire day. What happened next was related to me by Kasujja.

Minawa, to whom they were presented, was Amin's number one killer. He had terrible, glassy eyes and a vast belly. He never smiled except when a prisoner was being tortured. The tools of his trade included the following: hippo-hide whips, metal canes, electric cables, Zippo lighters, matches, knives, hammers, lighted cigarettes, broken Coca-Cola bottles and rope. Minawa took his job seriously, and often brought his children with him to work so they could watch him. He was so powerful, and so mad, that he would even order the torture of one of his own soldiers if he felt the man had been derelict in his duty of inflicting pain. Once he made me watch him torture a prisoner from Cell One. This prisoner was beaten horribly and suspended from the ceiling by his feet. 'Now,' said Minawa, 'he'll be able to admit he wanted to overthrow the Government.' Which, in due course, is what happened. The prisoner was killed that night.

Minawa's interrogations followed a pattern. A diesel generator was turned on in the next room so that French Embassy officials would not be disturbed. Prisoners were showered, so that Minawa would not be bothered by their stench. They were then brought in, lectured, invited to sign a confession, and tortured, sometimes by Minawa himself, often by the notorious Palestinian, 'Faizal of the Nile'.

On this occasion Major Kimumwe, Ssekalo, Kasujja and Mutumba entered Minawa's room, and were invited to sign a confession. This was the routine. What followed was not the routine: Major Kimumwe, Ssekalo, Kasujja and Mutumba agreed to the invitation. They felt that, yes, they should sign the confession. They went further: they invented other crimes.

'Minawa grew very excited,' Kasujja told me later. 'He even smiled. He promised to take us to see the President himself, and he was certain that a pardon would be arranged. Minawa chided us for being obstinate for so long. "Look at those scars on your poor bodies," he said, touching our skin gently. "Now you know how unnecessary this unpleasantness has been."'

Kasujja could read Minawa's thoughts. Minawa knew this would give Amin the chance to show the world's press that those killed by the Ugandan regime genuinely deserved to die; after all, they were self-confessed traitors. The arrangement could only reflect well on Minawa.

And then, Kasujja said, he couldn't resist. '*Effendi*,' Kasujja said, 'my Lord, we are treated badly. May we have cigarettes?'

Major Faruk Minawa was appalled by the notion that anyone in his custody should be treated badly. He ordered cigarettes. He ordered that all food for Cell Two should in future be brought from the Standard Hotel.

In his confession, Major Kimumwe was asked to list the reasons for his being unhappy with the Amin government. Major Kimumwe obliged. The reasons included the following: the brain-drain of professionals; the promotion of individuals on a tribal basis instead of merit (leading to the dominance of the Kakwa and Lugbara tribes at the expense of efficiency); the acute shortage of salt, sugar, soap, cooking oil and other various essentials; the consequent black market and price inflation; the collapse of Uganda's currency; the universal disregard of the constitution and the established laws; and a regime of military brutality.

Kimumwe described the list as a modest one, one that would interest the Mighty One.

As it turned out, the four were summoned to appear before the Mighty One that very day. Each was given a new shirt and a new pair of trousers, though Kasujja was denied a walking stick. Perhaps they thought he would try to attack the President with it. Minawa escorted them into a waiting car and they were driven through the centre of Kampala, out towards Amin's villa at Cape Town. Minawa was pleased and proud. He gave the group a tour, pointing out the charms of the palace, the statues, the fruit-trees, the works of art. The palace swarmed with sentries. Patrol boats crossed the lake constantly, and in every corner there seemed to be a man with a pair of binoculars. It seemed that Amin was expecting another coup attempt. At one point Amin appeared, gestured to a beautiful home across the lake, noted that it was a danger to presidential security and said, 'Bomb it.' Then he went back inside.

The four waited for two-and-a-half hours. Amin was apparently haranguing lawyers and church leaders, organizing the resignation of Sheikh Mufti, leader of the Moslem Council, and his replacement by a member of Amin's own tribe.

Eventually they were shown into a small circular room. Amin was seated at the far end, surrounded by TV cameras, journalists and various henchmen. Minawa was there, so was a woman from the government newspaper *The Voice of Uganda*. Kasujja described how he was repelled by the grotesque bulk of the man he and the others had wanted to kill: and still wanted to kill. Amin weighed over 310 pounds.

Amin ordered the prisoners closer, so the cameramen could film them for the television news. He then spoke to them in Swahili and Luganda and sometimes in English.

He spoke to them about their crimes. He put on a terrifying show. His eyes bulged. He banged the arms of his chair with his fists. He made as if to grasp Major Kimumwe by the neck and throttle him. He pulled out a gun and wondered out loud if he should shoot him in the head. 'It was then,' Kasujja said, 'that we thought we had made an awful miscalculation about the President's wish for a show trial. We thought we would be shot on the spot.'

Photo: Alain Nogues (Sygma)

Amin thrust the pistol under Major Kimumwe's chin. He said, 'You are the one who organized and supervised the killing of all the Acholis and Langis around Kampala. Why did you do this? Tell me now. Did you do this so the world would say, "Amin is a murderer"?'

This was the first Major Kimumwe had heard of the killings of the Acholis and Langis.

Amin pushed the gun closer and then turned to a journalist: 'Did you get that? This fellow wished to spoil my name. He wanted to take my good name. I knew I would get hold of him eventually. I fear no one, except God.'

The journalist glanced sideways to a colleague, a look which apparently convinced Major Kimumwe that his death was imminent. Amin continued, berating him first in English, then Swahili, then English once more. 'Fool!' he screamed. 'Idiot! Instead of commanding your forces as you should, you planned to kill me. You are obviously mad.'

Major Kimumwe started to speak, 'Your Excellency . . .' but Amin was in full swing, and had now turned on Mutumba, telling him that he must surely remember the time they went together to check the border, that time they put up such a good show against Nyerere.

Amin said, 'Mutumba. You were one of my favourites. I liked you because you were a revolutionary. Why do you think I promoted you so many times? I trusted you. I trusted you implicitly. What made you turn against me? What more did you want? Did you think these people would give you better things? You fool. You also are mad.'

Kasujja, who had been standing unaided on his one foot, now began to jerk convulsively. Amin switched his attention. He asked Kasujja to remember the time he had saved his life. The soldiers had wanted to kill Kasujja. He had merely ordered the removal of Kasujja's leg. This had been merciful. He could now, if he chose, order him a new one. Didn't Kasujja know how powerful he was? 'Stop fidgeting, man,' he barked.

Amin now turned to Ssekalo. He said, 'And you are one of those I personally recruited when Obote . . .'

Ssekalo interrupted. He started speaking to Amin. He spoke in a quiet voice. He said that Amin was a butcher. He said that Amin was a tribalist. He said, 'We had a very good plan. You would be dead now if it hadn't been for that Sergeant.' The Sergeant was Sergeant Dick, so called because of his fondness for the expression 'every Tom, Dick and Harry'. Sergeant Dick had known about the assassination plot and had betrayed those involved (for money, or a woman, or both) only hours before the planned ambush.

Nobody expected Ssekalo's outburst. And nobody expected the calm that characterized Amin's response: 'You'll face a firing squad and be killed by your own guns, the Chinese guns you imported from Tanzania to kill me and my ministers.'

Amin issued orders. They were to be taken back to prison via Nakasero market, where they would have the opportunity to admire the splendid range of goods now available in the Uganda of President Idi Amin Dada, and then via a bar in Bokassa Street which belonged to Sergeant-Major Peter Mulefu. They understood the point of visiting Mulefu. Besides being a bar owner, Mulefu was also the chief executioner at Nakasero. He was a member of the Kakwa tribe. The Kakwa were superstitious. They feared the spirits of revenge. To fend off these spirits, the Kakwa killer followed the practice of eating the vital organs of his victims. Mulefu's method was to rip open the chests of those he killed with a bayonet, and eat the heart while it was still pumping.

The group was led to Mulefu's bar. 'He inspected each man carefully,' Kasujja told me, 'and then he reached out his hand and tapped Major Kimumwe gently on the chest. He actually tapped him on the chest.'

It is difficult to express the relief I felt when I saw the familiar face of Major Kimumwe coming down the stairs.

Thursday night. The story of Thursday night is the story of Warrant Officer John Okech.

Warrant Officer John Okech was both saviour and potential death warrant. He saved us at midnight, risking his life to divert the attention of a guard who came into the cell to inspect the shirt hanging in front of the ventilator. We thought we'd had it, but Okech positioned his bulk in front of the guard and refused to budge. The guard went away. And yet an hour later Okech was endangering us all because he delayed the escape.

Since the fluorescent light was put out at nine o'clock, we had worked relentlessly on bending the bars. Most of this work was done by Okech himself. His strength was enormous; so, too, was his desperation: he knew that, after the others had confessed, we had very little time left; he knew that tonight, Thursday night, was his—and our—last chance for escape. But, hours later, he still could not squeeze through.

There was an argument. The thin ones demanded that Okech be left behind. Ssekalo made a break for the bars and had to be restrained by Major Kimumwe. There was bad feeling, and it was growing worse. Nambale and Mutumba then joined with Ssekalo: they did not see why their lives should be endangered by Okech's weight.

It was Major Kimumwe who pointed out that it was precisely one hour ago that Okech's weight had saved all of us.

Mutumba said nothing.

'One more day,' Major Kimumwe said. 'We owe it to Okech. Without him the bars would never have been moved in the first place.'

Finally, Mutumba said: 'Tomorrow is the last day. I will not die here like a dumb animal. Tomorrow I'm going. Nobody will stop me.'

Okech said nothing.

Friday, 23 September 1977. We attacked the bars early, at about seven a.m. Work was progressing when I looked through one of the other ventilators and saw a pair of improbably dressed legs just outside. The legs were wrapped in pink trousers and tucked into shoes with platform heels. It must have been a State Research boy. He was standing right next to 'our' ventilator. We gently removed the stand, closed the hole and hung up a shirt. We waited. The fellow stood there, motionless. We were certain he must have heard our noise. He moved away, and we expected guards to burst in at any moment. We knelt and prayed. Major Kimumwe told us the story of Jesus and Peter and the cock crowing three times. No guard came. It seemed a miracle.

By eleven a.m. the bars had opened much more. Major Kimumwe was convinced that Okech would be able to get through. We measured the diameter of the hole with a piece of cable and

Photo: Yves-Guy Berges (Sygma)

compared it against Okech's chest. 'You'll be all right,' Major Kimumwe assured him.

That day we were brought lunch. The usual cattle-head stew. We tried to eat, but we were too excited. The rats had a feast. We talked in low voices. We played draughts. We longed for the night.

At one point, Okech posed the question that had so far gone unstated: 'Gentlemen,' he said, 'suppose I fail to go through. What happens then?'

Nobody replied.

'Gentlemen, what then?'

Nothing.

'I'm not convinced I will go through.'

'You will,' said Major Kimumwe.

'But suppose I don't.'

'I'm sure you will.'

'You think so?'

'Of course.'

It was clear that even Major Kimumwe was determined to go that night.

We discussed escape routes. Our ideas were vague. Ssendawula and I planned to travel together. Kasujja wanted to join us. We didn't think it was a good idea. He understood. He would make it on his own, he said.

At eight p.m. soldiers came down to the cell area. One was fat and bare-chested, wearing only a pair of shorts. He carried a rifle in one hand and held a machete in the other. He laughed and scraped the machete across the concrete floor. '*Hi itakula nyinyi leo,*' he repeated: 'This will cut you tonight.' He was crazed and had been smoking *bhang*, African cannabis. It was common for the soldiers to smoke *bhang* before an execution.

He led the soldiers back upstairs. We heard them assemble outside, as if on parade. Then cars began to arrive, including one with an engine that chugged like a train: it was the Austin Cambridge of Sergeant-Major Peter Mulefu, the Kakwa killer. This meant one thing: executions.

'We're going to die tonight,' I said.

Prisoners were taken from Cell One. There was the familiar wail for mercy. And then there were shots. We heard bodies being thrown on to the back of a lorry. I panicked. I said we should escape now, immediately, take our chances outside.

'Cool down,' said Major Kimumwe. 'Keep calm.'

More soldiers appeared. Galabuzi Mukasa was taken from cell one. He was not a coffee smuggler or a rapist or a thief. He had written a play, one that Amin himself had seen and approved, but had later taken against because he was told it was a satire on his own character. So: Mukasa was to die. I wondered if I was next.

I said, 'We must get out.'

Then, unbelievably, the cars began to leave. First one, then another and, last of all, the noisy Austin Cambridge. The prison was silent. From outside we heard music from a distant night-club, the barking of dogs. At first no one dared say it. I felt ashamed for having panicked. We had been spared for another night.

But this was also, clearly, our chance. At one a.m. we sat in a circle and prayed. This would be the last time we prayed together. We prayed for courage and good luck. We asked God to bless our escape.

Okech said, 'Let us go in the name of Our Lord Jesus Christ.'

We removed our handcuffs. We were all rather solemn. We shook hands and hugged each other. We opened up the hole in the ventilator. The moon was bright, and we waited until clouds passed in front of it.

Okech was to be first. He turned and said, 'I'll see you on the outside.'

This was it: the moment of the escape. Okech climbed on the wooden crates and we pushed him into the hole, head first. But then he stopped. We pushed harder and harder. It was no good. He came down again.

Major Kimumwe smiled. He said we would have to push Okech through feet first. That way would work. We could twist his body round as we pushed.

We tried it, but this, too, did not work. We pulled Okech back out again.

'Now what?' he said.

Nambale said, 'What do you mean, "Now what?"? We're going.'

Okech was grim. 'Do that and I'll make sure you don't get very far. I'll make sure you get shot outside.'

Silence.

'So what do we do?' said Kasujja.

We tried again. We pushed Okech until we thought that his collarbone would crack and that he might suffocate. He was just too fat.

'Mr Okech . . .' I began to say.

'Don't say it,' Okech said. 'The rest of you are not going. We'll have to work tomorrow and remove one of the bars. They're loose enough.'

Ssekalo said he couldn't believe this was happening. Did he have to sacrifice his life for Okech? Mutumba buried his face in his hands. The others lay on their backs, and stared at the ceiling.

I knew what had to be done. I moved over to Okech. I slid an arm over his shoulder. I asked him to listen to me like a brother. I said he must stay.

Okech explained his position. He said he had been arrested only because his friend Ssendawula had refused to stop his car for the State Research boys one night after the assassination attempt. Now it was Ssendawula who wished to leave him to die, alone. Was that justice?

I knew that Okech was speaking the truth. If we left him alone in that cell he would die. But I told him he must be a good statesman. I told him he would be pardoned. His innocence was well-known. He needed only to invent a story which would dissociate him from the escape. He could say that he had been asleep. Or that unknown soldiers had stormed the cell and refused to take him along. He would be OK.

There was silence. Okech looked at me for a long time. He took a deep breath and shook his head. Silence. The sound of dogs barking.

He said, 'Very well.'

The relief we felt was overpowering.

Okech said, 'You may try your luck. You know I will not be pardoned. So please remember, I am going to die for you.'

Each of us embraced Okech. We told him we owed him our lives. Okech nodded, and said nothing.

It was nearly three a.m. when we lifted Ssekalo to the bars. He struggled and was through, giving the thumbs up to the rest of us below. Major Kimumwe was next, followed by Ssendawula, then me. It wasn't easy, even for a man of my medium build. I lifted myself off the floor by pulling on the bars. Nambale then lifted my body so it was level with the ventilator. I pushed my right arm through, and my head, and twisted on my side so that my shoulders were vertical, and received another push from below. With my chest already outside, and my hands on the ground, pulling my legs and hips through was easy. I signalled to Nambale, who followed. Mutumba was the last, helped through by Okech.

Okech watched through the bars. He asked me to give a message to his wife and children. He said, 'Good luck, gentlemen. Go well.' He was crying.

Out

The night was cool, bright, silent except for the barking of dogs. For some reason I thought of my wife, and the night of our honeymoon. I thought I was as good as reunited with her. Then a burst of laughter came from the guardhouse, and booming voices. I realized how much we had concentrated our energies on getting out of the cell, and how little we had thought about what would happen afterwards. It was another story.

We had agreed, however, that there would be no talking, except in an emergency. We would follow the orders of Major Kimumwe as though we were on a military operation. He would communicate by hand signal. He motioned, and we began to crawl along the side of the cell block.

At the corner of the building we came to an area that was brightly lit. Ssekalo peered round, to see if all was clear. It was. There were no soldiers. We crossed quickly to a wall. This was about seven feet high, and we had to climb it to get up to the level where we could tackle the fences. We lifted Ssekalo, and he pulled up Major Kimumwe, who in turn helped Kasujja, and so on.

We moved along the first perimeter fence. The security lights were dazzling. We could be seen easily. So we went along and found a darker spot. Kasujja followed us with astonishing agility.

Now we faced a much bigger fence. We couldn't climb this one, and we also feared it was electrified. Major Kimumwe signalled us to stop. We waited while Ssekalo searched for a place to crawl through. It was some minutes before he returned to report that he had found a spot, but that it would mean going *over* the fence and into the compound of a neighbouring house. There were problems. The guardhouse was close by. And there were two large dogs in the compound. Kasujja suggested that two of us go on ahead, get through the fence and strangle the dogs. We argued. The plan wasn't practical. What about the noise? Wouldn't the guards be alerted?

A soldier came round the corner. We were silenced. We watched as he walked round the side of the building. He stopped, as though he'd seen the hole in the ventilator. We waited for him to raise the alarm. Instead he dropped his rifle on the ground and lit a cigarette. He smoked for a while, turned round and went back round the corner.

Major Kimumwe found a hollow in the ground at the bottom of the fence, probably there for drainage. It looked possible to crawl under. But someone would have to lift the fence. And this, of course, was the one we thought was electrified. Someone would have to try it. Major Kimumwe began to scan our faces just as Kasujja hopped forward and grasped the wire.

Kasujja turned, smiling.

We wriggled through. Now we were outside the second perimeter fence, but still in a corridor surrounded by a roll of wire. We thought there would be a way out to the east, through the French Embassy. This meant we had to go round the front of the building, where the guards were. We crawled slowly, heads down. Ssendawula followed Major Kimumwe, and I was third. We were now in front of the reception area at the front of the gaol, and about to walk into an area that was brilliantly lit. We had come the wrong way. There were scores of soldiers, some on a veranda, some in jeeps, and others at attention, holding rifles to their shoulders.

'We must go back,' whispered Major Kimumwe.

We worked our way back. It was slow work. I waited for bullets to smash into my body. The dogs in the compound of the house were barking constantly. Why had no guard been sent to check on them?

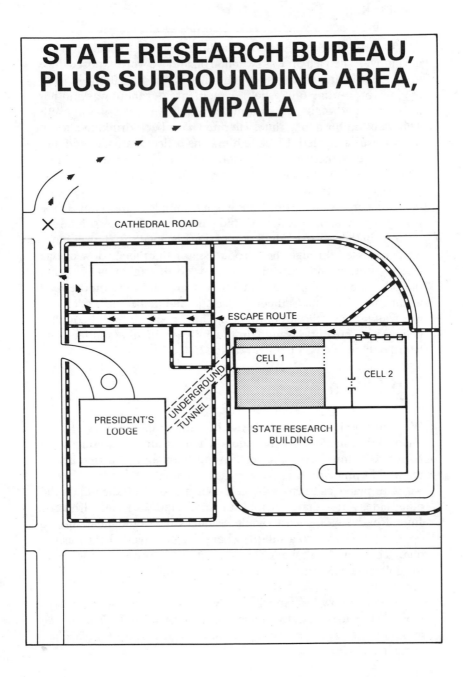

STATE RESEARCH BUREAU, PLUS SURROUNDING AREA, KAMPALA

CATHEDRAL ROAD

ESCAPE ROUTE

CELL 1

CELL 2

UNDERGROUND TUNNEL

PRESIDENT'S LODGE

STATE RESEARCH BUILDING

We were back in the dark, huddling together to decide on our next move. Then a light was switched on and we were exposed once more. A woman officer was in the toilet on the first floor, in front of a mirror, putting on lipstick. A moment later there was another light. In an adjoining room a male soldier was relieving himself. This went on for a long time. He must have been drinking a lot of beer. Kasujja giggled. I kicked him. The officer, satisfied with her appearance, turned away. We waited. The dogs were still barking. At last the soldier finished, and turned off the light.

Again, darkness.

We were retracing our steps when Nambale found a hole in the wire. It was as simple as that. Could it have been used by soldiers to smuggle in their girlfriends? I don't know. But within a few minutes we had passed through the wire, crossed from the shadow of one tree to another and then another, crawled through a gap beneath the side gate of the presidential lodge itself, and were on the road leading to All Saints Cathedral. Kasujja had picked up a stick and was walking fast. Stones on the road hurt my bare feet; I couldn't believe we were out. I waited for the noise of pursuing soldiers, and heard only the dogs. I felt light-headed.

Up Country

We split up at the crossroads by the cathedral. We hugged each other and wished each other luck. Then Kasujja was gone. And Major Kimumwe. And the rest. Ssendawula and I hurried across the well-lit junction.

Our plan was to cross the golf course and climb the hill on the other side. After that, I would turn right and walk until I hit the Jinja Road heading east, while Ssendawula would head in the opposite direction, to a suburb where a friend lived. That was the plan. The plan didn't work out. We got lost as soon as we were on the golf course. Worse: we were up to our thighs in a marsh, falling repeatedly.

I don't know how much time we wasted. An hour? Perhaps more. When we extricated ourselves and moved on down a hill, we found that we were on a road, back where we had started. We had come in a circle.

Ssendawula and I agreed to part, and I went back on to the golf course, this time making sure I kept parallel to the road. My home was in south Kampala. I knew I couldn't go there; it was the first place that would be searched. I'd decided to make for Nairobi, 450 miles away, in Kenya.

I guessed the time to be about five a.m. when I heard the cars. I knew it must be the State Research boys. No one else dared drive in the city at that hour. I hurried on.

I was on the Jinja road, somewhere between Nakawa and Kyambago, when a white Peugeot came up behind me. I turned off the road and ran into the bush, running for my life, making sudden turns—right, left, right, right, left—hoping to throw them off my trail. I didn't think I had much chance.

I hid in a half-finished building. It was made of red brick but had no roof. Perhaps an Asian family had been building it and had then been forced to leave the country. Trees and grass as high as the walls of the house had grown inside. I went in through a window frame so as not to leave any marks around the door, and hid, deep in the grass. I tried to keep quiet. I tried not to think of the snakes that were probably all around me.

Some time later I heard a man's voice. He was asking a woman if she had seen anyone. I knew it must be a State Research boy. I held my breath and prayed, praying for myself, praying for my survival. The woman said she'd seen no one, and the boy went away.

I waited. I tried to make plans. Instead I found myself thinking of irrelevant things: cold beer, buttered toast, the time one of my children had chicken pox. I dozed. Hours must have passed, and there was a rainstorm. It left me soaked again but at least, I reasoned, it should have washed away most of my scent, making it more difficult if they came after me with dogs.

I heard a helicopter overhead. I burrowed deep into the grass. I didn't need a prize to guess that the helicopter was looking for us.

Later in the morning I heard gunshots. I was relieved because they were a long way off. Then I was ashamed: it meant one of the others had probably been shot. I felt sure it must be Kasujja. He was the most vulnerable. Poor Kasujja. They'd got him. The Soviet training had not saved him after all. Kasujja: then I saw movement

113

in the grass. It was what I feared: a snake. It was a mamba, very poisonous. I kept still, telling myself that snakes attacked only moving things, and then only because they are afraid, not because they are aggressive. Snakes are not violent animals. I hoped the mamba would remember this. It had seen me, raised its head, lowered it again, and then raised it once more, tongue flickering, as if preparing to strike. I don't know how long this went on. It seemed like hours. Then the mamba decided it didn't like the look of me, executed a sinuous turn, climbed a wall and was gone.

I decided I'd risk the State Research boys, after all.

I was hungry and thirsty. I found a row of houses and from a dustbin scavenged a sodden crust of bread and half-full bottle of beer. I made my way to an open air market. The crowd was good cover. I followed two old men, one carrying a sack of flour on his head. White powder leaked on to his shoulders. I was close enough to hear their conversation, about the day being the worst business of the year. It was a pleasure listening to their concerns.

I spotted a middle-aged woman carrying a rattling bunch of saucepans, and decided it was best to walk beside her, as if I was with her. We walked for some time along the road when I flagged down a car, an ancient Austin. The car was blue. The man was grey: grey hair, grey overalls and grey bushy eyebrows. He was about sixty.

'Won't your wife come too?' he asked.

I told him the woman wasn't my wife. He shrugged, and I closed the door.

He said, 'Where do you work?'

'The Ministry of Agriculture,' I said. The lie came from my mouth before I'd really thought about it.

'That's interesting,' he said. 'What do you do?'

'I've been showing some people round here the advantages of mixed farming.'

'Which crops?'

This man was full of questions.

'Corn and coffee,' I said. I was beginning to panic. 'And there was a lot of manure. That's why I don't smell so good.'

'And is that why you're barefoot?'

'W-e-l-l,' I said, my mind racing. 'My shoes were stolen. One of the workers on the farm.'

'I see.'

The conversation faltered. I was relieved. He stopped to buy sugar, bread and milk. I sat in the car. He was gone for five minutes. I didn't like the way he'd been asking all those questions, and thought about making a run for it, but that would arouse even more suspicions. When he returned I decided I would ask the questions.

'And what do you do?' I said.

'I work at Naguru, the State Security Prison. I'm a policeman.'

I looked at him, trying to show no surprise. Was he joking? Or playing a game? Perhaps he had guessed who I was, and was driving me to the nearest station. I thought about throwing myself from the car. I waited a few minutes, humming a tune, Frank Sinatra's 'My Way'. We were on a deserted stretch of the Kampala-Jinja road.

I said, as casually as I could, 'You can let me out now.'

He said, 'But there's nothing here.'

I said, 'You can't see it from the road. A path goes through the bush to a village. My uncle lives there.'

'Right over there?' He pointed.

'That's it. Right over there.'

'Will you be safe?'

'I'll be all right, thank you.'

'It looks wild. Perhaps I should come with you.'

'That's very kind. But I'll be all right.'

'I think I'd better come with you.'

The man was either stupid, stubborn or a terrible sadist. I said, 'Really, no. Thanks.'

He looked at me, assessing me. I thought he must know. I waited for him to say he was arresting me.

Instead, he said, 'Suit yourself.'

He dropped me at the side of the road. It was pitch-dark. I watched the red tail-lights of the Austin disappear. I was back in the bush. Now I was faced with the highway robbers and the wild animals. And the snakes, of course.

I walked for days. I slept at night in the bush. I ate little. I'd concocted a story for anyone I met. I'd been released from Mulago Hospital and had no money. I was walking to Jinja. The story worked. I used the story on two old women, who gave me a meal, and an old man, who gave me clothes.

My next problem was crossing the River Nile. There were two bridges, both swarming with soldiers. I waited for a day. The bridges were quiet much of the time, except in the morning and evenings when workers were coming on and off shift. I overheard two men talking about the escape. It had been on South African radio. Some of us had apparently reached Germany. One of the men mentioned the Israelis.

The Israelis? I wondered what they were talking about.

The next morning I chanced it. I went with the morning shift across one of the bridges. I kept my head down, expecting to hear shouts from the soldiers. They didn't come. I crossed the Kenya/ Uganda border in the bush, avoiding the paths in case I ran into one of Amin's anti-smuggling patrols. I reached a big road around midday and calculated I was already well into Kenya. I'd made it. I felt that God existed after all. I jumped for joy. I thought that must be the end of the story. It wasn't.

There were police road-blocks.

It seemed unlikely that they could be looking for me. But it was possible. And if it was possible, then I could be caught, judged an undesirable and repatriated. I invented a new story: I was an employee of the East African Community, working in the research institute near Busia, and had been on my way home when thieves robbed me of everything, including my identity card. I retreated into the bush, expressing all my thoughts in Swahili.

The nights were freezing. I dined on the usual dustbin leftovers and gashed my foot on a broken bottle on the side of the road. I came down with malaria. My temperature rocketed. I told myself this was ridiculous. I hadn't expected this. I had escaped from Nakasero, got out of Uganda and was now going to die from malaria by the side of the road in Kenya. In despair I went to a police station and told my story, trusting to luck that they wouldn't send me back to Uganda. They told me I was a drunkard, and chased me away.

I joined a group of night-watchmen. I slept by their fire. In the morning I felt better. I didn't have malaria after all, just a bout of fever. One of the men told me his friend was driving a lorry to Nairobi that day. I could have a lift. The lorry broke down.

But at least the driver gave me fifty shillings. I had to walk from Kericho. I walked through Nakuru, Naivasha and the Rift Valley and finally Limuru. The sun was setting when I reached the suburbs of Nairobi. I had some change remaining: I took a bus.

At 8.45 on the night of 30 October 1977 I knocked on the door of a friend's house in Nairobi. His children answered. They said daddy was in the shower. They wouldn't let me in. They thought I was a thief. Then I saw my friend, coming down the stairs, wearing a towel round the waist, and heard his wife shrieking with surprise. They embraced me, saying at first they'd thought I was a ghost. They'd heard I was dead.

I drank tea. I ate mountains of buttered toast. I had a bath, my first in two months, and slept. On a mattress.

In Nairobi

I remained in hiding. If Amin or his henchmen discovered I was alive my relatives in Uganda would certainly be killed. I remained in exile until Amin's fall, in 1979.

I learned what had happened to my friends. One got out across the southern part of Lake Victoria. Another crossed Lake Kioga in a canoe. Miraculously, they all made it, even Kasujja. I saw him in Nairobi. He teased me about the fact that Ssendawula and I had not allowed him to come with us. I felt ashamed. Kasujja just laughed, and demanded that I buy him lots of vodka, Russian vodka.

I learned also about John Okech. When the guards came down into the cell area, he told them the rest of us had escaped while he slept. The guards inspected the cell with disbelief. They knew they would be blamed and became terrified for their lives. They ran away, and even left Okech with a gun when he told them he wished to kill himself rather than undergo torture. Some time later another six guards appeared. Okech shot them all, threw the gun into the corridor alongside the bodies, put back on his handcuffs, and waited in the cell. Soon there were more guards.

'*Effendi*,' said Okech. 'Some soldiers, they were white, they came down in the middle of the night, opened the cell and took the others. They wouldn't take me. I wasn't on the list.'

'What nationality were they?' said one of the guards.

'I don't know, *effendi*,' said Okech. 'I think perhaps they were Israeli.'

Okech's story was reported to Amin. It seemed that the Israelis had humiliated him once more. He ordered the immediate arrest of Major Faruk Minawa. Okech was summoned, and told to repeat his story. Amin became suspicious, demanded more facts, picked at the flaws in Okech's story, ordered an inspection of Cell Two. When the wrecked ventilator was discovered it became obvious, even to Idi Amin Dada, that Okech had been telling complex lies.

John Okech was transferred to Makindye prison, and killed there after a month of torture.

This story is written in his memory.

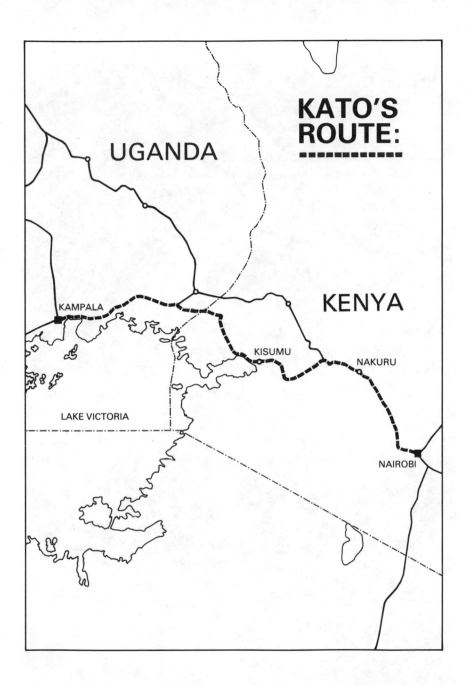

KATO'S ROUTE:

UGANDA

KENYA

KAMPALA

KISUMU

NAKURU

NAIROBI

LAKE VICTORIA

1962	Uganda gains independence from Britain.
1965	Milton Obote abrogates the constitution and names himself President.
1967	Idi Amin becomes Commander-in-Chief of the Ugandan Army.
1971	Amin, with the backing of British and Israeli intelligence, seizes power while Obote is attending the British Commonwealth Conference.
1972	Amin expels Uganda's Asian population.
1979	Amin is overthrown by an invading Tanzanian Army, and a coalition government is established.
1980	Milton Obote returns to power following a disputed election. Yoweri Museveni and his National Resistance Army begin a guerrilla war north of Kampala.
25 January 1986	Museveni and the NRA depose Obote, fifteen years to the day after Amin seized power.
June 1986	Since 1962, 500,000 Ugandans have died because of political upheaval of one kind or another: most have been killed by the intelligence agencies of each successive government.
January 1987	Uganda reports the highest incidence of AIDS in Africa. It is calculated that one in ten of the remaining Ugandan population is infected with the AIDS virus.
September 1987	A construction company renovates the former headquarters of the State Research Bureau for use as government offices, but, to date, has refused to open a basement room that has been sealed since Amin was deposed from power.

Yoweri Museveni

A child with AIDS

JAMES FENTON
THE TRUCE

Sotero Llamas was proud of the price on his head. Ten thousand dollars. This made him the most wanted man in the Bicol region. The rumour was that Sotero, or Teroy, or Nognog, was the NPA Commander of Southern Luzon. It was as a spokesman for the NPA that he was due, one Saturday late in 1986, to go down from the hills into the town of Legaspi, to help set up the regional cease-fire committee.

On the whole Teroy thought that the military would respect the cease-fire, but he was worried about Colonel Abadilla, a notorious killer and inquisitor of the left, who had been sent down to Bicol after his involvement in the Manila hotel coup (the first of the military attempts to get rid of Cory Aquino). Abadilla just might use the occasion to bump him off.

So Teroy asked me if I would mind accompanying him in the first car of the motorcade. 'If they see you there,' he said, 'that would make our precautions more iron-clad.'

The car belonged to the local radio reporter, who sat in the front seat giving a live commentary. In the back were two guerrillas,

---

The New People's Army (NPA) is the armed wing of the communist party in the Philippines, with 23,500 members, and has been active for eighteen years, and is reputed to control about twenty percent of the country's provinces. Even though Rodolfo Salas, seen by many as the commander-in-chief of the NPA, was arrested in October 1986, the NPA, represented by Anthony Zumel and Satur Ocampo of the National Democratic Front, agreed to a sixty-day cease-fire with the government that began fifteen days before Christmas. For many, it was the first time that members of the NPA had been seen in public, and *Liberation*, the monthly paper of the communist party, described the truce as a festive occasion. But two months of negotiation between the NPA and the government produced no results, and the cease-fire ended on 8 February 1987. On 11 February 1987, Cory Aquino announced that 'armed forces will resume operations against the rebels.'

Opposite: Sotero Llamas.

Photo: Vin Toledo

aged about fifteen or sixteen, called Marlon and Archie. When Teroy and I joined them first, we sat by the window. I thought: Good, he's sitting by the window.

Then we had a flat.

When the wheel was changed and we were getting back into the car, Teroy asked if I would mind swapping places. 'Not at all,' I breezed, taking the exposed position.

So now, if Colonel Abadilla's men wanted to shoot Teroy, he was protected on one side by innocent-looking kids, and on the other by a foreigner. Teroy offered me a sandwich, but I refused. I could see that he was a charming man who was used to getting his own way and involving other people in slightly larger adventures, perhaps, than they had bargained for.

'The trouble is,' said Teroy as the car moved off, 'we have not yet received our safe-conduct passes.'

All over the Philippines the NPA had been coming down from the hills. In the Southern Tagalog region, they had even been allowed to bring their weapons into Lucena. But here, Teroy said, they were not to be armed.

So the two heavy bags he had placed in the car were innocent after all. I decided they probably contained exceedingly heavy sandwiches.

Sotero had not been into Legaspi since 1971, he said. He had been an activist at Aquinas University, where he studied law. But after he had disclosed some irregularity in the University's affairs he had been black-listed. He had taken to the hills where he had helped to form the first generation of Bicol NPAs. Thirty-three people had been in that group. Many gave up early on. Others were captured, others killed. Of those who stayed with the NPA, only three are still, as he put it, 'vertical'.

When Teroy uses words like this, he laughs disconcertingly. He relishes the disconcerting. He keenly watches the effect his words have on the listener, and he is always happy to talk. This is partly because he knows very well how much he is at liberty to say. He's in command after all.

But there was something else, during this period and on this occasion particularly. Teroy the university activist, the clever and funny public-speaker, who had gone underground a decade and a half ago, was coming out, dropping his disguise. Before that day, even within his own group, there were people who did not know who was the legendary Nognog. But from now on anybody could have his photograph and anybody could know that Nognog, and K.A. Willy (for 'Wily'), and Teroy were the same person. Short, jovial, with a face like Socrates and a peaked cap like Castro, Teroy was going public.

When the NPA first began work in Bicol, they acquired arms by confiscating them from the private security men of the local landlords. Then 'enlightened elements in the middle class' had helped them, after which they began to recruit among the peasants. In the late Marcos years it had been easy to identify the enemy (Marcos = fascism) and to gain support from the peasantry. True, the beginnings had been hard, and there had been black years in 1974 and 1975. But all in all, according to Teroy, the basic issue was simple to understand and put across.

Since the February revolution things had changed, and in Bicol the situation was complicated. On the one hand, there was a popular government—reactionary, in the view of the NPA, but not fascist. There were still fascist elements in place among the military, in Teroy's analysis, with all kinds of pressures creating a new situation. This meant that there had to be intensive political work among the NPA and their supporters—but still, cease-fire or not, they had to be prepared for the resumption of armed struggle.

But the Bicol NPA needed arms. They needed explosives. They had just managed to buy an anti-tank weapon, but they needed more of these, and mortars—and they couldn't get such supplies without outside support.

They also needed doctors. Nothing demoralized them, Teroy said, so much as having a comrade wounded and being unable to get medical help for him. Finally, they also needed uniforms. They wanted fatigues, and they had asked their supporters to give them these as Christmas presents. After today's events, they had home-printed T-shirts, with a design of the Mayon volcano.

That morning, representatives of the clergy and the cause-oriented groups had come up into the hills from Legaspi, to meet the NPA and escort them down into town. A service was held on a basketball court. The Assistant Bishop of Legaspi was full of memories of Teroy when young. Nuns handed out boiled sweets. Peace-workers stuck flags into the NPA guns. The local radio interviewed Teroy as our lad from Tabako (a town noted for the manufacture of excellent scissors and unnerving knives). When Teroy spoke, it was to make people laugh—and I could see he must have been an excellent student leader.

When his colleague Celso Minguez tried to speak, he wept instead. He had been seventeen years in the movement. He was another of the three remaining members of the founding group. And then there was Alberto David, Jr, from the second intake. It had been a moving scene in the barrio, with people greeting each other ecstatically. Some of them were friends who had left the underground, but now had come back to meet their old colleagues. I had seen several of the NPA-organized events since the truce had come into effect, but none of them had quite this emotional, provincial intimacy.

'Is it really fifteen years since you've seen Legaspi?' I asked Teroy, as we drove down. He claimed it was, but it was amazing how often, along the route, he would point out areas as being particular strongholds of the NPA, and how little seemed to surprise him in the landscape.

I asked him how it felt, coming down.

He said he was still worried.

Would he see his family?

Teroy said he hoped they wouldn't be there. His children and his wife, whom he rarely saw, would cry—and then he would cry too.

We passed a military camp, where he used to do his reserve officer's training. 'I'm a reserve officer,' said Teroy with what seemed a touch of pride.

'You mean, you're *still* a reserve officer, officially?'

'Yes,' he said, 'but the question is—reserved for whom?'

People at the side of the road, hearing the loudspeaker van announcing the motorcade and its purpose, waved in a somewhat surreptitious way. I saw one man, for instance, who was definitely waving with the four fingers of his right hand, but with his thumb he was pretending to scratch his scalp. There was something intense and circumspect about the response along the way.

Fred and Bing, who were working with me at the time, had taken up a position by the first check-point into town. When the motorcade came close, a constabulary captain told them he was going to search every vehicle.

Fred asked him: 'Who's the NPA big shot here?'

'It's Nognog,' he said, 'Sotero Llamas.'

Would he recognize Nognog?

'No,' he said, 'that's the problem—sometimes we are even talking with them and we don't know who they are.'

The captain was a sympathetic man. His great hope for the cease-fire was that it might allow him to rejoin his family. He hadn't seen them for two years and he was afraid his children wouldn't recognize him any more.

Now the captain tried to stop the loudspeaker-van, waving it down. But people waved back at him and not a car in the queue stopped. Then he seemed, simply, to give up the idea of searching every vehicle.

Inside the vehicle with Nognog, I thought the captain was waving us on. He peered at us for a moment. Instinctively I moved back my head a little to allow him to kill Nognog instead of me. Just half an inch, but enough to make me feel a little ashamed afterwards.

Nognog/Teroy said to me again: 'I hope my children aren't there, or I'll cry.'

'There's nothing wrong with crying in public,' I said. I was thinking: if *he* starts, I'll start.

We reached the Cathedral precinct, and waited for a while to disembark and for Teroy to make his face known to the public. The NPA surrounded us in their T-shirts. Then we got out and marched in close formation to lunch, Teroy holding my hands tightly. And there were Bing and Fred again, retreating in front of us, clicking away among the press.

At lunch, a small crowd watched us through the slatted windows of the *cursillo*, asking each other which was Teroy. Among the onlookers, he recognized his drama professor from university days. I met her later. She was floating on air. She said: 'I taught them both, Sotero and Alberto David!'

I said: 'They used to act?'

'Yes,' she said.

'What did they play?' I asked.

She said: 'It was in 1970! They both played leading roles!'

I bet they did, I thought. I was relieved my minor role was finished, and relieved too that, when my photograph appeared the next day in the national press, I was clearly identified as the Bishop of Legaspi.

2

Teroy actually owed me a favour, which he was keen to repay. Several days before, on the eve of the official cease-fire, Bing and I had come down to Bicol on the understanding that we would be able to interview the NPA, photograph them and even accompany them down from the hills, if all went according to plan. Because there had been doubt about the last bit, and because I needed a fail-safe arrangement in order to have a story on offer to my newspaper (*The Independent*), I had chartered a plane. I had half a page of newspaper waiting to be filled, and I had visions of a truly elegant operation: Jojo was in Mindanao, Fred in northern Luzon—between us all we should see something of interest.

Everything went according to plan: we were met at the airstrip and taken from place to place, made the inevitable river-crossing and before too long were walking through a coconut plantation to meet the NPA. And we met the NPA, and they said, we're very sorry, but the man you were going to meet is not here and we have no authorization to talk to you. But this is absurd, we said. You've already brought us here—you must know the arrangement was official. They knew that all right, but because of a missing link in the chain of command they could do nothing about it. We had been promised access to a company-sized camp. We must have been a stone's throw from the place. But we were not to be allowed in.

Well, we said, could we at least interview some red fighters about their attitude to the cease-fire? Could they come out of the camp and talk to us? But that too was not to be. No provision had been made for such a thing. The red fighters were *there* all right, and sat in embarrassment at the edge of the conversation. But we couldn't talk to them, not even about the weather.

Hopelessly I began to explain through Bing the lengths to which we had gone to secure an original story, with photographs, how we had the space waiting, the plane waiting, the enormous expense (600 dollars), the hole in the budget, the necessity of cancelling the page . . . everything. But reasoning was useless. One act of authority was lacking.

Fury and despair overcame me. I left the conversation and began pacing around the trees beyond the scope of the lantern. Bing was being lectured on democratic centralism. I could tell he was becoming irritated: he was trying to say, Yes, I understand about democratic centralism, but it's not supposed to be a shield for stupid and petty behaviour; while the voice that was lecturing him turned gelid—this is a revolutionary struggle, discipline is everything and so forth. I was glad that, however trivial the issue, we had stubbed our toes against democratic centralism, for much of the NPA propaganda recently had made the insurgents seem amiable to the point of insipidity. The foul-up in our plans had killed my story, but at least I was seeing how things worked. I was seeing one of those *displays of discipline* which form such a profound component of communist culture.

Such displays can be over great things or small. I met one woman, an early member of the NPA, who had been taking part in the trial of a comrade. The man had been voted guilty and the death sentence chosen. The woman had been in the minority who believed that the comrade should be given another chance. But once the decision had been taken, she had *volunteered* to execute the sentence. She had wanted, she said, the experience of executing a sentence with which she had disagreed.

It is a terrible thing to want an experience in this way. It is a desire that arises not out of the practical necessities of membership of a guerrilla movement, but out of a pathological need for an obedience. Killing a comrade is anticipated as a supreme test of belonging, and there is a parallel here with another Filipino underground: that is the criminals. It is standard practice for the criminal gangs to demand of a new recruit that he commit a murder. The fact of having killed a man seems to be a kind of social glue.

3

News spread rather quickly through the underground about a foreigner who had chartered a plane to visit the NPA and been turned away at the last moment. Teroy said to me later: 'We're very sorry about what happened that night'—and here the mischievous look broke through—'and they tell me you even cried because you couldn't get your story.'

I laughed. I wasn't going to contradict him. Faced with a petty display of discipline by one of his *apparatchiks*, I had given a tenebrous display of rage and frustration. I could easily have cried. And afterwards, when I was offered the chance of free access to one of his areas, to meet and talk to whomever I pleased, I took care to point out that it would not be free access, and nor would conversation be free. Democratic centralism would not permit that—and nor would the normal security precautions taken by any guerrilla movement. I might have access, but it would not be free access.

Teroy agreed. It is under his controlling influence that the Bicol NPA has become notoriously strict on discipline. He is the original democratic centralist. Every year there is one—but only one—month of discussion. It takes two months to organize the meeting, and fifteen days for the comrades to arrive. They can't descend on a barrio like delegates on a conference hotel. Roads are watched. Unusual movements would be noticed. And so arrivals must be staggered. Then they go through everything: organization, military, financial and personal matters. Political decisions are made, and for the rest of the year they must be faithfully carried out.

It's a tried and tested system: recruitment, discipline, organization have all been worked out and can be explained, neatly, point by numbered point. When Teroy said he would explain the whole thing to me when we had our interview together I did not feel it necessary to tell him that the interview began the moment we first met, and had continued through those early weeks of the truce, as we drove around Bicol to public meetings, sleeping in schools and seminaries, being ministered to by nuns.

When the NPA went to mass I refused to join them. Teroy was amused and intrigued. Why not? 'Because *I'm* an atheist,' I said, affecting a certain superiority. There followed a deal of eyebrow music between us: Teroy of course is a non-believer, but . . . diplomacy . . . and he enjoys humouring the nuns.

Here we are, then, guests of the Augustinized Sisters of Our Lady of Consolation, eating and sleeping in the science room of the Consolation Academy, among the bottled specimens and retorts. A banner on the wall reads: 'If I have seen further than other men, it is by standing on the shoulders of giants.' Some of the young guerrillas are learning a song, set to a beautiful tune which sounds Spanish or even Neapolitan in origin. The tune became popular in Filipino prisons: it was a song of the underworld. Now the tune has taken to the hills, with new words:

> We are the poor people, with no strength except our industriousness,
> No wealth at all except our strength—sweat, blood and honesty.
> What happened to this creative force?
> Why did the others steal and leave nothing over?
> Since we joined the bloody uprising
> Our aim is liberty with the broad masses.
> Firmly, valiantly, shouting and struggling
> We'll carry the flag right on to total victory.
> We'll carry the flag right on to total victory.

I imagine that the tune began life as a love-song, travelling round the Mediterranean in the seventeenth century. Then perhaps it was press-ganged and found its way out here.

Teroy is writing notes. The *apparatchik* is doing the accounts. At an adjacent table, the red fighters are practising drawing the hammer and sickle—a task they are finding difficult. The wrong paint was used on their silk-screened NPA special truce T-shirts, and the Mayon volcano is flaking off after the first wash.

Teroy starts telling me about sex, which can be a problem in the NPA. Rape is a capital crime, and I've heard it said that in the early days of the movement comrades were killed for illicit affairs. Teroy says that ordinary sexual abuses are carefully investigated and that demotion is the discipline. He has taken care not to fall into any sexual trap himself. And he has, of course, a system, which he explains to all his men.

The first thing is: never to be alone. Secondly, when you go to bed, try not to sleep near female comrades. Thirdly, keep active— it's when you're idle that you begin to think about these things. Write poetry. Read a book. Play Scrabble. Teroy and Celso Minguez are extraordinarily good at Scrabble, although Teroy has a way of laying down a faintly improbable word and quickly removing it at the first sign of objection. Once we acquired a Scrabble set which turned out to have only two vowels represented. But this seemed to cause no difficulty: the whole was played with Os and Us.

Another way of coping with the sexual problem, of course, is conjugal visits. In wartime these are classically dangerous moments, if one partner is in the underground and the other not. The truce was a sexual boon for the NPA. On Christmas Eve, in the Legaspi classroom where we have been billeted, Teroy points with pursed lips (Filipino-style) towards the *apparatchik*, who has been padding around all evening, inconspicuously getting things done. Now he's opening a briefcase and producing shirt and trousers, perfectly pressed. 'You can always tell,' says Teroy, 'if someone is carefully getting his work done, like that. It means he's got a conjugal visit.'

Now other wives, including Teroy's, arrive, and the senior comrades retire, leaving us to listen to the fireworks in the town. The guerrillas have no relish for fireworks. Their ears are trained to react swiftly to all kinds of explosives—except fireworks. It is a disturbing sound.

For the twentieth time that day, a young guerrilla picks up the guitar and sings 'Boulevard'. We read. We keep busy. We do all the things Teroy has recommended to keep our minds off sex. We are woken after the midnight mass by the nuns who come with carols and a cake. Then a group of pretty girls from the town arrive with sweetmeats. We drink hot chocolate and feel a little sorry for ourselves, like seminarians.

4

One thing Teroy regrets is the lack of opportunities for reading. He carries a lot of books around with him (that was what was in the heavy bags we took down into Legaspi), and I noticed that he is currently dipping into John Reed's *Insurgent Mexico*. This was perhaps on some central committee reading-list on insurrection, which has been very much a topic for debate.

In February, as the snap election turned into a revolution, the NPA were completely left out of events, and not surprisingly there was debate and discontent afterwards. People were saying: We should have been in there; we should have staged an insurrection. So Teroy asked the central committee to prepare a study of insurrections—ones that have succeeded, ones that have failed. Within three months a paper on insurrections was distributed, together with books for Teroy. But he is a busy man.

He has difficulty reading ten pages before falling asleep.

There is something enviably out-of-touch about the Filipino guerrillas. Books are hard enough to come by in the cities anyway, let alone in the hills. And those political contacts with the outside world that the NPA maintains are not necessarily the most useful: Teroy was able to explain to me at some length what had happened to the Canadian Maoists. And what had happened to them? They had split. Over what had they split? Over the women's question, and over the language question. So much for the Canadian Maoists.

He also began to tell me that what had happened in Cambodia had not been nearly as bad as has been made out. And from what he started to say I soon worked out that he had received a visit from an old friend of mine, a Japanese photographer who was apparently never able to face up to the truth of what happened.

The Cambodia question is a hard one for the NPA, partly because of the effectiveness of *The Killing Fields*, which was widely distributed here. 'Black propaganda!' the leftists tended to say, although I never heard one of them find serious fault with the film's presentation of events. Just before Marcos fell, an article in *Commentary* by Ross Munroe depicted the NPA as being the

Khmer Rouge of the future, and referred to their increased ruthlessness and brutality.

The man cast by Munroe in the role of Pol Pot, Rodolfo Salas, had been arrested by the military during the truce negotiations. As for the negotiators themselves, Satur Ocampo and Tony Zumel, it would be hard to imagine them in the Cambodian context. Nevertheless the stories of brutality told in the article are not to be dismissed. The NPA admits that it has thorough phases of paranoia in which massacres have occurred.

These are referred to as infiltration periods, when 'Deep Penetration Agents' (DPAs) were causing havoc in the movement: 1974 to 1975 and 1982 to 1983 are two periods mentioned by Teroy, the worst areas being Mindanao and Southern Tagalog.

Anyone will tell you that, in the attempt to root out the DPAs, good comrades were killed: when the truth of the matter finally became clear, those responsible for the killing of innocent comrades were shot in front of their own men. The responsible cadres might themselves have been fine comrades—Teroy in some cases sympathized with them. But they had let their reason be ruled by their emotions. Justice had to be given to the dead.

Teroy's guidelines for the detention of DPAs:

1. They often have relatives in the military.
2. They have 'lumpen experiences'—criminal backgrounds.
3. They have unresolved personal problems.
4. They are extremely active within the movement.
5. But they regularly visit their families—which is when they have a chance to contact their friends in the military.
6. And finally, the army follows closely the units in which they work.

Just as you can see the thinking behind these indicators, so you can see the scope for paranoia. The presence of a DPA is suspected when some particularly bitter disaster has befallen a unit—they realize they were being fired on from behind, for instance, or that a carefully laid plan has been leaked.

But imagine an NPA unit which is being successfully shadowed by the military. How many of its members are likely to have no relatives in the army, to have no 'lumpen experiences' or unresolved personal problems? Most of them will be 'very active in the movement'. But that's also the ethos. Keep active. (If only to keep your mind off sex.)

So the detection of DPAs could be a very bloody business indeed. There's another thing. While nobody doubts that the military has its agents, and that some of these get well-entrenched in the NPA, you would have to know a great deal about what went wrong in, say, Southern Tagalog before you could be sure that the problem had been created by DPAs. In most communist movements, power struggles or ideological purges have at some time or another been presented in similar terms. Unfortunately, despite all our vigilance, we were sabotaged by foreign agents, fascists, crypto-fascists, DPAs . . .

The DPA phenomenon seems to recur. I heard of a recent case in Surigao which sounded like the field of dragon's teeth. A whole company destroyed itself with imprisonment, torture and executions. If such an event can be provoked by the presence of government agents in a unit, then the government has a truly awesome power at its disposal, and the guerrilla movement an awesome susceptibility. Mistakes were made, they will say, or excesses were committed, and those responsible have been 'severely' punished.

But one must always ask why the NPA should be prone to this kind of 'mistake'.

5

To begin to understand the success of the NPA, its fearful strengths as well as its fearful weaknesses, one might begin with the question of justice. Not justice in the abstract, but concrete justice at the end of the remote, dusty road. You can stay in the Philippines—you can be born and bred there—without ever getting a sense of life in the distant barrio: the devastating helplessness and defencelessness.

It might be that you are at the mercy of the weather or of disease. It might be a mortgage or a loan on a crop. It might be cattle-rustlers or land-grabbers. The cattle sleep beneath your hut—you live with them for safety. Every night you tie the *carabao*'s rope around your neck, so that you will feel its every movement.

But one morning you awake—the rope is cut and the animal is gone. That, they say, 'is like losing a limb.'

A local landlord allows his fences to fall into disrepair. When you complain that his animals are destroying your crop, his men come and rebuild new fences taking part of your land. At this point you know that if you complain further you may be killed.

An illness in the family sends you straight into debt, a debt into a mortgage, a mortgage into a foreclosure and a forced sale of land. It can all happen slowly. More likely it will happen very fast. As with a man I know who lost four children, in just over a week, during an outbreak of measles. Then his wife had to go into hospital . . .

At any moment the trapdoor may open under you. You are responsible for your own physical protection: the long knife—the *bolo*—you carry with you to the fields is more than a knife—it is a sword. You have some reason to visit the next village. You strap on your sword and you take a companion.

You can drive the length and breadth of Luzon, sticking to the main road, and get no feeling for this. The roads attract houses and small sums of money. They are ribbons of enterprise. You can observe their economy very clearly from the air. Beyond the ribbons, the fields. Beyond the fields, the plantations. An hour's drive from busy Laguna de Bay, a silent town with not a single private car. On the plains of Mindanao, hidden Muslim villages still living in fear of the last Christian massacre.

On a bleak, typhoon-swept shore, a community settling down to the knowledge that for the next three months there will be strong winds and no work.

There is the justice of the state—a complicated algebra of money, petrol, influence, luck and time. There is the justice of the gun—but who owns the gun? There is the justice of the sword in this world, and of God in the next—and the two are not exclusive, not at all. There is a Christ for the pickpockets, a Christ for the cut-throats, a Christ for the communists and a Christ for their sworn enemies.

And the enmities go deep. Once, during the truce, I saw a police spy being caught during a peasant demonstration. The stewards surrounded the man while his ID was checked, and sure enough he was some kind of agent. The stewards kept the crowd at bay, but once or twice people slipped through the cordon, punched him once or twice and slipped away again. Finally, the stewards took the man to the police and handed him over, minus his ID. The police were at first uncertain what to do. But suddenly the man, who had hitherto looked only very frightened, remembered his pride. He wanted his ID back. He demanded it. He broke away from his captors and lunged into the crowd. He was going to get his ID even if they killed him.

At that point, the police assumed responsibility. And if they had not taken him away, I could well believe that the man would have been killed. As it was, he was left with a burning sense of honour unredeemed. Maybe that night he would go out and kill someone.

Spy, informer, traitor—imagine the words on the lips of the distant village where you live. I know a group of friends among the poor fishermen of Quezon. They were an inseparable gang of mates—always joking together and amusing themselves with a highly developed comic routine. One day I arrive at the village and Balolov's hut is empty. All that is left of his possessions is a light anchor made of stone and rattan, hanging in a tree.

'Balolov is dead,' laughs a woman, 'No more *Kapitbahay*.' I called him *Kapitbahay*, or neighbour, because his hut is next to the cottage I am renting. It turns out that, according to the village, Balolov has made wholesale accusations against his friends, involving the illegal sale of milkfish fry. Now neither he nor his family can show their face in the village. As long as they stay where they have gone, three miles or so along the coast, they can remain non-persons. All the old friends shake their heads and smile. Beyond the smile lies something absolute. 'It's a shame.' I say. Yes, they concede, it's a shame—no more *Kapitbahay*. Balolov was so poor he had not yet even been able to have his three-year-old daughter baptized.

This preyed on his mind. He must have felt that he was being undermined by the other fishermen—he was working for the legal concessionaire; some of them weren't. But he must also have known that his protest was a kind of suicide, a suicide protest against the injustice in his life.

6

Teroy and I are sitting within sight of the Mayon volcano. It is an object of national pride—a perfect cone. The smoke from the crater streams a short way down one side, then disperses horizontally into the atmosphere. It is as if people were standing on the edge emptying bags of feathers, which roll in lumps for a while until the air currents lift them off. Teroy has just explained how, in his system, you organize and consolidate a group of barrios.

'The next phase,' he says, 'we call cleaning.'

Cleaning is when you kill the informers. 'You get the masses with their *bolos* and you go to the informer's house and you say: "Comrade, you have something to pay." '

As he explains this, Teroy, in an instant, demonstrates his technique, and I am his model. He is coming at me, with one hand outstretched to grasp my shirt and the other holding aloft the imaginary *bolo*. Teroy smiles during the demonstration. I flinch. I can easily see him coming up the garden path with his *bolo*-men.

I ask him how he can be sure who the informers are. There are three ways. First, most of them don't know how to keep a secret— they give themselves away. Secondly, the military doesn't know how to take care of its informers—they are seen with them.

Lastly, the NPA have their own informers among the military.

And what happens to the families of the informers? Don't they become implacable enemies of the NPA?

Teroy points to a tall young man from his group. He is one of the best of his soldiers, has led several successful raids. This man's father was an informer, and from what Teroy said I concluded he had been executed on Teroy's instructions.

But such a strange case of transferred loyalty must be exceptional. On another occasion I was told that the best way with informers was to exile them from the village—precisely because of the reactions of the families.

But still, in general, revolutionary justice is marked by a series of strategic killings. When an area is being organized, the 'semi-legal team' of two or more people move through the barrios making their first contacts and an ocular survey of secret trails and escape routes. They stay one night only in each barrio, moving backwards and forwards across the area setting up their initial organizations, the 'Barrio Liaison Group', who begin the social investigation. They are looking for the poor or 'lower-middle' peasants. The middle-middle, the upper-middle and the rich peasants are not good recruiting material. In a mixed group, the poor peasants will defer to them. What Teroy looks for is the peasant whose initiative and leadership qualities can be released from his lowly background. He will discover his own abilities—as it were, invent himself as he goes along. It is precisely the opposite approach to that of the Philippine Military Academy, which begins with the élite as its material.

Only when an area has been consolidated, with a complex set of groups, will the 'cleaning' begin, and only when the cleaning has been achieved will the land reform be effective. For the land reform is like a surreptitious strike: all the peasants unite to report bad crops to their various landlords. Everyone has the same story, everyone will stick together. And thus the land rent is reduced.

You do not abolish the rent overnight, or take over the land. To do so is to ask the landlord to bring in the military or the private armies. Instead, you have quietly to let the landlord know that you are now an organized presence to be dealt with: 'Time has changed, comrade. You can no longer have the deal you once enjoyed. But if you want to play straight with us, we'll play straight with you . . .'

The NPA often say that when they first move into an area it is the killing of cattle-rustlers that wins them the decisive support. After that they are greeted like heroes. A man's family's way of life can change. Instead of living with the cattle they can put them in the pen overnight. The thieves are eliminated—the hoodlums go.

At the same time the NPA have acquired a monopoly of firearms, for among the first of their actions is the confiscation of guns from the farmers, and it is only after the consolidation has been completed that these may be handed back to their (trusted) owners.

But once an area has been consolidated it may soon receive the attention of the military. At this point the NPA makes a calculation about the level of activity they themselves will indulge in. If they go too far, they will 'destroy their own mass base.' There will be reprisals, mass evacuations, hamlettings.

And thus begins a period in which the advantages and disadvantages of being 'consolidated' will be bitterly contrasted. If the regime works peacefully enough, it may look like a kind of justice. But if not, you will find that the answer to the question 'What has the NPA done for you?' is a sharp 'You mean, what have we done for them?'

7

Teroy is an extrovert—a revolutionary more in the Latin American than the South-east Asia mode. He may use euphemisms like 'cleaning', but he, basically, tells you what he is up to and why. By the time this article is published he will be the overall NPA commander for southern Luzon. The boast of his group is that it is they, the Bicol troops, who will in the end take Manila. And Teroy is a power-broker already, not just on the military fronts. During the truce he told me that traditional politicians of every shade of opinion approached him for this, that or the other deal. The constitution has been voted in (the NPA would have nothing to do with it) and that meant that there would be elections, first national, then local. Everyone was interested in the fact that people like Teroy had come out of hiding for a while, but the people most interested were the traditional politicians. Businessmen, landlords and politicians have all been keen to deal with the NPA—for a strict, perceived advantage. If you wanted evidence that the truce was working to the advantage of the NPA, Teroy would be evidence.

Jeff Tugawin, who comes from northern Luzon, is very different. Again, he was one of those leaders chosen to surface and make themselves known during the truce, but this was against the better judgement of men in his area, who had been fighting a hard battle in the Cagayan Valley and believed they were winning. Jeff and his group arrived late in Metro Manila: they too had trouble with their safe-conduct passes, and trouble in believing in their validity once they had them. If Teroy had feared Colonel Abadilla, the man Jeff didn't trust was Colonel Rodolfo Aguinaldo—as it were, his opposite number in the Cagayan region. (Both of these colonels have since been stripped of office after coup attempts, and are now on their own *maquis*.)

By the time Jeff arrived in the capital, the talks which had taken so long to set up were proving something of a barren exercise. Each side felt that the other had nothing to say or offer. And in the meantime the military became increasingly outraged at the presence of the communists—on television, on the streets, even joining demonstrations, and with their own office in the National Press Club.

Jeff went on television and gave some interviews. In public he stuck to the agreed line. In private he was never expansive. I had known him for quite some time when he suddenly, to my surprise, asked if I would like to hear a song. He picked up a guitar and sang 'Suicide is Painless' from *M.A.S.H.* He is a good guitarist singer—you can easily imagine him as a Methodist youth leader, which he once was. When he had finished his song, and I asked him for an NPA song, he looked at me as if I was mad. Jeff in the city—truce or no truce—was underground.

After 22 January, when a group of protesters for land reform were massacred at Mendiola Bridge, everybody else went underground. The talks were finished. The office in the National Press Club was closed, and word was put out that all the communist delegates had gone to the hills.

Actually they didn't all go at once. They had a month left of safe conduct, for what that was worth. And a mass exodus from the capital would have made them particularly vulnerable.

Jeff had a long journey up north ahead of him. He was going first to a wedding of some comrades, and he invited me along to see a communist wedding. Nothing would arouse my curiosity less, in normal circumstances, but I did wonder if, one day, Jeff would actually talk.

He said of Teroy: 'I like him—I wish I'd had more chance to meet him in Manila. He's amusing and full of ideas.' Jeff's style was so different, so quiet and reserved, and I thought that in what he said about Teroy he was implying a comparison with himself.

We eventually went up north, and Jeff hardly spoke along the way. But at the end, somehow, he seemed to explode. He said that now the truce was over he could speak his mind, whereas before he had wanted to do so but had been constrained by party discipline. Jeff was dismayed at the sacrifices they had made for the truce—they had even released hostages they were holding—whereas his wife, a prisoner of the military, had not been released. In Cagayan they had been winning against the military—why stop fighting now?

Indeed, as Jeff warmed to his theme, he said, Was it not a terrible thing that Salas, Rodolfo Salas, had been arrested in the course of the setting up of this truce? Salas had been right all along—said Jeff. 'I even dare to say,' he said, his eyes bright with outrage, 'that the boycott in the snap election was right.' When Cory stood against Marcos they had been right to have nothing to do with it. And after Cory's victory, Salas was demoted, but, when asked to admit his mistakes, he had been defiant: 'History will absolve us,' he had said. And Jeff agreed. He is the convinced hardliner—have nothing to do with Cory or that junk about a truce.

There was only one thing that made people respect the NPA, he said, in all their struggle in Cagayan, and that was guns. 'Politics is guns, guns, guns and it is nothing else.' The idea that they could enter some kind of junior partnership in politics was rubbish. Until they had a leading position (fifty-five percent was how he put it) there was no point in talking to anybody.

'Guns, guns, guns and nothing else.' 'Guns, guns, guns—and nothing else.' I remember vividly how he spat the words out.

I asked him: 'If it comes to the point where the communists take Manila, whose troops will do it? Will it be the guys from Bicol, or will it be the ones from Cagayan?'

Jeff laughed.

'You mean,' he said, 'will it be Teroy or me?'

'Yes.'

'What do they say in Bicol?'

'They say they'll be the ones to do it.'

Jeff said: 'If Teroy gets to Manila first,' slight pause, 'I'll be very happy for him.'

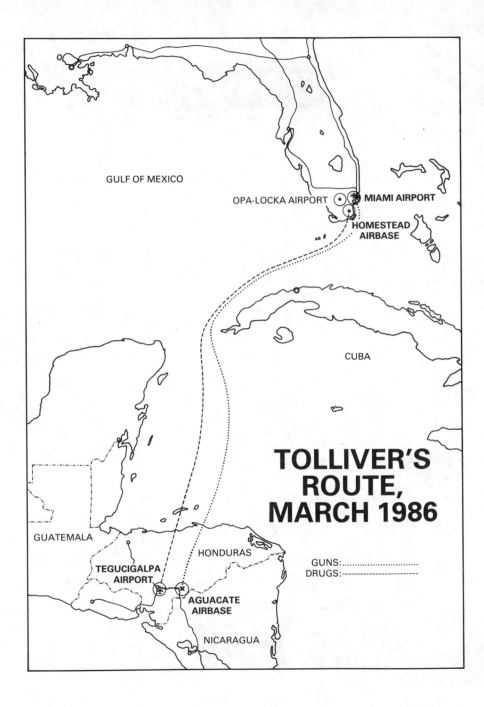

GULF OF MEXICO

OPA-LOCKA AIRPORT   **MIAMI AIRPORT**

**HOMESTEAD
AIRBASE**

CUBA

TOLLIVER'S
ROUTE,
MARCH 1986

GUNS:................................

DRUGS:------------------------------

GUATEMALA

HONDURAS

**TEGUCIGALPA
AIRPORT**

**AGUACATE
AIRBASE**

NICARAGUA

The current holder of the record for the fastest time in a powerboat between New York and Miami is a Columbian-American named George Morales. Morales achieved this honour in 1985, when he raced a catamaran with four 635-horsepower engines from one city to the other in nine hours and thirty-four minutes, earning him a prize of half a million dollars. Powerboat racing is so expensive, however, that even this amount of money would not have financed Morales's sporting activities, which culminated in three successive years as Miami's unbeaten, off-shore powerboat champion. He had, in addition to powerboats, seven or eight vehicles valued at more than 30,000 dollars each, five or six maids and hangers-on, and an elaborate security system that included closed circuit television and electronic gates. What made it all possible was Morales's line of business, the importation and sale of very large quantities of cocaine.

Morales is well-dressed, elegant, self-assured and was very good at his business. He had his own airline, Aviation Activities Corp., and kept an impressive fleet of planes right next to Hangar One at Opa-locka Airport, outside Miami. He had a stable of pilots with years of experience. Also on the payroll were presidents and generals throughout the Caribbean and Central America. His enterprise kept dossiers on south Florida's Drug Enforcement Administration agents, and there were law enforcement officials at home and abroad who could depend on him for generous bribes.

But both business and pleasure came to a halt on 13 June 1986, when Morales was gaoled and eventually sentenced to sixteen years in prison.

Morales's troubles began in the spring of 1984, when he was indicted for conspiracy to import and distribute cocaine. It was this awkward development that made him particularly receptive to the proposal he received from a delegation of Contras and a CIA man that turned up at his Opa-locka office soon after the bad news.

According the Morales, the delegation proposed a trade: it would see that his indictment was 'taken care of', slowed down, perhaps dropped entirely. In return, Morales would donate 250,000 dollars every three months to the 'cause', train Contra pilots and put his planes at the disposal of those fighting the war. The Contra pilots would also, however, be available for Morales to use on occasional runs from Colombia to Costa Rica and points north. Morales was no stranger to the Contra movement, having bought and leased safe houses for the Contras in Miami, and having shared his expertise in off-shore banking.

The CIA man who came to see him was Octaviano Cesar, a Nicaraguan exile based in Costa Rica, who later took the position of 'Director of International Relations' for a Contra faction called the Southern Opposition Block. Morales says that Cesar became his regular contact and assured him that 'high-level Washington people' would keep him out of gaol. Cesar 'had spoken with Vice-President Bush about my situation,' Morales remembers, and that 'the indictment was dying away. It was the sort of situation where the DEA [the US Drug Enforcement Administration] got into bed with the CIA just to the point where I was in the middle. The CIA knew I was working with them full-time. The CIA knew what was going on. They needed the support.'*

As the relationship developed, Morales says, he donated a total of three million dollars in cash and provided, in addition, pilots, houses and planes. The money itself reached the Contras through off-shore banks, and sometimes was delivered in 'boxes, suitcases, bags' stuffed with hundreds of thousands of dollars in cash. In October 1984 Cesar actually accompanied Morales on a trip to the Bahamas to pick up a donation—400,000 dollars in cash from a local bank.

In early 1987, Cesar admitted knowing Morales, and soliciting aid from him. He remembered going to Morales's Opa-locka office, but he was somehow unable to recall the trip to the bank. Cesar's hand shook violently as he stumbled through his version of the Bahamas jaunt. 'We took one of those old taxis they have there. We went to a place where supposedly they have excellent

---

*Eight sources, ranging from senior Contras to high-level administration officials in Washington, attest that Cesar was indeed an operative of the Central Intelligence agency.

hamburgers . . . We had a couple of beers. We had a hamburger, and then we came back.' Cesar maintained that he had absolutely no knowledge that Morales was an indicted drug dealer. The US Customs Service discovered, however, that Cesar had noted the 400,000 dollars on a signed customs declaration form dated 13 October, 1984.

By August 1984, Morales was doing a brisk business with the fledgling FDN Contra group in the south, and the hub of the operation was the 8,000-acre ranch of CIA operative John Hull.* The arrangement was this: Morales's pilots would ferry guns down to Hull's ranch, and would then return with substantial quantities of narcotics. Hull not only got his guns; he got money: Morales remembers paying Hull 300,000 dollars a flight, a percentage of the value of the cargo.

I met one of Morales's pilots, Gary Betzner, who spoke about two runs he made to the ranch: 'I took two loads—small aircraft loads—of weapons to John Hull's ranch in Costa Rica and returned to Florida with approximately a thousand kilos of cocaine, five hundred each trip.' At the time of our meeting, Betzner, like Morales, was in the Metropolitan Correctional Center in Miami, which—with its landscape gardening and condominium

---

*Hull, born in Indiana, was a field agent at the end of White House chain of command overseeing the southern front of the Contra War: he answered, that is, to both CIA station chief Joe Fernandez and Lieutenant-Colonel Oliver North.

The FDN Contras (the Nicaraguan Democratic Force) have dominated the northern theatre of the Contra War. The strategy of the North and his colleagues was to build up an FDN faction in the south, and thus squeeze the Nicaraguan Sandistas between co-ordinated fronts. Such a build-up required sabotaging the efforts of rival Contra factions, such as the one led by Eden Pastora, whose fractious relationship with the CIA led it to commandeer his aircraft, encourage the defection of his commanders and spread rumours that Pastora's group was responsible for the narcotics-trafficking in the south.

architecture—is also known in select circles as the Miami Country Club. Betzner was serving fifteen years on a drug charge unrelated to his Contra mission—'I was fairly tried, fairly convicted and fairly sentenced'—and was famous for a dramatic escape attempt involving a helicopter landing in the flower beds to collect him. Unfortunately, federal agents had infiltrated the scheme and were on board.

Gary Betzner had five other names and passports: 'Whatever I had in my pocket is who I was, and that person was legitimate. He had a business, he had insurance, he was like a real person. That was just the paperwork that I needed to be able to move freely in the world.' He has been flying drugs for years, after having started out as an Arkansas crop-duster. He had also taken part in other covert government activities. In 1983, prior to the mining of the Nicaraguan harbours, he picked up a DC-3 that had been confiscated from a drug dealer at Boca Chica Naval Air Station in Key West. It was loaded with six ship mines, which he flew to Ilopango, the big military base outside San Salvador. The mine delivery, as Betzner describes it, was part of a package deal, and he and his co-pilot went on to Colombia where they picked up '6,000 pounds of pot', sanctioned as a payment for the delivering the mines.

When Morales approached Betzner with what sounded like a similar 'package', Betzner was ready to sign on. Morales, according to Betzner, 'was working with the Contras and it was sanctioned by the CIA . . . and it went all the way from George Bush down'—which, unsurprisingly, is denied by George Bush's office.

The going rate for Morales's 'package' was quite handsome, paid in cocaine. 'I took twenty kilos each trip. It came to about 350,000 dollars a trip. John Hull's strip is a little short, you know. I thought it was kind of dangerous with the load I went down there with.' Otherwise, the trip was fairly easy, with landing and take off at both ends in broad daylight. On one trip he picked up a load of weapons at the Fort Lauderdale airport. 'There were some C-4 explosives, M-60 machine guns. It was stacked all the way to the ceiling. I was way overloaded.' Once he landed, the 'people working for John Hull loaded the aircraft. In both cases, John Hull was there,' and 'saw the the weapons coming in' and 'saw the bags' of cocaine loaded for the return trip to Florida. 'The cocaine was there when we off-loaded the weapons . . . I loaded the heavy bags forward and the boxes aft. One blond-headed kid was there, a couple of Costa Ricans. John Hull had on a baseball cap. I told him I was from Arkansas. He said he was from Indiana and asked me how I liked his place. I had some coffee.'

On Betzner's second trip, he flew into a different strip at the back of Hull's ranch, called Los Llanos, that he described as being near a sawmill and tall radio towers (the Voice of America relay station is indeed on a nearby dirt road). After the cocaine was loaded, Betzner set a course for Opa-locka Airport. Once he landed, he jumped off the wing. 'George was standing there, his hands in his pockets, talking to these guys, just real casual.' The 'guys' turned out to be agents from the Drug Enforcement Administration. Morales later clarified their roles: they were on his payroll.

There is absolutely no doubt in Betzner's mind that Morales had the full protection of the CIA. 'George Morales is a very, very careful man. There would be no way in the world that he would ever risk a 300,000-dollar airplane and his friend—myself—and his own life, his own business and everything to be so foolish as to fly into Opa-locka Airport with 500 kilos of cocaine right in the middle of a drug war when there's an agent on every corner. There's security on the airport and he's being watched all the time. Taxi right up in front of his place and unload? I mean, that's ridiculous.'

Betzner's understanding of what he calls the 'guns-for-drugs program' is that the cocaine would be converted into cash for more weapons. 'It wasn't the private guns that went down that were that important; it was what was coming back. That could buy much larger and better and more sophisticated weapons, and it was unaccounted-for cash.' Betzner believes that Contras must have garnered 'around forty million' from such drug flights. 'Probably more than that. I mean, why get into the business if you're just going to make a few million dollars? You can buy a few helicopters; it won't feed a big army very long.'

According to Morales, the purpose of the US government's involvement in drug trafficking is very simple: 'They needed the

157

financial support for the Contras and it was one more way for them to obtain that financial support. The word came down from Washington, from the top, that no matter what had to be done in order to get money to supply the Contras it had to be done.' Morales got involved, however, for complicated reasons: apart from the prospect of being protected by the CIA and the appeal of lucrative drug runs, Morales considers the enterprise to be one of patriotic duty: 'To fight for freedom, to fight against the communists.' He calculates that he and his peers made a notable contribution to the southern front. 'I would say that seventy to eighty percent of the money went to the south.'

Morales also claims that the drug money performed an additional, less lofty purpose: it was used to fill the gap left by legitimate funds disappearing into Miami real estate or off-shore bank accounts at the expense of the Contra troops. 'Some of the money got stolen before it ever got out of here [Miami]. They had to come up with some idea, some sort of way, to reimburse that money and also to supply more to the Contras.' By late 1985, Morales says, echoing the private sentiments of Oliver North's Contra liaison Robert Owen, the Contra war had become all 'business'. The fight for freedom had gone by the wayside: 'They were just fighting for profit. It was not necessary to prove how you spent the money. No questions asked. No receipts.'

2

I visited John Hull on his *finca* in 1986. Hull stoutly denies any involvement of any kind at any time with drugs or arms shipments. 'We're not involved in drugs,' he says, 'we're not involved in arms movements.' His employees keep careful logs on the 'five or six' operable airstrips he controls, 'not for me but for the Costa Rican narcotics people'—which amuses George Morales; he confided that a top official of the Costa Rican narcotics force was one of many on his payroll.

The local US Drug Enforcement Administration agents have a different view. When I talked to them in San José, they said that the San Carlos Valley, the region of John Hull's ranch, was a 'problem' and that that part of Costa Rica had become a major transshipment point for cocaine, but they had been instructed by the head office in Washington not to discuss the subject of Contra drug-trafficking. Similarly, Pat Korten, spokesman for the US Department of Justice, admitted in March 1987 that John Hull had been under suspicion 'for years' for cocaine trafficking, but that federal agencies, including the FBI, simply had not been able to amass enough evidence for a criminal prosecution, even though George Morales, Gary Betzner and others had produced abundant testimony.

But the authorities display a curious reluctance to accept their evidence, routinely dismissing Morales and Betzner as convicted criminals spinning tales in the hope of lighter sentences. Leon Kellner, the US Attorney in Miami went further, actually dissembling in order to discredit Morales, and—to the annoyance of the Senate Foreign Relations Committee that was about to call Morales as a witness—told one reporter that George Morales had failed a lie-detector test: in fact, Morales had never taken, much less failed, any such test.

In the event of being called before Congress as witnesses, the best that either Morales or Betzner could realistically hope for was immunity from prosecution for the Contra drug runs they were now disclosing. When the Drug Enforcement Administration found out that Morales would be testifying before Congress under oath, one of its agents made him an offer: a shorter sentence for an agreement not to take his story to Capitol Hill. Jack Blum, the chief drug investigator for the Senate Foreign Relations Committee, learned of the Drug Enforcement Administration's offer, and shored up Morales's resolve to appear before the Senate and forego the Drug Enforcement Administration's offer. Morales testified without immunity.

3

It is also reported that there is another airfield in Costa Rica being used for drug trafficking. This is the airfield at Santa Elena. The airfield was top secret, had been authorized by Lieutenant-Colonel

Oliver North and was constructed as a strategic part of North's enterprise. It is also, according to several sources, a transshipment point for cocaine.

Geraldo Duran, described by Morales as one of his top pilots, is reported to have used Santa Elena for drug runs. Duran is also a friend of John Hull's, and in fact, in July 1987, the Senate Foreign Relations Subcommittee on Narcotics and Terrorism released copies of fuel receipts, confirming several trips taken by Hull and Duran to Colombia in 1983.

Another source is 'Tosh', who has never been behind bars. Tosh said that in June 1986 he had made at least two cocaine runs through Santa Elena. His claim is all the more interesting because, at the time, Santa Elena was such a tightly-guarded secret that its existence was not known to either the press or Congress.

'**M**ickey' Tolliver is the Nick Nolte of the drug-pilot set. His father had been in the US Air Force and had instilled a love of flying in all his sons, expressed in Tolliver as an attraction to the danger, fast women and huge sums of cash that went with a career as a top-of-the-line drug pilot. By 1987 he had chalked up seventeen years of experience carrying unconventional freight, largely guns and drugs.

In August 1985 Tolliver received a call from his colleague Barry Seal, well-known in the trade for his ties with the CIA. Seal asked him if he would be available for 'interesting flying'. The interesting flying, thought Tolliver, could be 'anything from Campbell's soup to dead babies, but knowing Seal it involved drugs.' He had no idea that he was stepping into the middle of the secret Contra supply network, and that his control agents would include, according to Tolliver, at least one high-level operative in the Oliver North-CIA operation: veteran CIA agent Rafael Quintero.

Seal told Tolliver to go to Miami and call a particular number. A voice at the other end said, 'We'd like you to go down to Tegucigalpa, Honduras, to talk to our people down there . . . Everything will be explained when you get there. You'll meet a guy there named Wayne Westover. Just go out to Opa-locka, Hangar

One, and someone will be waiting for you and they'll take you down there, no problems.'

Tolliver was accustomed to doing business with people whose identities were never fully explained. 'That's the way things work; you meet people you never met before and they'll have suitcases full of money. It's a big equalizer, you know. A guy comes up to you, says, "Hi, my name is John Doe and I don't know you but here's half a million dollars."'

Tolliver made his way to the airport at seven the following morning. 'We flew to Tegoose [Tegucigalpa] and I should have figured something right there—somebody was doing something— because there was no customs, no immigration, no nothing. We just walked right outside the terminal, got in a car, and went to the Maya Hotel.'

Wayne Westover was introduced as 'our liaison man from northern Honduras, but he's here now to tell you what to do.' Actually, Westover's role appears to have been limited to introducing Tolliver to another 'liaison', José Ferrer. Ferrer explained the mission, which would be flying military supplies. Tolliver agreed. He was told to go home and wait for a call from a 'Mr Hernandez'.

It took a month for 'Hernandez' to get in touch. 'He started talking about specifics, dollars and cents, what the merchandise was: guns, ammunition, things like that, for the Contras.' Hernandez then threw in a sweetener. 'As an extra added bonus, we could either free-lance on our way back, meaning we could bring back our own cargo, or we could bring back their cargo, without ever having to worry about interception, arrest or anything like this. Everything would be taken care of.' The cargo was drugs.

His new employers were flexible about the kinds of drugs Tolliver could carry. 'Whatever you wanted,' he recalls them saying, 'marijuana, cocaine. It was my understanding that they would make sure we wouldn't get caught. They were providing not only the cargo but the landing areas, crews, everything: for drug runs.' As it happened, it was 'they' rather than Tolliver who provided the drugs for the first trip from Honduras.

Tolliver professes not to know who benefited from the trafficking. 'That's not my end of the business. Never has been.

Believe it or not, the entire business is compartmentalized. I'm like a teamster, I'm in transportation. You've got people who are in off-loading; you've got people who are in distribution; people that are in sales. It's like IBM.'

In December of 1985 Tolliver says Hernandez introduced him to Rafael Quintero. The meeting took place at the Sheraton River House in Miami.

Tolliver assumed that Quintero was CIA. 'If he wasn't, he was very heavily connected with someone; either that or he had a direct line to the Lord. They were talking about where they wanted to land down there and the protection we'd have and don't worry, everything's taken care of.' The pay, 75,000 dollars, was less than Tolliver's usual rate. 'There's the inherent God-and-country deal. I gave them a GI discount.'*

Finally, in March 1986, the flight was set to go. Tolliver, with 10,000 dollars in expenses and a phoney ID card that read 'Pacific Air', made his way to Butler Aviation at Miami airport. A Latin crew was waiting, and a DC-6 loaded with 28,000 pounds of 'guns, ammunition, things like that.' The plane, painted an elegant silver with a distinctive red stripe down the side, had been obtained from a man Tolliver remembered only as 'Mike', who he had heard had subsequently suffered the embarrassment of a drug charge in Detroit.

The destination was Aguacate air base, another Contra supply base in Honduras established by the CIA. Security was tight, and uninvited guests were not welcome. Tolliver spotted one American, an 'aloof, tall, slender blond'. There were no customs agents. Contra troops unloaded the plane while Tolliver was bundled off to Tegoose for a three-day furlough at the Holiday Inn. Later, his co-pilot moved the DC-6 to the airport at Tegucigalpa, and when Tolliver returned, the plane was fully loaded. This time the cargo

---

*The following month, Tolliver says, Quintero summoned him all the way to Ecuador to give him a message he refused to transmit over the telephone: Tolliver should not talk to Barry Seal anymore. A month later Seal, a professional informant, was murdered in New Orleans on the orders of a Colombian cocaine cartel.

was 'twenty-five thousand [pounds] and change pot. The piece of paper they gave me said twenty-five, I think, three-sixty.' That is, he was carrying 25,360 pounds of marijuana. Tolliver described his return trip this way:

'We take off from Tegucigalpa, Honduras, and we leave.'

'To?'

'South Florida.'

'Where in south Florida?'

'We landed at Homestead.'

'Homestead?'

'Air Force Base.'

'You brought 25,000 pounds of pot and landed at Homestead Air Force Base?'

'That's correct.'

Clearance was no problem. 'I was given a discrete transponder code to squawk about two hours south of Miami. I received my instructions from the ground, from air traffic control for traffic separation. I told them we were a non-scheduled military flight into Homestead Air Force Base.' It was the middle of the night. 'We landed about one-thirty, two o'clock in the morning, and a little blue truck came out and met us. [It] had a little white sign on it that said *Follow Me* with flashing lights. We followed it.

'I was a little taken aback, to be honest with you . . . I figured it was a set-up, or it was a DEA bust or a sting or something like that.' Yet nothing happened. 'The little guy in the truck puts us in the pickup truck and takes us out. I got in a taxi-cab.' Tolliver was paid his 75,000 dollars.

'Every time something happens, I become more and more inured to it. No more surprises; there can't be any more surprises.' He assumes that this operation had to have been sanctioned at a very high level. 'It has to be someone that high up, because who else can you get that's going to pick up a phone and say, "Let this happen?"' He neither knew nor wanted to know what happened to the twelve tons of marijuana—'as long as I got paid. I mean, I'm not callous, I'm just, you know, basically a whore. I'd say that I am one of the very few people who'll stand up and say, "Yes, I did it." You have myriads of people who have done the same thing, and they won't say it. So 25,000 thousand [pounds of marijuana] is the tip of the iceberg.'

4

In late April 1987, US Customs Service said that it and the CIA had begun to investigate 'whether drugs were smuggled into the United States by traffickers who had learned that routine customs inspections were suspended for the officially sanctioned flights' by the CIA to and from Central America. According to custom officials quoted in the *Boston Globe*, 'Between fifty and a hundred flights that had been arranged by the CIA took off from or landed at US airports during the past two years without undergoing inspection . . . The system provided for the CIA to notify the Customs Service that a certain flight was about to leave from or land at a US airport.' As one customs official put it, 'Our inspectors took that to mean hands off everything. And they stopped checking everything, personal belongings as well as cargo . . . It was an invitation for problems.' No one seems to have asked what the 'officially sanctioned flights' were for at a time when Congress had barred CIA aid to the Contras.

One official admitted that Tolliver's account of his epic trip to Homestead 'had credibility. We think he did land at Homestead.' But, he added, Tolliver must have been a 'free-lancer. Unless you believe that the CIA is involved in drug trafficking, which I do not, then the only reasonable explanation is that he knew from his contacts there was an inspection-avoidance system in place there and bluffed his way through it.' Of course, had Tolliver bluffed the air force and customs personnel on the ground he would have had an interesting time trying to explain the presence of twelve tons of marijuana. Someone had to unload that cargo, and it is hardly a speedy job off-loading and warehousing 25,360 pounds of pot.

But there were more clues to be found in the aircraft Tolliver had used, the DC-6 with its distinctive red stripe, traced to a company called Vortex, which an administration source had told us before was being used to ship arms to the Contras in violation of the Congressional ban. On 25 February 1986, Vortex had received a contract of 96,961 dollars to ship supplies to the Contras from the Nicaraguan Humanitarian Assistance Office (the humanitarian assistance office at the State Department). The Vortex vice-president who signed the contract was Mike Palmer.

Palmer's career had been in the grand tradition of the Contra supply effort: three months in gaol in Colombia in the spring of 1985 after he was caught trying to pick up a plane-load of marijuana. Four months after signing the State Department contract, he was in trouble again, indicted in Detroit for conspiracy and drug possession. Vortex was dissolved in 1986, when the Contra supply effort was much in the news, only to be reborn as Vortex International.

It seems that Palmer, the man indicted in Detroit, must be the same 'Mike' who had supplied Tolliver with the plane for the trip to Aguacate in Honduras. Thus the State Department had been issuing cheques to Vortex in February 1986, just one month before Tolliver flew tons of guns and drugs between Florida and Central America in a Vortex plane obtained from an indicted drug smuggler. (The success of Vortex in feeding off the Nicaraguan Humanitarian Assistance Office while apparently air-freighting narcotics is paralleled by another State Department contractor, Dioxa, which received a 38,000 dollar contract and whose boss was subsequently indicted on charges relating to half a ton of cocaine.)

After Tolliver's flight, his DC-6 was then re-registered to a new front company, though, in a slip typical of covert operations, the new firm had the same address as the old.

On 1 April 1987 Vortex was involved in an inter-agency squabble. A Vortex plane on its way back from Central America, with Mike Palmer at the controls, was stopped for customs inspection. Palmer said he was flying for the State Department. Customs agents then ran Palmer through their computer, which raised the issue of his Detroit indictment and extensive drug connections. They detained plane and pilot for further investigation. An exasperated CIA official then called customs to rescue both plane and Palmer, and to demand that customs stop meddling in their business. A customs agent raised the drug question with the CIA, but was firmly told to let the matter drop.

Even though the CIA has openly admitted that the indicted drug smuggler Mike Palmer was its man, customs officials continue to insist that the drug shipments were the work of 'free-lancers'

Leslie Cockburn

rather than operators sanctioned by the agency. As a custom official put it: 'These people, these free-lancers, took advantage of our [inspection-free CIA] programme. That's bad enough and it happens to be true.'

However, there are those in the Administration who acknowledge what is taking place: that the drug connection exists and it is considered to be 'business as usual'. The story is not without precedent. The flow of heroin from South-east Asia on to the

An instructive example of Lieutenant-Colonel Oliver North's fitness for a central role in US foreign policy is evident in his relationship with a man name Kevin Kattke.

Kattke was not a seasoned covert operator; he was not an old hand from South-east Asia days; he was not anything of the kind. His base of operations was the building maintenance office at Macy's Department Store, Hampstead, Long Island. Kattke led a hum-drum life. When his duties allowed, Kattke liked to take vacations in the Caribbean, particularly Jamaica. He nurtured ambitions for a career in espionage. Thus, in the course of his Jamaican excursions he made a point of buying drinks for the local constabulary and then transmitting items of 'intelligence' to the local US Embassy. Prior to the invasion of Grenada in October 1983, Kattke contacted the National Security Council, claiming, according to a subsequent FBI report, to represent a 'Grenedian [sic] student group who were contemplating an overthrow of the communist-leaning government of Grenada.' The official to whom he spoke was the then Major Oliver North. The two were made for each other. North referred to him as a 'rogue CIA agent'. Kattke returned the compliment. He called North 'the Compass'.

Kattke's contacts were not limited to the Caribbean. Back in Long Island he had a Lebanese friend who sold insurance for Equitable Life. At a meeting in a Brooklyn bar in the late spring of 1985, the insurance salesman confided to Kattke that the man holding the hostages in Beirut happened to be his cousin. For a mere 300,000 dollars, the cousin would disclose the prisoners' whereabouts.

166

American market increased dramatically during the 'secret war' in Laos in the early seventies. The anti-Castro CIA team in Florida were already drawing attention to their drug-smuggling activities by 1963. There is evidence of covert co-operation with the drug trade as far back as the early 1950s. It may have been that then, as now, those who sanctioned the unwholesome alliance believed, like George Morales, that 'it doesn't matter what we have to do in order to obtain the money to fight the communists.'

This vital intelligence, quickly relayed to 'The Compass', prompted North's rescue plan, which Robert McFarlane approved. The money was raised by a phone call to millionaire Ross Perot, whose interest in such affairs dated from a successful operation to extract two of his employees from a Tehran gaol during the Iranian revolution. The Drug Enforcement Administration men whom North had asked to be assigned the mission were duly despatched (to the bemused irritation of their superiors), knapsacks bulging with Perot's cash. The mission went awry. The insurance salesman's cousin was happy to accept the 300,000 dollars. Unfortunately he produced no information concerning the hostages.

This was not Kattke's only impact on high policy. In early February 1986 he was monitoring events in Haiti, where the regime of Baby Doc Duvalier was crumbling. Prowling around the presidential palace late one evening, Kattke noticed that the upstairs lights were not on. He immediately called the National Security Council to report that Duvalier had fled. Soon after, a contact emerged to say that Duvalier was in fact playing ping-pong in the basement. By then it was two a.m., and Kattke thought it would be an inconsiderate hour to call Washington so late. He, therefore, kept this latest news to himself. Thus White House spokesman Larry Speakes went on record with the statement that Duvalier had left, a week before he actually did.

In the spring of 1985, I sat in a Connecticut coffee shop with an elderly nun. She belonged to the Maryknoll order, whose members were scattered throughout Central and South America. The nun was on leave from her post in the village of San Juan de Limay, a collection of whitewashed houses at the end of a dirt track in northern Nicaragua. There had been heavy Contra activity in the surrounding hills. The road from Estili was marked with painted crosses.

The nun told me how she caught a lift one day on a pick-up truck full of farmers and housewives. When the Contras attacked, some of the passengers were killed. The sister was released, and hurried back on foot to warn others in the village not to take the road. She was captured en route by another band of Contras, who took her prisoner. She remembered that some of them had a patch sewn on their uniforms: '*Soldier of Fortune Convention*'. She asked if I knew what it meant. I explained that it was a memento of an annual gathering organized by *Soldier of Fortune* magazine where mercenaries and would-be mercenaries gathered to swap stories and fantasize about war.

The nun asked the men why they had attacked San Juan de Limay some days before and burned the town's only bus. She explained that it had taken a very long time to raise the money for that bus and for many it was the only means of transportation. If they won the war, she asked would they buy the town another bus. 'You won't need the bus,' a soldier replied. 'After democracy comes, everyone will drive a big car.'

■ METHUEN MODERN FICTION ■

KEN KESEY
DEMON BOX
The author of the great *One Flew Over the Cuckoo's Nest*
explores the rich territory of his own experience. 'Very
fine writing indeed' *New Statesman*
£3.95

MICHEL TOURNIER
GILLES & JEANNE
A provocative and vivid retelling of the relationship
between Joan of Arc and Gilles de Rais. 'Beautifully
realised . . . Alan Sheridan's translation picks up the
echoes of the past and the very modern chill analysis.'
Sunday Times
£3.50

NAWAL el SAADAWI
SHE HAS NO PLACE IN PARADISE
Subtly sharp stories on sexual politics by the author of
Woman at Point Zero and *Death of an Ex-Minister.*
£3.95

JOHN LAHR
THE AUTOGRAPH HOUND
'A funny, moving, terrifying portrait of the dream life of
America – haunting, beautifully written. I think it is a very
important book.' Arthur Kopit
£3.95

SIEGFRIED LENZ
THE HERITAGE
'A colossal achievement' Salman Rushdie 'Deserves
comparison with *Dr Faustus* and *The Tin Drum* as a
comprehensive analysis of Germany's cultural
disintegration.' *TLS*
£4.95

methuen
PAPERBACKS

ADAM MARS-JONES
REMISSION

Y*ogurt*. Yogurt taught me something yesterday. I was eating a yogurt, not one I'd bought, something one of the lovers picked up for me, a really creamy one with a crust of fat, not at all my usual style of yogurt. Maybe it was the creaminess, or maybe it was the absurd clashing of the fruits (apricot and mango, of all combinations), but I could really taste it; first thing I've really tasted in months. The fruit was only there in shreds, but there was enough juice in those shreds, juice or sugar or something, electricity for all I know, to give my mouth the feel of something vivid. And I thought—first thinking I've done in months, too, I dare say—I thought, illness is a failure, that's obvious. You don't have to be well to know that. But what is it a failure of? And at that moment, the answer seemed to be: imagination. It seemed to me then, reeling as I was from the impact of the fruit in the yogurt, that with a little effort, with a little imagination, I could taste anything, take pleasure in anything.

The yogurt didn't stay down, of course; it wasn't such a new beginning as all that. But what it had to teach me it taught me on the way down; on the way up it had nothing to say. And even that was a lesson of sorts. It was no more unpleasant to vomit that yogurt than it was to throw up my usual watery potlet. Its curds were no viler as they rose in my throat. I suppose I've been following a policy of appeasement with my stomach, and that's always a mistake. I've been behaving as if my insides were just being temperamental, and if I could find some perfectly inoffensive food for them, they would do the decent thing and hang on to it. And it just isn't so. I might as well eat what has a chance of giving me pleasure. My stomach will lob it up indifferently.

At the end of all that, after I had vomited, I was—I imagine—just fractionally weaker than when I had started. I had used some energy (vomiting is hard physical work) and I hadn't managed to get any nourishment. Trying to break down the yogurt had been, as it turned out, a costly waste of gastric juice. But in spite of that, I had had three distinct phases of pleasure—one, the taste of the yogurt itself; two, the long, incredulous moment when it seemed that it would stay down; three, the euphoria, after it came up, of having expelled poison, of knowing it wouldn't be fizzing in my guts for the

Photo: Susan J. O'Connor

rest of the day—and only one phase of unpleasantness when it was actually coming up. In some strange way it seemed that I was ahead on the day's transactions. That's when I thought of making this tape.

It's only a cheap, little secretarial Sony, this machine, but it's got everything I need. The controls are very simple; you don't even have to look at them. When things get bad, I can curl up with it under the bedclothes, a muttering foetus that can't get comfortable. [   ] If I get a coughing fit, I can edit it out, like that, by using the pause button. I've just got the two tapes, so I can change them over very easily, with the minimum of fumbling around.

There's the shits-and-vomits tape, which I'll use when I'm making the same old complaints, when I'm sicking up the same old record of bodily disasters. I'm never going to play it back. I'll just record on top of it, same old rant anyway. It's not for listening to, just for getting out of my system.

This tape is different. I've written the word *remission* on the spine of the cassette, and that's what I mean to concentrate on, every little quantum of forgiveness I can find in my body or my circumstances. I'll play it back eventually, but I'll wait as long as I can, so that I have a real hoard of positive moments to refresh myself with.

It's a bit odd, using the same channel to get rid of some experiences and intensify others. But I don't have to look further than my underpants to remember a similar arrangement.

And if there's a medical breakthrough soon, very soon—in the next twenty minutes, say—then I may not have to go back to the shits-and-vomits tape at all, just steam on with my remission. But I'll still go on thinking *remission*, however long it lasts; I'll never say *cure*. I can't be doing with that word. It makes everything impossible. It's a real obstacle to getting on with things.

What else fits the requirements for the remission tape? *The video.* Sleep is sweeter than it ever was, and I resent time wasted on anything else. But my video has taken all the angst out of insomnia. I sleep quite a lot in the day, so I'm likely to wake up in the middle of the night, quite suddenly, as if there was someone flashing a torch an inch away from my eyes. Television will have packed up hours before, the sleepy-head announcer yawning after the late film (it's past midnight, imagine!), wishing all the other sleepy-heads out there good-night. There's a programme on before close-down that has the nerve to call itself *Night Thoughts*. It's on at different times depending on the schedule, but always before one. *Night Thoughts* indeed! Can you beat it? The tube trains are hardly tucked up in their sheds for the night, and there's a lot of thinking to be done before morning, unless you have a video.

I bought the video quite a while ago, and it was one of those bits of self-indulgence that turn out to be good resolutions in disguise (having said that, I can't think of any others). I thought I'd turn into an addict, and I certainly taped a lot of programmes, but I never got round to watching them. I'd just buy more tapes as they got filled up. I never got into the habit of labelling the cassettes, so now I never know what I'm watching. I watch episodes of *Hill Street Blues* from two different series, and the only way I can tell them apart is by seeing whether Henry Goldbloom has a moustache or not. Promotions and romances don't help me much with the chronology, but with Henry's moustache I know where I am. I always did like moustaches. On top of that, Henry Goldbloom is always talking suicides down from their high places, reasoning with them through his megaphone of good intentions, and I suppose that's bound to strike some sort of chord.

The great thing about the video, of course, is that I can play things as fast or as slowly as I want. The other night I watched an old episode of *The Avengers,* in which John Steed was meant to dispose of a bomb by lobbing it into the bell of a euphonium. The detonation made the euphonium uncoil, like one of those irritating party-blowers. Except that the actor was too clumsy, or too drunk, to throw the bomb properly, and it rolled under a chair. The euphonium blew up all the same, of course, but if you rewind the video and play the sequence again you can see that it had no reason to. I found the whole thing extravagantly amusing, the other night, and I played it again and again, perhaps because it was one of the few things I'd come across in some time that was in no way a metaphor of my present condition.

That can't be right. Surely I can do better than that. With the

175

explosion, all the instrument's brass knitting unravels. What remains on the carpet is revealed as an intestine, tarnished and smoking. Good. Do better. What *The Avengers* was telling me, in an episode made around the time of my puberty, is that euphoniums end up unrolled and in ruins, even if they don't take a bomb in the bell. That's just what happens, with euphoniums. Good thought. Hang on to that.

Change the subject. *The lovers.* I have two lovers at the moment. *Lovers* is the wrong word, but then it always is. All I can say is, these two do everything for me a lover could do, and that's pretty amazing. We treat each other as if we had a history of sex, but that isn't the intimacy that binds us. I've had half-lovers before, even three-quarters lovers, once or twice, but these two are somehow fully loving towards me, and that's worth putting down on this privileged spool of tape (chrome dioxide for a longer life).[

]*Dead parents.* Anyone whose doctors are not cheerful should try as a first step not to have parents alive. I'm not being unduly oriental here; it's not that I think it's disrespectful in some way to turn in while your parents are still around and about. But I'm sure it confuses things. There's a touch of the bailiff about parents, I've always thought, as if they were waiting for you to fall behind with the payments on your life, so they could repossess it. What a terrible thing to say.

I'm not always so cynical, but I try. Anyway, I'm sure it makes it worse, having your parents around. Not my problem. Having your parents die is unpleasant in its own right of course, and not only in the expected ways. Example: my father had this terrible rightness about him. From his hospital bed he corrected the doctors' pronunciation and finished their sentences for them. I always hated that. It makes me think, now, how robust he was in his dying, how reliable his vitality was right up to the moment that it fell away from him. But the point is that while he was alive, I didn't realize that I have a scarcely less terrible rightness myself, though everyone I've known must have noticed it. I finish people's sentences for them too—I just interrupt them later on in their flow—so I've always fooled myself I'm a good listener. And compared to my Dad, I *am* a good listener, but the people I've shut up over the years didn't know that.

The lovers are going to get a bit of a shock, when I get some strength back and start bossing them about. I think they deserve an entry of their own, while their patience has yet to be tested, while my character is still blurred by my powerlessness.

The lovers. I had a lover, of a sort, when I was diagnosed, but I soon got rid of him. I'd already placed a small ad which defined me as a Lonely Heart, which was my way of serving notice to myself that I was going to serve notice on him, and then I was diagnosed. I thought at once, that settles it (that was my first thought), I've got to get rid of him and I did. He thought his health made him necessary to me, and I had hell's own job convincing him it made him even more of a nuisance than he was before, more of a menace, more of a pest. I couldn't carry him and illness too.

So when the magazine forwarded the replies to my ad, everything had changed, and they were replying to someone who didn't exist any more. There were only two replies, perhaps because I was never the world's most beautiful man, and my advert wasn't exactly raging with self-esteem. But I thought they deserved an explanation, and I arranged to meet them, both of them together so I didn't need to repeat myself.

By treating these strangers well after behaving so badly to someone who thought he was close to me, I think I was exercising in some final way the prerogatives of vigour. That's how I've worked it out since then. It was a choosing spree, and now my choices are made.

All the same: it wasn't as easy as I thought. I felt a terrible lurch when I started talking, and I had something like an anxiety attack. Perhaps it was simply grief for the person who had placed the ad, and wasn't around any more. It's hard to be sure what it is you're having when you know your body is scheduled to fail you piecemeal—and your mind doesn't have a lot to look forward to, come to that—and you experience a sensation of intense heat and horror. Whether it was only an anxiety attack or what, I wasn't able to stay as long as I'd meant to, and I stumbled out while their drinks were still half finished. And a couple of hours later they phoned, the two of them, to ask how I was, and to say they'd like to help me in any way they could, if I'd let them.

If I try, knowing them as well as I do now, I can probably reconstruct the conversation that led up to their phone call. But I don't care to analyse something that has become so necessary to me. I answered. They offered. I accepted. We've developed some useful routines.

Diagnosis broke me up, the way a plough breaks earth, and all the recent growth, rooted so lightly, was pulled right up. But I was left all ready for seeding. When they phoned—it was Rory actually holding the phone and doing the talking—I remember I said, 'Let's get one thing straight. I have never depended on the kindness of strangers.' Then I had to break it to them that what I was saying was Yes.

The lovers. Leo and Rory, my lovers, my lions. They pay their visits separately; I know they meet up at least once a week to arrange their timetables. They used to visit in the day, but now they know that day isn't really the time they're most useful. They used to be great soup-merchants, the pair of them, but they soon got sick of eating their own soups. Rory now helps me with housing benefit, which is much more important. Leo has a car, and Rory doesn't, so it's Leo who stays the night, assuming he's free, when I have a clinic appointment in the morning. If it's Rory keeping me company, we take a taxi.

The taxi costs money, of course, but I prefer Rory's company at the clinic. Leo gets very tense, and I more or less have to look after him. Rory is different. I've been particularly unwell for a few weeks, and the hospital wanted a stool sample. That's not easy when your stools move at a hundred miles an hour, like mine do at the moment. With a straight face they gave me a little pot with a screw top, as if what they wanted collecting was a butterfly and not a bowel movement. Rory wasn't with me that day. Anyway, I tried. Day after day I'd go to the lavatory with my little pot, but I was never quick enough. It was as frustrating as my train-spotting days as a boy, when I would stand by the main line in the early morning mist as the express thundered by, trying to read the number on the engine. Anyway, I got my sample at last, and took it along. After a week, I went back for the results, and they told me the sample had leaked and couldn't be used for analysis. They hadn't phoned me, of course, to say so. Didn't want to depress me, I dare say. So they gave me another pot and sent me back home again, to wait for the express.

These grumbles shouldn't be on this tape at all—they're classic shits-and-vomits stuff—but it all leads up to Rory and why he's good to have around. When I'd got my second sample to the hospital and they'd analysed it at last, the doctor prescribed Dioralyte, which she said I have to take every time I have a loose bowel motion. She added, 'It comes in three flavours, avoid the pineapple,' and I could catch Rory's eye and know that he was feeling the same tickle of amusement at her phrasing. The doctor pinched the skin of my arm to see how dehydrated I was, and we both watched the little swag of raised flesh she left, which took a good long time to fade. If they'd told me about Dioralyte earlier on, of course, I wouldn't be dehydrated in the first place, but you can get it from the chemist even without a prescription, so it's not the sort of thing that holds a highly-trained person's attention.

Or she can be explaining about *cryptospiridion*, the guest in my gut, and be saying, 'It produces nausea in the upper tract and diarrhoea in the lower, you see, because the whole intestine is implicated.' I can look at Rory and know he's thinking what I'm thinking: *Implicated? It's up to its bloody neck.* Leo would just sit there squirming, willing her to change the subject and talk about something nice.

I wish I'd had Rory with me when the doctor—the first doctor—asked me his three little questions.

Did I receive anal intercourse?

On occasion I did.

He made a note. Had I visited Central Africa?

On occasion I had.

He made another note. Had I received blood there, by any chance?

I seemed to remember something of the sort, when I was weak and confused from hepatitis. As I came out with the last of my answers, I could see the doctor's lips framing a word that looked like *Bingo,* and it would have been handy having Rory's eyes there for mine to meet.

Not that Rory's perfect. When we first heard about *crypto*, he and I, when she first mentioned the name, he blurted out, 'Oh dear, that's a stubborn one, isn't it?' I couldn't resist saying, 'Thanks a bunch, that's all I need,' just to see him flinch, though it really doesn't make any difference to me. In fact I'm glad he knows what he's about, if he does, so I don't have to worry about him the way I worry about Leo.

It's at night that Leo comes into his own, and not because he sleeps in the buff. He has a beguiling little body and all that, hairless and pale-skinned, but it's really only memory that tells me so. I let him sleep on the side of the bed away from the window, otherwise he thinks he won't sleep. It doesn't bother me which side of the bed I sleep, but with Rory I pretend I have a preference for lying away from the window. That way I know who it is that's staying over, even when I'm half asleep, just by our positions, just by feeling which side the warmth's coming from.

I couldn't really be in any doubt, anyway. Leo may wear no night-clothes, but he keeps to his side of the bed, and he turns his back on me—slowly, quietly, as if I'll be offended—when he's going to sleep. Rory sleeps in a night-shirt, but all the same he hugs me and holds me to him, which is all very nice. Just as he's dropping off to sleep, he's been known to stroke my nipple absent-mindedly with his thumb, but my nipple, quite unlike itself, inverts instead of stiffening.

There can't be much doubt in their minds about who they're sleeping with, that's for sure. The guest in my gut, the gate-crasher in my gut, sends out smells beneath the duvet. And when I have my sweats, I can't think it's pleasant for them. The sheets spread my wetness pretty widely.

I cheat them both, I suppose, by sleeping so much in the day. But it makes such a difference having a lover installed and snoring if I'm not doing much sleeping at night. And Leo is perfect, regularly breathing, just the minimal presence I need. Leo's snoring is my night-light. Sleep works on him like a humane killer, stunning him before it bleeds the consciousness out of him. If he stays up too late, he slurs his words, and then starts to doze with his eyes open, and I expect he's replying to my conversation in his head, and doesn't realize he's making no sound.

In the morning it works the other way round. He opens his eyes when I bring him a cup of tea, but it's a minute or two before he can properly hold the cup. Till then he blinks, yawns, changes position, groans and scrabbles at his hair. I know he's embarrassed that I bring him tea in the morning, but I'm solidly grateful that he sleeps so soundly, and I'll reward him in any way I can, even if it involves effort.

Rory is a much more partial sleeper, and when I get up he often joins me in front of the video. Or he'll go to the kitchen and mix up some Complan, with bananas and honey, the way I 'like' it, the way I can sometimes even tolerate it.

As he pads in, Rory asks me which series we're in, that is, are we escaping to 1982 or 1984? Does Henry Goldbloom have a moustache?

I tell him what year it is in the violently reassuring world of *Hill Street Blues*. Sometimes Rory seems to be doing a Henry Goldbloom himself, but all it means is that he's skipped shaving for a day or two. He gets rid of the growth before it has a real prospect of changing the balance of his face. It's a shame, he's got a great thick growth of hair right up his neck—what we used to call a poor man's cravat—so he actually looks a little odd clean-shaven.

It's wonderful of him to keep me company, I know, but I wish he'd go back to bed. Sometimes I put on a yawning routine, and we both go back to bed again, then I sneak out and go back to the video. It's not him I mind, it's the company he brings with him. If I can slide out of bed without waking him, I can get half an hour uninterrupted in front of the video. But when he gets up, and especially when he starts moving with a sort of muffled purposefulness round the kitchen, a gnawing and a churning wake up too. The gnawing is hunger and the churning is nausea, and wouldn't you know it, the gnawing is exactly in the middle of the churning, so there's no way I can get to it. So what with Rory and the Complan and the gnawing and the churning, it gets to be too much of a huddle round the video, and my view of the screen gets blocked off.

L *ower levels of illness.* I'm supposed to have mellowed; that seems to be the general verdict. I don't believe a word of it, myself. What really happens is different. There's an awkward interval, when you're ill but not yet conditioned by illness. You're far enough down to be spending all your time below ground, but every now and then you come across shafts of something very like daylight. That makes you impatient and hard to deal with. Things get easier, for other people at least, when you don't have moments of real vitality to show up the false. By now it's second nature for me to follow the cues I get from Leo and from Rory, and not to hang around waiting for my own spontaneity. Only if that draining away of impulse is mellowing can I take credit for it.

The new, eroded me—but for form's sake we'll say *mellow*— the new mellow me has learned to put up with a lot of goodness from people lately.

Rory tries to get me to lie down when I eat, as if that was going to help me hang on to my food, when all it means is more trouble being tidy when I throw up, but I forgive him for that. I know he means well even when he mixes me up some Dioralyte the moment I've had my *loose motion,* though I'm quite capable of throwing up the Dioralyte on the spot, before it's even properly gone down, just to make it clear that my system discriminates against digestion impartially, from both ends of the process.

Eroded as I am into mellowness, I've even learned to have mercy on Leo. We were in bed the other night, but for once he wasn't sleeping, for the very good reason that every time I lay down in bed I was having an attack of coughing. I tried sitting up in bed for a while, and then gradually sliding down to horizontal, but you can't fool a cough that way. I was trying it one more time just the same, when there was a knock on the door. It was very late, and we were both surprised. Leo put on a shirt and went to answer it. When he came back, he took off the shirt and got back into bed without explaining. I asked him who it was, and he said it was someone delivering pizza who'd got the wrong address.

'At this time of night?' I asked him.

'Yes.' I didn't even know you could have pizza delivered around here.

'What address was he looking for?'

'Don't know.'

'Did he find where it was?'

'Don't know.' We lay there for a moment, and Leo turned slowly over in bed, away from me.

I then had the idea that what I wanted most in the world was pizza. A sudden flow of saliva even soothed my cough for a moment. I suppose it was partly because it was so late, my nausea was deeply asleep, and for a moment I had a clear view of my hunger. And then the pizza seemed so near, so ready on the other side of the door. So I said, 'Leo, this may sound silly, but could you go out and see if that pizza man is still around? If he is, tell him I'll take it off his hands. I'm not fussy about toppings. I'll even pay full whack.'

Leo dragged himself slowly out of bed, put on the shirt again, his trousers and his shoes, and stumbled across the room towards the door. Then he came back and sat on the bed. He told me then that he'd made it up about the pizza. When he'd opened the front door there was a man there in dressing-gown and slippers, holding out a bottle of Benylin, that heavy-duty cough stuff, and saying, without a lot of warmth, 'Try this.' Leo hadn't wanted to tell me. He put the Benylin somewhere where he was going to pick it up the next morning and take it away with him. He hadn't known what else to do.

Nor did I for a moment, and then I asked him to fetch me the bottle, I'd have a swig anyway, just to be friendly. The nausea was wide awake by then, so it didn't cost me a lot to be generous, just a little. Leo undressed again and fell asleep soon after that, and so did I, I think, though I woke up towards morning for a little practice hacking, which Leo slept through, and I hope everybody in the street did too.[   ]

*S*almon sperm! What's the word? Milt. It's unbelievable! They just told me today. It turns out that milt is clever stuff. It has a Suppressing Effect. What it Suppresses is Replication. It's such clever stuff. And what that means is, salmon sperm is on my side. Milt loves me! And I love milt.

They're very dour about it. They say, don't build up your hopes too high. They never said that about fears. They never said don't build up your fears too high. And I'm not getting carried away. All I say is, milt loves me and I love milt! I don't even need to fellate the fish to get at it, though God knows I'd do it if I had to. They've synthesized it for me. They say, warning me, that it'll taste like metal. I say, you're wrong, it'll taste like Life. And they say, warning me, that I'll have to take it every four hours at first, day and night. And I say, nursing mothers have to put up with a lot more than that. I'll set the alarm for the middle of the night, and when it goes off I'll know what makes it worth while waking; there's no sleep so deep that I won't know. I'll know it's my Life waking me for its four o'clock feed.

They tell me it isn't a cure, as if I didn't know that. I tell them I know it could only be a poison, that's all doctors can ever give you, poison; you just have to hope that it hates you less than it hates what you've got. They tell me salmon sperm can attack your red cells, and your white cells come to that, so it might help to take some iron and vitamin B. I tell them I've always liked spinach. Oh, I've got all the answers. I just want to be able to put off the questions a bit.

*R**emission.* Maybe I'll be able to move over to this tape for good. Shut away the shits-and-vomits tape in its little case and never need to pull it out again.[

]Remission. I had my remission.[

]I had my remission, and I didn't record it. I didn't even write anything down.[

]When I listen back to this tape, I hear myself explaining what I'm going to use it for, but I never do. I never do.[

]Some things I don't need help remembering. I remember getting the first prescription for my salmon sperm, and going along with it to the hospital pharmacy. Rory was with me that day, but he was shutting up for once. The new twist my case was taking seemed to have robbed him of his small talk. The Aussie I've always hated was on duty in the pharmacy, with his usual tan, only more so, and the stupid bleach-streaked hair, only more so. And of course the awful voice! When you're waiting your turn, eyes down or looking at the warnings on the walls for innocent things like whooping-cough, and he's bellowing instructions to the customers before you in the line, you can think he must have picked up an old copy of *Punch* from the table, and rolled it up to make his voice so deafening. Then when it's your turn you find it's even worse. He *roars* at me as he passes over the box of Dioralyte, 'Make up a sachet after every loose bowel movement,' and then tells me how many times a day I need to take my antibiotics, as if it wasn't written on the container. He seems to have a heroic notion of his job, as if he was still a life-guard back in Australia—though I think you need broad shoulders for that—striding across toasted sand and warning red-heads not to sun-bathe. Then he pushes across the salmon sperm. I'd expected it to be a liquid, somehow, a heavy metallic liquid, what with its being so new and precious and rationed. I must have been thinking, too, of cod-liver oil. So I was disappointed for a moment when it was just ordinary capsules, like the timed-release symptom-suppressors you take for a cold, except with a different paint-job, white with a thin blue belt at the middle. Then I was impressed all over again by the size of the bottle, it wasn't really big, but bigger than I'm used to, so it looked like a sweetie-jar in an old-fashioned corner shop. For a moment I thought, almost tearful with gratitude, *All that, for me?* £250 for a fortnight's treatment isn't peanuts, but why should I have been so surprised to be worth it? Then the Aussie booms out, 'You have to take these every four hours, day and night, do you understand? The best thing is to take 'em at four, and eight, and twelve. That way you only need to get up once in the night.'

And I thought, this idiot knows *nothing;* if I was sleeping eight hours at a stretch I wouldn't be needing the salmon sperm, would I? I'd be holding down a job, wouldn't I, the way a paper-weight holds down a pile of prescription forms, the way you hold down yours. The week before, I'd just have let it wash over me, but this time it was as if the salmon sperm was giving me strength already, just by sitting there on the counter, so I said, 'Oh, I think I'll miss the four o'clock dose, get a full night's sleep.' I tried to make my voice campy. 'I'm not really an early morning person.' I could see Rory out of the corner of my eye, trying not to giggle.

But of course the Pharmacist From Bondi Beach looked really concerned, and he even lowered his voice, and he said, 'You really should, sir, it's important.'

If I'd had more than just the sight of the salmon sperm to give me strength, perhaps I'd have said something really crushing. But I couldn't think of anything anyway, so I just lowered my voice, all

185

the way down to a whisper, and said, 'Just to please you, then.'

There was no holding me. I nipped into the waiting-room on my way out, flashed the nurse a big smile and asked, 'Would it be possible, do you think, to trace the kind person who brings along all those back numbers of opera magazines?' Then, just as she got launched on the sort of smile that says you've made someone's day, I said, 'because I'd really like to push him off a small cliff. That would make my day.'

I remember that day because I had had a premonition of health. I was still outside the world of the well, that world which I understand so little of now.

I have to reconstruct those weeks, those (admit it) months, from what they have left behind, like a pathologist reconstructing a dead person's last meal. I remember looking at my first capsule, with a tiny animal printed on it in blue, like the little lions that used to be stamped on eggs, and what I took to be the world WELCOME in tiny letters. I remember thinking with real fervour, *Welcome yourself,* before I saw that the L in the word was double.

I know I became impatient with Leo and Rory almost instantly. They seemed so petty and nannyish, so ignorant of the real business of life. They nagged me to take my salmon sperm, as if it was something I'd forget just to be annoying. In fact I became very good at waking up seconds before the alarm went off for the three o'clock and seven o'clock feeds—I just had to be different, didn't I?—as if there really was a baby in the room, screaming. It should have struck me as funny when Leo struggled out of sleep at ten past seven one morning and started shaking me, convinced that I'd missed the seven o'clock feed and probably the three o'clock too, which of course he'd also snored through. It should have seemed funny, but it didn't. I suppose it was hard for them. They had suited themselves to me by an effort of will; it must have seemed ungrateful on my part to discharge myself—and so suddenly—from the intensive care I had demanded from them. But that didn't stop me from thinking what my mother used to say, poor bitch, of a piece of furniture that no longer pleased her: I'd rather have your space than your company.

Something peculiar must have happened. I stopped being feverish all the time, in that low-level way that becomes your new normal after a few months. But I entered another kind of fever; I was in a fever of health. That must be the explanation. I know I took a lot of trouble to repeat, in my new health, experiences that I'd had in sickness. That must be a very sophisticated pleasure.

I know, for instance, that in my sickness I had made a trip to Highgate Ponds. I needed to be driven, by Leo of course, and I needed to take a little rest at the unofficial gay sun-bathing area before I tottered down to the nudists' compound.

Leo and I laid out our towels on the concrete. I'd brought along a blanket and a pillow (which Leo was carrying, of course) for a little extra padding, but at least I laid the towel on top. I wasn't ashamed to strip off, though of course I was worried in case I had to run for the dingy lavatory, under the eyes of the ghastly crew by the weight-bench. But shame didn't get a look in. As far as I was concerned, this was strictly between me and the sun. I wasn't going to be done out of our date just because I could hardly walk.

I was surprised to see that Leo was shy, and kept a pair of swimming trunks on. I wanted to tempt him out of them, so I could at least look at the label and see whether they were bought from C&A or the British Home Stores.

After a while I struggled into a swimsuit myself, and walked weakly through to the pond. I was hoping that I would feel strong enough for a dip at least, which was a pretty bizarre hope. Perhaps I thought that, all other sources of energy having failed, I would turn out to be solar-powered. I lay down on the diving-board. I had been there about ten seconds, feeling the wind on me almost warm, and watching the people sprawled on the raft in the middle of the pond, when a man came out of a hut and shouted at me that sun-bathing was not allowed in the swimming area.

The trip I made in my health, I seem to think, was very different. I took bus after bus to get there, by myself. I strode past the sun-bathing area, and straight into the compound, though this time I was reluctant to take off my underwear. By then I had a little roll of tummy fat which I was very proud of, and which showed to best effect above the waistline of a pair of underpants, and I wasn't in any hurry to have it vanish the moment I took my briefs off and lay down. I expect I was waiting for someone to call out, 'Wonderful! I can't see your ribs. Well done!'

Before the sun had properly got to work I was standing up again and pulling my swimming trunks up. I went out into the swimming area, but I wasn't quite brave enough for the diving-board. The water looked cloudy, but I knew it was supposed to be pure and clean, equally free of pollution and disinfectant. I let myself down an iron ladder that had a lot of weed attached to it. The ladder wasn't full-length, as I had assumed, it stopped only a little below the surface, so I slipped into the coldest water I have ever touched. My body gasped and went on gasping. The water was unexpectedly deep, too, considering it was so near the edge of the pond. I set out to swim to the raft, which supported what looked like the same group of sun-worshippers, but I found myself swimming instead in a tight circle back to where I had started. I wanted to strike out for that floating island of health, but my body wasn't having it. My feet had no memory of the ladder, and scrabbled for purchase where the rungs were imaginary. Then I remembered, and felt for the actual bottom of the actual ladder, and managed to pull myself out.

I slumped on the jetty to recover. Not even the most officious attendant, seeing me there flat out and wheezing, could imagine I was having a sun-bathe on the sly, but the men on the raft set up a round of ironic applause that I could hear even through the numbness of my ears.

I wasn't going to give up. I didn't hang around until my skin had dried off and my trunks felt cold and clammy. I went back down the ladder and swam out through the cold. The water got warmer after a while, or else it stayed cold and I got used to it. The raft was only fifty feet or so away, but that was quite far enough. I could feel the special uneasiness of swimming in water of unknown depth. As I got near the raft, all I could see above the edge of it was the soles of someone's feet, those odd sort of feet with the second toe longer than the big one.

The ladder by the raft was even shorter than the one on the jetty. In my memory, it has only two rungs. I know I had to pull myself up with what felt like the last of my strength. But when I looked round at the raft, which rocked under my weight and wasn't as securely tethered as I'd expected, it was covered with shit. I don't mean that the men there were lying in it; they were too fastidious for that, with their uniform tans, as if they'd all chosen the same shade from a paint card. But there were substantial little turds scattered all over the raft. They were bigger than anything I've known a bird do, but I couldn't imagine what beast could have got there to lay them. I was tired out from my swim, but lying in shit was too recent a memory—from nights when I improvised a pair of incontinence pants out of an old Marks and Sparks bag—for me to be able to stay on the raft. I climbed down the rusty ladder, losing my footing one more time, and swam back to the jetty. It may be that my strength was failing towards the end, but I think the water near the jetty was the coldest of all.

I know I did all that. I even remember it all, in the sense that I still bear traces of those thoughts and sensations. I remember what my body felt in its health, what it touched, how it reacted. But I have no sense of how my body felt to itself. It was just one more thing that happened to me, and I have kept nothing from it. The tape is blank for all those weeks and months.

And now I am back in my siege of fevers. What it feels like, as always, is shame, as if this raised temperature was nothing more than a hideous extended blush, which I could get rid of if I just did the right thing. I find myself wondering what it was I did wrong, what crime my body remembers with this heat of shame. They didn't lie to me about the salmon sperm. I knew it could nibble away at my cells. I knew there was a price to be paid for the job it did. I knew it wasn't a medicine so much as a protection racket; I just hoped we could get along. I took vitamins, I took iron, I took supplements. Was there one night when I passed up a dish of green vegetables, in my feverish health, snubbing all those B vitamins, and went out instead? There must have been.

How can I put it, to make myself feel I have made heroic choices? Health for me is more than being not-yet-dead. It's not something you patrol; it's something you must forget to patrol or it's not any sort of health at all. That should do it. That sounds right. That must be why I didn't use this tape to hoard up bits of my health, so I could live off them at a later date.

And here I am with a body that's ashamed of itself, that's

burning with remorse for something it did or didn't do, and with the word *surge* beating at my ears. They warned me what would happen when I came off the salmon sperm. A surge of virus. Virus replicating uninhibited. *Surge* is a word that sounds overwhelming even on the smallest scale, down on the cellular level. What chance do I have, against a *surge*?

Every time I went to hospital for some more salmon sperm, and they took blood, I must have known they were monitoring my levels. Fourteen. Twelve and a half. Eleven. Nine. It was more than a pit stop. And when I went below nine, and they started giving me transfusions, I knew what they were about. But I tried to think, closing my eyes when the prick came in my arm, and then the slowly growing ache in it, that I was giving blood rather than getting it, that from my overflowing health I was giving freely of my surplus. Nine and a half. Nine. Eight. I tried to think I was paying my taxes, when all the time my bloodstream was being heavily subsidized. On long car journeys as a child, I remember, to stop from feeling sick—from motion, from too many boiled sweets, from my father's Senior Service and my mother's Piccadilly—I would close my eyes and try to interpret the sensations in terms of movement backward, though I don't quite know why that was comforting. I could produce a surprisingly strong and consistent illusion until I opened my eyes at a bump in the road, or when my mother asked if I was asleep, and the world came crashing back at me.[

]The lovers are back. They can deal with me again. And I suppose that really means that I can deal with them. Rory has that handsome look in the face that means he's certain to shave in the morning, and Leo smells so strongly of soap he must wear a bar round his neck.[   ]

They've done something very tactful with the key. I'm not very steady on my feet just at the moment, and my neighbour has a spare set of keys. She's always been a hypochondriac, can't bear to be in the room with anyone who has a cold, so I suppose it's something of a miracle that she's not returned them, or that they don't reek of disinfectant. This I noticed today, and it qualifies for inclusion on this tape. That's what this tape is supposed to be for, isn't it? Sometimes my neighbour even leaves groceries outside the door. Anyway, when Rory last came by he let himself in, and explained that he had happened to run into my neighbour outside the house. Then *Leo* let himself in next time he paid a visit, and he looked all tense and startled, as if at any moment he might be called upon to lie. So my guess is they've made a policy decision not to make me walk any more than I have to. They must knock on my neighbour's door every time they come round. For all I know, they get her to leave the key under the mat when she goes out. I think they're waiting for me to twig and get angry, but they'll have to wait a little while longer. I'll either keep it to myself or let it hitch a ride on a real grievance. 'And another thing,' I'll say, 'about the keys . . .' [

]We've started taking baths together, the lovers and I. Rory lifts me into the tub very competently, which is so reassuring it's *sinister*, but at least he climbs right in with me, like no nurse in the world who wants to remain in employment. Suddenly I wonder if he answered my ad—poor idiot—to get his life moving again after grief, and has to keep his teeth clenched on his knowledge. So I'm more than usually grateful that he gets into the bath with me. He sits behind me with his knees bent, so I can rest my head on his chest, and he strokes me a little awkwardly with a sponge. It's a posture I like anyway, and now in particular I'm glad of it because it's not a position that encourages talking. We can't really see each other's faces. I think he closes his eyes in the steam, and from time to time he seems to drift off. He doesn't seem to mind that the water gets cold; perhaps he doesn't even feel it.

If there was just a little more water in the bath I'd be floating. As it is my head bumps softly against Rory's chest. Here and only here, in this limbo inside another, I remember my lover, the lover I disposed of so efficiently, dumping his body in an acid bath of resentment. What I remember isn't the friendship, which I resisted, or even the sex, which I wanted only when I wanted it, but the game we used to play when we were out together, the game he taught me and that he may even have invented, the sweetly innocent game he called *compelled*-to-fuck. One or other of us would say, 'If you were *compelled* to fuck a set number of people—under pain of death, mind . . .' (or later just, 'If you were *compelled* . . .'). Then the other would say, 'How many?' And the answer would be, 'One on this bus,' or 'Two before we leave the Food Hall,' or 'Three before the next traffic light.' Then he would say, 'Three? You'll be lucky. That one, at a pinch. Another one? No chance. All right, the thinner of these two bobbies, the less fat I mean. That's the lot. That's my last offer. One more? Do I really have to? Let it be the one with the tie, then. Cancel that. The other bobby. If I have to.' What I remember best is the grudging lust in all its variety that he could call up on his face, as he made his protesting selections.

Sooner or later I have to tell Rory that it's time for me to get out. I start shivering, even in the water, even against his skin. He doesn't risk trying to lift me out while he's wet and slippery, so he dries himself as quickly as he can and comes back for me with a hot towel. By now I'm really shivering. He helps me stand up and pulls the plug out. He wraps the towel round me and rubs away until at last a tingle passes to me from the towel. By then I'm likely to be exhausted, and once he even had a shot at carrying me to the bed. He was staggering by the time we got there, and he didn't so much lay me down as fall with me down on to the mattress.

Leo is different, of course. He has a hard time lifting me into the bath, so I hang on to the towel rail just in case—though I'm not sure I could support my weight for more than a second or two, if he lost his grip. He puts stuff in the bath so that it's full of nutty-smelling bubbles by the time I arrive in it, which relaxes me and relaxes him too, because he doesn't have to see me naked for more than a few moments. I'd rather he joined me in the bath—the edge of the tub is hard against my shoulders—but he likes to stay where he is. Still, he's become something of a pro as a back-scrubber, and that's something. At first he used a nail-brush, but one day he couldn't find it so he used my toothbrush instead, and we've never gone back to the nail-brush. He's even brought along a toothbrush which is specifically for scrubbing my back.

He starts on my left shoulder, pressing hard with the bristles, moving his wrist in tiny circles. It's extraordinary how—even the first time he did it, and much more so now—my skin anticipates the sideways progress of the brush as he moves it across my back, so that I develop a roving itch that is always just a fraction ahead of the scrubbing. When he has reached the outside edge of my right shoulderblade, he drops his hand an inch or so and scrubs steadily back to the left again. I try to concentrate all my attention on the itch, which moves ahead of the toothbrush all the way. It's as if there was a poem written on my back that I learnt by heart in childhood. I have wholly forgotten it, but each word that I am prompted to remember sparks the memory of the next. I close my eyes. The travelling itch holds still, for once, at the extremity of my back, until the brush comes to scrub it out.[

I lose the ability to talk. My voice unravels, and speech drops away from me like the mouthpiece of an instrument I am suddenly unable to play, a mediaeval instrument that I don't even recognize as a possible source of music.

When I open my eyes again, they are both there, both the lovers. Leo and Rory. Imagination is the last thing to fail me. I see them lying side by side on their fronts, their arms around each other, their faces pushed into the pillows. They turn slowly towards each other, and I see Rory trace a line with his finger down Leo's cheek. I can see a tear on Leo's skin by the tip of Rory's finger, but from my point of view I can't make out whether Rory is following its progress as it trickles, or drawing it out of Leo's eye with the gesture he makes. Rory leans over and kisses the tear where it has come to rest, and I flinch in spite of myself. Leo turns away from the kiss, so they are both on their sides now, facing the same way.

Rory sets up a gentle motion of the hips, which Leo's hips take up. A terrible rattle of protest and warning bursts from me, behind clenched teeth. Their hips are in rhythm now, and Rory's face is pressed against Leo's neck, just as it was against the pillow a few moments ago.

I turn my head away, and see the cardboard box that contains all my medicines in their varied containers. I see also the little piles of Leo's and Rory's clothes. Their two pairs of trousers have fallen in an oddly symmetrical pattern, forming a sort of star, and I can see among the keys attached to one belt-loop a new pale-silver copy of a familiar shape. I glance at the keys on the other trousers, to locate the twin of it. But I forgive my lovers their ability to comfort themselves and each other, and I forgive myself for bringing them together, as I cross the room as quietly as I can and open the door, as quietly as I can. Then I close the door after all, walk back across the room, not worrying any more about whether I make any noise, and sit back down on the edge of the bed.

NADINE GORDIMER

A SPORT OF NATURE

'Gordimer's virtuosity has never been more apparent than in this novel.'
THE LISTENER

'Throughout <u>A SPORT OF NATURE</u> Nadine Gordimer marshalls her formidable powers to describe the revolution she believes must come.' **THE GUARDIAN**

'A genuinely picaresque novel ... excellent, often funny, always intriguing.' **THE TIMES**

'This is an exhilarating book ... Nadine Gordimer is as good on the comic incongruities of human behaviour as on injustice and outrage.' **THE OBSERVER**

JONATHAN CAPE   £10.95

NADINE GORDIMER
SPOILS

In the warmth of the bed your own fart brings to your nostrils the smell of rotting flesh: the lamb chops you devoured last night. Seasoned with rosemary and with an undertaker's paper-frill on the severed rib-bones. Another corpse digested.

'Become a vegetarian, then.' She's heard it all too many times before; sick of it, sick of my being sick of it. Sick of the things I say, that surface now and then.

'I want no part of it.'

We are listening to the news.

'What? What are you going on about. *What?*'

What indeed? No: which. Which is it I choose to be no part of? The boy who threw a stone at the police, had both his arms broken by them, was sodomized by prisoners into whose cell he was thrown; the kidnapped diplomat and the group (men, as I am a man, women, as she is a woman) who sent his fourth finger by mail to his family; the girl doused with petrol and burned alive as a traitor; those starved by drought or those drowned by flood, far away; the nineteen-year-old son of Mr and Mrs killed by the tremendous elemental thrill of 220 volts while using an electric spray gun on his motorbike. The planned, the devised, executed by people like myself, or the haphazard, the indifferent, executed senselessly by elemental forces. *Senselessly.* Why is there more sense in the conscious acts that make corpses? Consciousness is self-deception. Intelligence is a liar.

'You're not having great thoughts. That's life.'

Her beauty-salon philosophy. Stale, animal, passive. Whether I choose or not; can't choose, can't want *no part.*

The daily necrophilia.

'Become a vegetarian, then!'

Among other people no one would ever think there was anything wrong. He is aware of that; she is aware of his being aware, taking some kind of pride in appearing exactly as they have him in their minds, contributing to their gathering exactly what his place in it expects of him. The weekend party—invited to a lodge on a private game reserve—will include the practical, improvising man; the clown who burns his fingers at the camp fire and gets a laugh out of it; the woman who spends her time preparing to feed everyone; the pretty girl who perks up the company sexually; the good-timer who keeps everyone drinking until late; the quiet one who sits apart contemplating the bush; one or two newcomers, for ballast, who may or may not provide a measure of serious conversation. Why not accept? No? *Well.* What else has he in mind that will please him better? Just say.

Nothing.

There you are!

He, in contrast to the clown, is the charmer, the wit. He knows almost everyone's foibles, he sets the anecdotes flowing, he provides the gentle jibes that make people feel themselves to be characters.

Whatever their temperaments, all are nature lovers. That is nothing to be ashamed of—surely, even for him. Their love of the wild brings them together—the wealthy couple who own the reserve and lodge rather than race horses or a yacht, the pretty girl who models or works in public relations, the good-timer director of a mining house, the adventurous stockbroker, the young doctor who works for a clerk's salary in a hospital for blacks, the clowning antique dealer . . . And he has no right to feel himself superior—in seriousness, morality (he knows that)—in this company, for it includes a young man who has been in political detention. That one is not censorious of the playground indulgences of his fellow whites, so long as the regime he has risked his freedom to destroy, will kill to destroy, lasts. That's life.

Behaving—undetectably—as one is expected is also a protection against fear of what one really is, now. Perhaps what is seen to be, is himself, the witty charmer. How can he know? He does it so well. His wife sees him barefoot, his arms round his knees on the viewing deck from which the company watches buffalo trampling the reeds down at the river, hears the amusing asides he makes while gazing through field-glasses, notices the way he has left his shirt unbuttoned in healthy confidence of the sun-flushed manliness of his breast: is the silence, the incomprehensible statements that come from it, alone with her, a way of tormenting her? Does he do it only to annoy, to punish? And what has she done to deserve what he doesn't mete out to others? Let him keep it to himself. Take a valium. Anything. Become a vegetarian. In the heat of the afternoon everyone goes to their rooms or their makeshift beds on the shaded part of the deck to sleep off the lunch-time wine.

Even in the room allotted to them, he keeps up, out of sight of the company (but they are only a wall away, he knows they are there) what is expected. It is so hot he and she have stripped to their briefs. He passes a hand over her damp breasts, gives a lazy sigh and is asleep on his back. Would he have wanted to take her nipples in his mouth, commit himself to love-making, if he hadn't fallen asleep, or was his a gesture from the wings just in case the audience might catch a glimpse of a slump to an offstage presence?

The house party is like the fire the servant lights at dusk within the reed stockade beside the lodge. One never knows when a fire outdoors will smoke or take flame cleanly and make a grand blaze, as this one does. One never knows when a small gathering will remain disparate, unresponsive, or when, as this time, men and women will ignite and make a bright company. The ceremony of the evening meal was a bit ridiculous, but perhaps intended as such, and fun. A parody of old colonial times: the stockade against the wild beasts, the black man beating a drum to announce the meal, the chairs placed carefully by him in a missionary prayer-meeting circle well away from the fire, the whisky and wine set out, the smell of charred flesh from the cooking grids. Look up: the first star in the haze is the mast-light of a ship moving out, slipping moorings, breaking with this world. Look down: the blue flames are nothing but burning fat; there are gnawed bones on the swept earth.

He's been drinking a lot—she noticed: so that he could stomach it all, no doubt he tells himself.

The fire twitches under ash and the dinner orchestra of insects whose string instruments are their own bodies, legs scraping against legs, wings scraping against carapace, has been silenced by the rising of the moon. But laughter continues. In the huge night, not reduced to scale by buildings, tangled by no pylons and wires, hollowed out by no street- and window-lights into habitable enclosures, the laughter, the voices are vagrant sound that one moment flies right up boldly into space, the next makes a wave so faint it dies out almost as it leaves the lips. Everyone interrupts everyone else, argues, teases. There are moments of acerbity; the grapes they are eating pop into sharp juice as they are bitten. One of the quiet guests has become communicative as will the kind who never risk ideas or opinions of their own but can reproduce, when a subject brings the opportunity, information they have read and stored. Bats, the twirling rags darker against the dark: someone suggested, as a woman cowered, that fear of them comes from the fact that they can't be heard approaching.

'If your eyes are closed, and a bird flies overhead, you'll hear the resistance of air to its wings.'

'And also, you can't make out what a bat's like, where its head is—just a *thing,* ugh!'

The quiet guest was already explaining, no, bats will not bump into you, but not, as this is popularly believed, because they have an inbuilt radar system; their system is sonar, or echo-location—

'I wear a leopard-skin coat.'

The defiant soprano statement from a sub-conversation breaks through his monologue and loses him attention.

It is the pretty girl; she has greased her face against the day's exposure to the sun and her bone-structure elegantly reflects the frail light coming from the half-moon, the occasional waver of flame roused in the fire or the halo of a cigarette lighter. She is almost beautiful.

'—D'you hear that!'

'Glynis, where did you find this girl?'

'Shall we put her out to be eaten by her prey, expose her on a rock?'

'No leopards here, unfortunately.'

'No, because people kill them to make fur coats.'

The wit did not live up to his reputation, merely repeated in sharper, more personal paraphrase what had been well said, no one remembered by whom. He spoke directly to the girl, whereas the others were playfully half-indignant around her presence. 'The coat would look much better on the leopard than on you.' But the inference, neither entirely conservationist nor aesthetic, seemed to excite the girl's interest in this man. She was aware of him, in the real sense, for the first time.

'Wait till you see me in it.' Just the right touch of independence, hostility.

'That could be arranged.'

This was a sub-exchange, now, under the talk of the others; he was doing the right thing, responding with the innuendo by which men and women acknowledge chemical correspondences stirring between them. And then she said it, was guided to it like a bat, by echo-location or whatever it is, something vibrating from the disgusts in him. 'Would you prefer me to wear a sheepskin one? You eat lamb, I suppose?'

It is easy to lose her in the criss-cross of talk and laughter, to enter it at some other level and let fall the one on which she took him up. He is drawn elsewhere—there is refuge, maybe, rock to touch in the ex-political prisoner. The prisoner holds the hand of his pale girl with her big nervously-exposed teeth; no beauty, all love. The last place to look for love is in beauty; beauty is only a skin, the creature's own or that of another animal, over what decays. Love is found in prison; this no-beauty has loved him while his body was not present. And he has loved his brothers—he's talking about them, not using the word, but the sense is there so strongly—although they live shut in with their own pails of dirt; he loves even the murderers whose night-long death songs he heard before they were taken to be hanged in the morning. 'Common criminals? In this country? Under laws like ours? Oh yes, we politicals were kept apart, but with time (I was there ten months) we managed to communicate. (There are so many ways you don't think of, outside, when you don't need to.) One of them—young, my age—he was already declared an habitual criminal, inside for an indeterminate sentence. Detention's also an indeterminate sentence, in a way, so I could have some idea . . .'

'You hadn't killed, robbed—he must have done that over and over.'

'Oh, he had. But I hadn't been born the bastard of a kitchen maid who had no home but her room in a white woman's backyard. I hadn't been sent to a "homeland" where the woman who was supposed to take care of me was starving and followed her man to a squatter camp in Cape Town to look for work. I hadn't begged in the streets, stolen what I needed to eat, sniffed glue for comfort. He had his first new clothes, his first real bed when he joined a gang of car thieves. Common lot; common criminal.'

Common sob story.

'If he had met you outside prison he would have knifed you for your watch.'

'Possibly! Can you say "That's mine" to people whose land was taken from them by conquest, a gigantic hold-up at the point of imperial guns?'

And the bombs in the streets, in the cars, in the supermarkets, that kill with a moral, necessary end, not criminal intent (yes, to be criminal is to kill for self-gain)—these don't confuse *him*, make carrion of brotherhood. He's brave enough to swallow it. No gagging.

Voices and laughter are cut off. You don't come to the bush to talk politics. It is one of the alert silences called for now and then by someone who's heard, beyond human voices, a cry. *Shhhhh* . . . Once it was the mean complaining of jackals, and—nearer— hawking from a hyena, that creature of big nostrils made to scent spilt blood. Then a squeal no one could identify: a hare pounced on by a wheeling owl? A wart-hog attacked by—whom? What's going on, among them, that other order of the beasts in their night?

'They live twenty-four hours; we waste the dark.'

'Norbert, you used to be such a night-club bird!'

And the young doctor offers: 'They hunt for their living in shifts, just like us. Some sleep during the day.'

'Oh, but they're *designed* as different species, in order to use actively all twenty-four hours. We are one species, designed for daylight only. It's not so many generations since—pre-industrial times, that's all—we went to bed at nightfall. If the world's energy supplies should run out, we'd be back to that. No electricity. No night shifts. There isn't a variety in our species that has night vision.'

The bat expert takes up this new cue. 'There are experiments with devices that may provide night vision. They're based on—'

'*Shhhhh* . . .'

Laughter like the small explosion of a glass dropped.

'Shut up, Claire!'

All listen, with a glisten on eye movements alone, dead still.

It is difficult for them to decide on what it is they are eavesdropping. A straining that barely becomes a grunt. A belching stir; scuffling, scuffling. But it could be a breeze in dead leaves. It is not the straw crepitation of the reeds at the river; it comes from the other direction, behind the lodge. There is a gathering, another gathering somewhere there. There is communication their ears are not tuned to, their comprehension cannot decode; some event outside theirs. Even the ex-political prisoner does not know what he hears; he who has heard through prison walls, he who has comprehended and decoded so much the others have not. His is only human knowledge, after all; he is not a twenty-four hour creature, either.

Into this subdued hush breaks the black man jangling a tray of glasses he has washed. The host signals: be quiet, go away, stop fussing among dirty plates. He comes over with the smile of one who knows he has something to offer. 'Lions. They kill one, two maybe. Zebras.'

Everyone bursts the silence like schoolchildren let out of class.

'Where?'

'How does he know?'

'What's he say?'

He keeps them waiting a moment; his hand is raised, palm up, pink from immersion in the washing-up. He is wiping it on his apron. 'My wives hear it, there in my house. Zebra, and now they eating. That side, there, behind.'

The black man's name is too unfamiliar to pronounce. But he is no longer nameless; he is the organizer of an expedition; they pick up a shortened version of the name from their host. Siza has brought the old truck, four-wheel drive, adapted as a large station wagon, from out of its shed next to his house. Everybody is game. This is part of the entertainment the host hoped but certainly could not promise to be lucky enough to provide; all troop by torch light the hundred yards from the lodge, under the mopane trees, past the bed of cannas outlined with whitewashed stones (the host never has had the heart to tell Siza this kind of white man's house does not need a white man's kind of garden) to Siza's wives' pumpkin and tomato patch. Siza is repairing a door-handle of the vehicle with a piece of wire, commanding, in his own language, this and that from his family standing by. A little boy gets underfoot and he lifts and dumps him out of the way. Two women wear traditional turbans but one has a T-shirt with an advertising logo; girl children hang on their arms, jabbering. Boys are quietly jumping with excitement.

Siza's status in this situation is clear when the two wives and children do not see the white party off, but climb into the vehicle among them, the dry-soled hard little feet of the children nimbly finding places among the guests' shoes, their knobbly heads with knitted capping of hair unfamiliar to the touch into which all in the vehicle are crowded. Beside the girl with her oiled face and hard slender body perfumed to smell like a lily, there is the soft bulk of one of the wives, smelling of wood smoke. 'Everybody in? Everybody OK?' No, no, wait—someone has gone back for a forgotten flash-bulb. Siza has started up the engine; the whole vehicle jerks and shakes.

Wit is not called for, nor flirtation. He does what is expected: runs to the lodge to fetch a sweater, in case she gets chilly. There is barely room for him to squeeze by; she attempts to take a black child on her lap, but the child is too shy. He lowers himself somehow into what space there is. The vehicle moves, all bodies, familiar and unfamiliar, are pressed together, swaying, congealed, breathing in contact. She smiles at him, dipping her head sideways, commenting lightly on the human press, as if he were someone else: 'In for the kill.'

It is not possible to get out.

Everyone will be quite safe if they stay in the car and please roll up the windows, says the host. The headlights of the old vehicle have shown Siza trees like other trees, bushes like other bushes that are to him his signposts. The blundering of the vehicle through bush and over tree-stumps, anthills and dongas has been along his highway: he has stopped suddenly, and there they are, shadow-shapes and sudden phosphorescent slits in the dim arch of trees that the limit of the headlights' reach only just creates, as a candle, held up, feebly makes a cave of its own aura. Siza drives with slow-motion rocking and heaving of the human load, steadily nearer. Four shapes come forward along the beams and stop. He stops. Motes of dust, scraps of leaf and bark knocked off the vegetation float, blurring the beams surrounding four lionesses who stand not ten yards away. Their eyes are wide, now, gem-yellow, expanded by the glare they face, and never blink. Their jaws hang open and their heads shake with panting, their bodies are bellows expanding and contracting between stiff-hipped haunches and heavy, narrow shoulders that support the heads. Their tongues lie like red cloth, the edges rucked up on either side by long white incisors.

They are dirtied with blood, and, to human eyes, de-sexed, their kind of femaleness without femininity, their kind of threat and strength out of place, associated with the male. They have no beauty except in the almighty purpose of their stance. There is nothing else in their gaunt faces: nothing but the fact, behind them, of half-grown and younger cubs in the rib-cage of a zebra, pulling and sucking at bloody scraps.

The legs and head are intact in dandyish dress of black and white. The beast has been, is being eaten out. Its innards are missing; half-digested grasses that were in its stomach have been emptied on the ground; they can be seen—someone points this out in a whisper. But even the undertone is a transgression. The lionesses don't give forth the roar that would make their menace recognizable, something to deal with. Utterances are not the medium for this confrontation. Watching. That is all. The breathing mass, the beating hearts in the vehicle—watching the cubs jostling for places within the cadaver; the breathing mass, the beating hearts in the vehicle, being watched by the lionesses. The beasts have no time; it will be measured by their fill. For the others, time suddenly begins again when the young doctor's girl-friend begins to cry soundlessly and the black children look away from the scene and see the tears shining on her cheeks and stare at her fear. The young doctor asks to be taken back to the lodge; the compact is broken; people protest, Why, oh no, they want to stay and see what happens. One of the lionesses breaks ranks and turns on a greedy cub, cuffing it out of the gouged prey. Quite safe; the car is perfectly safe, don't open a window to photograph. But the doctor is insistent: 'This old truck's chassis is cracked right through, we're overloaded, we could be stuck here all night.'

'Unreal.' Back in the room, the wife comes out with one of the catch-alls that have been emptied of dictionary meaning so that they may fit any experience the speaker won't take the trouble to define. When he doesn't respond she stands a moment, in the doorway, her bedclothes in her arms, smiling, gives her head a little shake to show how overwhelming her impression has been.

Oh well. What can she expect. Why come, anyway? Should have stayed at home. So he doesn't want to sleep in the open, on the deck. Under the stars. All right. No stars, then.

He lies alone and the mosquitoes are waiting for his blood, upside-down on the white board ceiling.

No. Real. *Real.* Alone, he can keep it intact, exactly that: the stasis, the existence without time, and without time there is no connection, the state in which he really need have, has no part, could have no part, there in the eyes of the lionesses. Between the beasts and the human load, the void. It is more desired and awful than could ever be conceived; he does not know whether he is sleeping or dead.

There is still Sunday. The entertainment is not over. Someone has heard lions round the lodge in the middle of the night. The scepticism with which this claim is greeted is quickly disproved when distinct pugs are found in the dust that surrounds the small swimming-pool which, like amniotic fluid, steeps the guests at their own body temperature. The host is not surprised; it has happened before: the lionesses must have come down to quench the thirst their feasting had given them. And the scent of humans, sleeping so near, up on the deck, the sweat of humans in the humid night, their sighs and sleep-noises? Their pleasure- and anxiety-emanating dreams?

'As far as the lions are concerned, we didn't exist.' From the pretty girl, the remark is a half-question that trails off.

'When your stomach is full you don't smell blood.'

The ex-prisoner is perhaps extrapolating into the class war?— the wit puts in, and the ex-prisoner himself is the one who is most appreciatively amused.

After the mosquitoes had had their fill, sleep came as indifferently as those other bodily states, hunger and thirst. A good appetite for fresh pawpaw and bacon, boerewors and eggs. Hungry, like everybody else. His wife offers him second helpings; perhaps he needs feeding up; there is a theory that all morbid symptoms are in fact of physical origin. Obsession with injustice—what's wrong with the world is a disease you, an individual, can't cure; that's life. The one who went to prison may be suffering from a lack of something— amino acids, vitamins—or an excess of something, over-feeding when a child or a hyperactive thyroid gland. Research is being done.

Siza confirms that the lionesses came to drink. They passed his house; he heard them. He tells this with the dry, knowing smile of one who is aware of a secret to-and-fro between bedrooms. After breakfast he is going to take the party to see in daylight where the kill took place last night.

'But is there anything to see?'

Siza is patient. 'They not eat all. Is too much. So they leave some, tonight they come back for eat finish.'

'No thanks! I don't think we should disturb them again.' But nobody wants the young doctor and his girl-friend to come anyway and spoil the outing.

'The lions they sleeping now. They gone away. Come back tonight. Is not there now.'

The wife is watching to see if she and her husband are going along. Yes, he's climbing, limber, into the old vehicle with the cracked chassis; he's giving a hand up to the hostess, he's said something that makes her laugh and purse her mouth.

The black women are thumping washing at an outdoor tub. Neither they nor their children come on this expedition. There is room to breathe without contact, this time. Everything is different in daylight. It is true that the lionesses are absent; the state that he achieved last night is absent in the same way, like them, drugged down by daylight.

Not a lion to be seen. Siza has stopped the vehicle, got out, but waved the passengers to stay put. The scrub forest is quiet; fragile pods that burst and sow their seed by wind-dispersion spiral slowly. Everybody chatters. The stockbroker leaves the vehicle and they shout at him. All right. All right. Taking his time, to show his lack of fear, he climbs aboard. 'Lions are not bulls and bears, Fred.' They laugh at this mild jeer which is the kind expected to sustain the wit's image—all are amused except the stockbroker himself, who knows the remark, in turn, refers to his image of himself as one whom no one would guess to be a stockbroker.

Siza comes back and beckons. The vehicle is quickly quit. And now the emptiness of the scrub forest is untrustworthy; all around, you can't see what's behind dead brush, fallen logs and the screens of layered branches that confine vision to ten feet. They talk only softly, in the sense of being stalked. The black man is leading them along what looks almost like a swept path, but it has been swept by a large body being dragged through dust and dead leaves: there is the carcase of the zebra, half-hidden in a thicket.

'No tyre-tracks, we didn't drive right into here! This can't be the place.'

'They pull him here for when they come back tonight.'

'What! To keep the meat fresh?'

'For the birds mustn't see.' Siza gives a name in his language.

'He means vultures. Vultures, eh, Siza?' A mime of the vultures' hunched posture.

'Yes, those big birds. Come look here—' The tour continues, he takes them a few paces from the carcass and stands beside a mound over which earth has been scratched or kicked. Flies whose backs spark tinny green and gold are settled on it. The black man has his audience: taking up a stick, he prods the mound and it stirs under dust like flour-coated meat moved by a fork.

'Christ, the intestines! Look at the size of that liver or spleen!'

'You mean lions can do that? Store things covered? How do they do it, just with their paws?'

'It's exactly the way my cat covers its business in the garden, scratches up earth. They're cats, too.'

The young jailbird and his girl and the antique dealer have made a discovery for themselves, having, in the confidence of excitement, retraced for a short distance the way along which the kill was approached. They have found the very pile of the contents of the zebra's stomach that someone noticed last night.

It is another mound. He has come over from the mound of guts they are marvelling at. There is nothing to watch in dead flesh; it is prodded and it falls back and is still. But this mound of steaming grass that smells sweetly of cud (it has been heated by the sun as it was once heated by the body that contained it) is not dead to human perception. What's going on here is a visible transformation of an inert mass. It is literally being carried away by distinctly different species of beetle who know how to live by decay, the waste of the digestive tract. The scarabs with their armoured heads burrow right into the base of the mound and come out backwards, rolling their ball of dung between their strong, tined legs. The tunnels they have mined collapse and spread the mound more thinly on its periphery; smaller beetles are flying in steadily to settle there, where their lighter equipment can function. They fly away carrying their appropriate load in a sac—or between their front legs, he can't quite make out. A third species, middle-sized but with a noisy buzz, function like helicopters, hovering and scooping off the top of the mound. They are flattening it perfectly evenly, who can say how, or why they bother with form? That's life. If every beetle has its place, how is refusal possible. And if refusal is possible, what place is there. No question mark. These are statements. That is why there is no point in making them to anyone. There is no possible response.

The mound is slowly going to disappear; maybe the vehicle is about to take the party back to the lodge, the weekend is going to be over. He is walking back to the rest of the party, still gathered round the carcass and the black man. For the space of a few yards he is alone; for a few seconds he is equidistant between those at the dung mound and those up ahead, part of neither one nor the other. A sensation that can't be held long; now he is with the group at the kill, again. There is some special stir of attentiveness in them, they crowd round and then herd back a step, where Siza, the black man, is crouched on his hunkers. He is business-like, concentrated, not taking any notice of them. He has given them all he could; now he has the air of being for himself. He has a knife in his hand and the white man who has just joined the group recognizes it; it is the knife that is everywhere, nowhere without the knife, on the news, at the dark street-corners, under the light that the warders never turn out. The black man has thrust, made his incision, sliced back the black-and-white smooth pelt on the dead beast's uppermost hind leg and now is cutting a piece of the plump rump. It is not a chunk or hunk, but neatly butchered, prime—a portion.

They laugh, wondering at the skill, curious. As if they can't guess, as if they've never sunk their teeth into a steak in their lives. 'What're you going to do with that, Siza?' Ah yes, put it in a doggy bag, take it home when you've already stuffed your own guts, taken the land (as the jailbird would say).

The black man is trimming it. Along with the knife, he has brought a sheet of newspaper. 'For me. Eat it at my house. For my house.'

'Is it good meat?'

'Yes, it's good.'

One of the men chides, man to man. 'But why not take the whole haunch—the whole leg, Siza. Why such a small piece?'

The black man is wrapping the portion in newspaper, he knows he mustn't let it drip blood on the white people.

He does it to his satisfaction in his own time and looks up at them. 'The lions, they know I must take a piece for me because I find where their meat is. They know it. It's all right. But if I take too much, they know it also. Then they will take one of my children.'

MAURIZIO CHIERICI
THE MAN FROM
HIROSHIMA

Colonel Paul Tibbets, Jr, pilot of the *Enola Gay*

The protagonists of Hiroshima have no nostalgia. Even those people only remotely connected with the event have had difficult lives. All except one: Colonel Paul Tibbets, pilot of the *Enola Gay*, the plane that carried the atom bomb. On TV, serene under his white locks, he was unrepentant: 'I did my duty; I would do it again.' Tibbets is the only one to have passed these years without so much as a shiver. One of the pilots in the formation which flew over Hiroshima that day was unable to participate in the victory celebrations; he took his life three days before the official ceremony.

I knew another pilot full of problems; it wasn't at all easy to arrange to meet him. Everyone said: 'You'll need patience. But if he gave you his word, you'll hear from him sooner or later.' For days I waited and no one came. Then the pilot called to apologize. There was fog at the airport: the plane couldn't take off. Or: he had no money and the banks were closed. He would buy the ticket tomorrow. Tomorrow came and went; there was always a different story. Eventually I made a proposal: 'Eatherly, in five days it will be Christmas. I want to be back home in Italy before then. So I'll come to see you. It's much warmer where you are than in New York, and I've never been to Texas. I'll leave this afternoon.'

'No, stay where you are,' Eatherly interrupted. 'It's hard to talk here. Being in Texas blocks me; the people inhibit me. They know me too well, and there's no love lost between us. I plan to spend the holidays in New Jersey with a friend—I'd go out of my mind staying in Waco for Christmas—so I'll come and see you.'

I waited. Hours and hours in the lobby of the Hotel St Moritz, Central Park south. Behind windows the city is grey. Great lighted clocks scan the seconds at the tops of skyscrapers. Soon it will start to snow. People rush past who have come to New York on business, and who are going home laden with presents in coloured packages, their ribbons fluttering to the ground. In this festive atmosphere I find it strange to be meeting a man who contributed to the deaths of 60,000 people and turned their city into a monument for all time.

Three hours later the man sits down on the other side of the table, a glass in his hands. He is thin; his eyes are deeply marked, making his glance look old. But his hands are calm. When we shook hands I could feel they were cold and dry. He speaks first.

'How do I look?'

'I couldn't say. I've only seen your photographs. In them you seem older. And more tired and down on your luck.'

'I'm not old, or tired; only tormented. But not all the time. They have taken care of my nightmares. Right there in Waco; a doctor by the name of Parker. Grey-haired man; thin. It was heavy treatment. I don't know if their methods have changed, but the one they used with me was useless. "Give it up, Claude," Parker said, "you're not guilty. It just fell to you to pilot a plane over Hiroshima. How many other Claudes were there in the air force who would have carried out an order as important as that one? The war finished; they went home. And what was the order anyway? Look at the sky and say: *Too many clouds here. Can't see Kokura and Nagasaki. Better do Hiroshima.*" Every day for fourteen months Doctor Parker gave me more or less the same speech. In the end I had to ask not to see him any more. I'd got worse.'

'There are a lot of stories, Mr Eatherly. Some people say you're a fake. Why?'

He doesn't answer immediately. Instead he asks if he can take advantage of my hospitality: would I have another drink with him? I wouldn't like to give the impression that Eatherly was an alcoholic. He could hold a bottle of whisky without any trouble and his eyes never clouded over. They remained alert and cold, just as they had been when he entered, bringing in a little of the wind from the city.

'You mean what Will Bradfort Huie wrote? He's a journalist who spent two days with me and then wrote a book—a whole book—about my life. Who am I? I don't know. But no one can describe himself in a minute. If I asked you point-blank: "Do you think of yourself as an honest person, or someone who works at giving others an impression to suit your own needs?" would you be able to demonstrate either in a minute? I doubt it. I didn't know how to answer him either.'

'Are you a pacifist as you've claimed for years?'

'I am, and sincerely so, as is any American of good will. If I were religious, I would say that pacifism springs from a Jewish or Christian consciousness, but I'm not religious, and I don't want to look a fool expounding my philosophy. I can't be religious after

Hiroshima. When someone makes a trip like mine and returns alive, he either kills himself or he lives like a Trappist monk. Cloistered; praying that the world changes and that the likes of Claude Eatherly and Paul Tibbets and the scientists who worked on the bomb are never born again.'

Claude grew up in Texas, where discourse is uninformed by Edwardian whispers from New England. Hearty laughter and loud voices; every sensation seems amplified. After the Japanese bombed Pearl Harbor, Texas offered more volunteers than any other state—the yellow devils had to be punished. Eatherly was among the volunteers. The youngest of six children, and a tackle on the Texas North College football team, he had a level head and a solid way of bringing them down. He didn't miss in the air either: he shot down thirty-three planes and his career took off. After three years he became a major, and a brilliant future seemed to await the handsome man with two bravery medals on his chest. The medals were what dug his grave. In the summer of 1945, he got orders to return home, but first he had to carry out one more mission. Just one.

You don't send a soldier home for the pleasure of giving him a little of the good life. In the letter he posted to his mother announcing his imminent return, Claude wrote, 'This will be the last cigarette they stick in this prisoner's mouth.' Nothing to get worried about. He went to New Mexico and joined a formation of supermen: the best, bravest, most famous pilots, all being trained in secret. They assigned him to a Boeing B-29 Superfortress that Claude christened *Straight Flush*.

The account of that morning some weeks later belongs to history. Three planes take off during the night of 6 August from Tinian in the Mariana Islands. Paul Tibbets is the group's commander. Eatherly opens the formation. There are no bombs in his plane; as for the others, no one suspects what a terrible device is hidden inside the *Enola Gay*. A bigger contrivance, they think, nothing more. Eatherly's job is to pinpoint the target with maximum accuracy. He must establish whether weather conditions allow for the centre to be Hiroshima, Kokura or Nagasaki, or whether they should continue towards secondary targets. He tells the story of that morning's events in a voice devoid of emotion which suggests that the recitation is the thousandth one.

'I had command of the lead plane, the *Straight Flush*. I flew over Hiroshima for fifteen minutes, studying the clouds covering the target—a bridge between the military zone and the city. Fifteen Japanese fighters were circling beneath me, but they're not made to fly above 29,000 feet where we were to be found. I looked up: cumulus clouds at 10,000, 12,000 metres. The wind was blowing them towards Hiroshima. Perfect weather. I could see the target clearly: the central span of the bridge. I laugh now when I think of the order: "I want only the central arch of the bridge, *only* that, you understand?" Even if I'd guessed that we were carrying something a bit special, the houses, the roads, the city still seemed very far away from our bomb. I said to myself: This morning's just a big scare for the Japanese.

'I transmitted the coded message, but the person who aimed the bomb made an error of 3,000 feet. Towards the city, naturally. But three thousand feet one way or the other wouldn't have made much difference: that's what I thought as I watched it drop. Then the explosion stunned me momentarily. Hiroshima disappeared under a yellow cloud. No one spoke after that. Usually when you return from a mission with everyone still alive, you exchange messages with each other, impressions, congratulations. This time the radios stayed silent; three planes close together and mute. Not for fear of the enemy, but for fear of our own words. Each one of us must have asked forgiveness for the bomb. I'm not religious and I didn't know who to ask forgiveness from, but in that moment I made a promise to myself to oppose all bombs and all wars. Never again that yellow cloud . . .'

Eatherly raises his voice. It is clear the yellow cloud accompanies him through his life.

'And what did Tibbets say?'

'Tibbets has nerves of steel, but the evening afterwards he explained how he spent those minutes. They had told him to be extremely careful: he was most at risk. So when the machine gunner yelled that the shock waves were on their way, he veered to take photographs; but the aeroplane just bounced like a ping-pong ball held up by a fountain. Calm returned and Tibbets felt tired; he asked to be relieved, and fell asleep. But he talked about it that evening when the number of victims was just beginning to be known. He kept on saying: "I'm sorry guys, I did my duty. I've no regrets." And I don't have his nerves. A year later I asked to be discharged.'

'What reason did you give?'

'Exhaustion. I was exhausted. And I wanted to get married. It's risky to bring matters of conscience into it when you're in the forces. They were astounded—how could I throw away such a promising future? The day of my discharge they waved a sheet of paper in front of me. It said I would receive 237 dollars a month pension. That was good money in those days, but I turned it down. And since the regulations didn't allow me to refuse, I put it in writing that the sum was to go to war widows. The end of my relationship with flying.'

He didn't tell the rest of the story willingly. He returns to Texas where his family doesn't recognize him: thin, nervous, irascible, 24 years old. He marries the Italian girl he met in New Mexico while he was training for the final mission. Concetta Margetti had tried Hollywood and finally been reduced to selling cigarettes in a local nightclub—not perhaps the ideal wife for someone in Claude's state. But they write to each other, they get married. A war story, yes; but the war had shredded Eatherly's nerves. In the middle of the night he wakes his wife, breathless and in tears: 'Hit the ground, the yellow cloud's coming!' It goes on like this for four years. His family finally convince him to enter the psychiatric hospital in Waco as a voluntary patient. He can take walks in the park any time of the day or night. He plays golf and receives visitors. Concetta keeps him company on Sunday. His brother brings him books and a pair of running shoes.

Then the problems start. Claude forges a cheque to send to the victims of Hiroshima. He enters a bank with a toy pistol; for a few minutes the employees are terrified until Eatherly bursts out laughing. One day his move succeeds; he threatens a department store clerk with a fake gun and makes her turn over the money, which he throws from a balcony before escaping. They catch him and take him back to Waco. He's no longer a voluntary patient: now they lock him in. They accuse him of behaving in an antisocial way.

(This euphemism is the last show of respect for his heroic war record.) He is confined to his room.

After fourteen months in the mental hospital he leaves, a ghost. His wife abandons him. His brother closes his bank account. Claude cannot look after himself or his money. And now the protest smoulders again. He enters a bar in Texas, armed. He threatens the people inside and gets them to put their money into the sack he is holding, just like he's seen in films. But it comes to nothing. He is handcuffed and taken to gaol in a police car. The sergeant accompanying him doesn't know who he is, only that he's an ex-pilot. I asked Eatherly how it felt to be facing a prison sentence for the first time.

'I should say terrible, but it wasn't. Nothing mattered to me. I'd been in prison all the time; the door was inside me. In the police car the sergeant was staring at me. He was curious. He was thinking about some famous criminal . . . It was a long trip. I was quiet, but his staring eyes bothered me. "Where do you come from, sergeant?" I asked him. "From Chicago." And I: "I knew you came from somewhere." I wanted to unfreeze the atmosphere, but he wasn't having it. He asked me: "It's not strictly legal, but can you talk, here in the car?" I made a yes sign.

'"Where are you from?"

'"From here."

'"Where were you based during the war?"

'"In the Pacific."

'"I was in the Pacific too. Where did they land you?"

'"Tinian, in the Marianas, special group 509."

'He looked at me, stunned. "I know who you are. You're Major Eatherly! Good God, Major, how did you end up like this? You're sick, right? I read that somewhere. I'll give you a hand."

'Then they locked me up in the loony bin again.'

His torment went on: a poor soul, incapable of getting on with the business of life. No one understands his drama. People's aversion to him grows. Let's not forget that Eatherly lived out this difficult period in the America of Senator McCarthy—the Grand Inquisitor of frustrated nationalism. McCarthy fomented a type of suspicion which reflected the cold war: the witch hunt. Eatherly becomes a witch. His passionate, if slightly naïve, criticism of the mechanisms of war is considered a threat to national security. The judges disagree over his case. The biography confected by William Bradfort Huie from less than two days of interviews weakens his defence. For Bradfort, the Major 'never saw the ball of fire, nor was he aware of the yellow wave. By the time of the explosion, he and his gunner were 100 kilometres from the site.' Returning to base he was surprised by the journalists and photographers crowding the runway where the *Enola Gay* had landed. 'If Eatherly is mad,' writes Bradfort, 'then his madness was hatched on 6 August, 1945, not from horror but from jealousy.'

'When I knew him,' Bradfort Huie continues implacably, 'he was already a fraud. Right off he asked me for five hundred dollars. He had never once attempted suicide. I spent a long time with him, and I looked at his wrists: there were no scars.'

'Is that true Claude?'

'These are not the kind of things you want to brag about. Look at my arms.' He turns up the sleeves of his jacket and unbuttons his cuffs. Two purple scars, deep and unpleasant, run towards his hands. 'I don't want you to pity me. I'm happy to have been able to talk. Now I've got to go.'

He disappeared as he had appeared, with the same suddenness. Before passing through the bar door and turning out into the hall he looked back, as if he had forgotten something. 'I want to apologize for being late. And thanks for these . . .' He gestured towards the row of glasses on the table.

'It was my pleasure to meet you. Merry Christmas.'

Fourteen months later Claude Eatherly took his life.

Translated from the Italian by Wallis Wilde-Menozzi

MARGIN 3

SUMMER 1987

Sorley MacLean on Hugh Macdiarmid;
David Mus Tunnelling out of Virgil;
Walter Perrie on Tribe, Class & Quarrel;
Neutron Photographs by Michael Judge;
and much more.

MARGIN 3 costs £3 from your bookshop
or direct from
The Square Inch,
Lower Granco Street,
Dunning, PH2 0SQ.

CARLOS FUENTES
THE DISCOVERY
OF MEXICO

I was born on 11 November 1928, under the sign I would have chosen, Scorpio, and on a date shared with Dostoevsky, Crommelynck and Vonnegut. My mother was rushed from a steaming-hot movie house in those days before Colonel Buendía took his son to discover ice in the tropics. She was seeing King Vidor's version of *La Bohème* with John Gilbert and Lillian Gish. Perhaps the pangs of my birth were provoked by this anomaly: a silent screen version of Puccini's opera. Since then, the operatic and the cinematographic have had a tug-of-war with my words, as if expecting the Scorpio of fiction to rise from silent music and blind images.

All this, let me add, took place in the sweltering heat of Panama City, where my father was beginning his diplomatic career as an attaché to the Mexican legation. Since he was a convinced Mexican nationalist, my father insisted that the problem of where I was to be born had to be resolved under another 'sign': not of Scorpio but of the Eagle and the Serpent. The Mexican legation, however, though it had extra-territorial rights, did not have a territorial midwife, and the Minister, a fastidious bachelor, would not have me suddenly appearing on the legation parquet. So if I could not be born in a fictitious, extra-territorial Mexico, neither would I be born in that even more fictitious extension of the United States of America, the Canal Zone, where, naturally, the best hospitals were. So, between two territorial fictions—the Mexican legation, the Canal Zone—and a silent close-up of John Gilbert, I arrived in the nick of time at the Gorgas Hospital in Panama City at eleven that evening.

The problem of my baptism then arose. As if the waters of the two neighbouring oceans touching each other with the iron finger tips of the canal were not enough, I had to undergo a double ceremony: my religious baptism took place in Panama, because my mother, a devout Roman Catholic, demanded it; but my national baptism took place a few months later in Mexico City, where my father, an incorrigible Jacobin and priest-hater to the end, insisted that I be registered in the civil rolls established by Benito Juárez. Thus, I appear as a native of Mexico City for all legal purposes, and this anomaly further illustrates a central fact of my life and my writing: I am Mexican by will and imagination.

Photo: Burk Uzzle (Archive Pictures)

221

All this came to a head when my father was counsellor of the Mexican Embassy in Washington, D.C., and I was growing up in the vibrant world of the American thirties, more or less between the inauguration of Citizen Roosevelt and the interdiction of Citizen Kane. When I arrived in the United States, Dick Tracy had just met Tess Truehart. As I left, Clark Kent was meeting Lois Lane. You are what you eat. You are also the comics you peruse as a child.

At home, my father made me read Mexican history, study Mexican geography and understand the names, the dreams and defeats of Mexico: a non-existent country, I then thought, invented by my father to nourish my infant imagination: a land of Oz with a green cactus road, a landscape and a soul so different from those of the United States that they seemed a fantasy.

A cruel fantasy: the history of Mexico was a history of crushing defeats, whereas I lived in a world, that of my D.C. public school, which celebrated victories, one victory after another, from Yorktown to New Orleans to Chapultepec to Appomattox to San Juan Hill to Belleau Wood: had this nation never known defeat? Sometimes the names of United States victories were the same as the names of Mexico's defeats and humiliations: Monterrey-Veracruz. Chapultepec. Indeed: from the Halls of Montezuma to the shores of Tripoli. Miguel Hidalgo, the father of Mexican independence, ended up with his head on exhibit on a lance at the city gates of Chihuahua. Imagine George and Martha beheaded at Mount Vernon.

To the south, sad songs, sweet nostalgia, impossible desires. To the north, self-confidence, faith in progress, boundless optimism. Mexico, the imaginary country, dreamed of a painful past; the United States, the real country, dreamed of a happy future.

Many things impressed themselves on me during those years. The United States—would you believe it?—was a country where things worked, where nothing ever broke down: plumbing, roads seemed to function perfectly, at least at the eye level of a young Mexican diplomat's son living in a residential hotel on Washington's Sixteenth Street, facing Meridian Hill Park, where nobody was then mugged and where our superbly furnished seven-room apartment cost us 110 pre-inflation dollars a month. Yes, in spite of all the problems, the livin' seemed easy during those long Tidewater summers when I became perhaps the first and only Mexican to prefer grits to guacamole. I also became the original Mexican Calvinist, and an invisible taskmaster called Puritanical Duty still shadows my every footstep: I shall not deserve anything unless I work relentlessly for it, with iron discipline, day after day. Sloth is sin, and if I do not sit at my typewriter every day at eight a.m. for a working day of seven to eight hours I will surely go to hell. No *siestas* for me, alas and alack and *hélas* and *ay-ay-ay*: how I came to envy my Latin brethren, unburdened by the Protestant work ethic, and why must I, to this very day, read the complete works of Hermann Broch and scribble in my black notebook on a sunny Mexican beach instead of lolling the day away and waiting for the coconuts to fall?

The nation that Tocqueville saw was destined to dominate over half the world realized that only a continental state could be a modern state; in the thirties, the USA had to decide what to do with its new power, and Franklin Roosevelt taught us to believe that the United States had to show that it was capable of living up to its ideals. I learned then—my first political lesson—that this commitment to its idealism is the true greatness of the United States, not (the norm in my lifetime) material wealth, not power arrogantly misused against weaker peoples, not ignorant ethnocentrism burning itself out in contempt for others. As a young Mexican, I saw a nation of boundless energy and the will to confront the great social issues of the times without blinking or looking for scapegoats. It was a country identified with its own highest principles: political democracy, economic well-being and faith in its human resources, especially in that most precious of all capital, the renewable wealth of education.

I saw the United States in the thirties lift itself from the dead dust of Oklahoma and the grey lines of the unemployed in Detroit, and this image of health was reflected in my life, in my reading of Mark Twain, in the movies and newspapers, in the North American capacity for mixing fluffy illusion and hard-bitten truth, self-celebration and self-criticism: the madcap heiresses played by Carol Lombard co-existed with Walker Evans's photographs of hungry migrant mothers, and the nimble tread of the feet of Fred Astaire did not silence the heavy stomp of the boots of Tom Joad.

My school—a state public school, non-confessional and coeducational—reflected these realities and their basic egalitarianism. I believed in the democratic simplicity of my teachers and chums, and above all I believed I was, naturally, in a totally unselfconscious way, a part of this world. It is important, at all ages and in all occupations, to be 'popular' in the United States; I have known no other society where the values of 'regularity' are so highly prized. I was popular, I was 'regular' until a day in March—18 March 1938. On that day, a man from another world, the imaginary country of my childhood, the President of Mexico, Lázaro Cárdenas, nationalized the holdings of foreign oil companies. The headlines in the North American press denounced the 'communist' government of Mexico and its 'red' president; they demanded the invasion of Mexico in the sacred name of private property, and Mexicans, under international boycott, were invited to drink their oil.

Instantly, I became a pariah in my school. Cold shoulders, aggressive stares, epithets and sometimes blows. Children know how to be cruel. And this was not reserved for me or for Mexico. At about the same time, an extremely brilliant boy of eleven arrived from Germany. He was a Jew and his family had fled from the Nazis. I shall always remember his face, dark and trembling, his aquiline nose and deep-set, bright eyes with their great sadness; the sensitivity of his hands and the strangeness with which he appeared to his American companions. This young man, Hans Berliner, had a brilliant mathematical mind and he walked and saluted like a Central European. He wore short pants and high woven stockings, Tyrolean jackets, and had an air of displaced courtesy that infuriated the popular, regular, feisty, knickered, provincial, Depression-era little sons of bitches at Henry Cooke Public School on Thirteenth Street N.W.

I discovered that my father's country was real. And that I belonged to it. Mexico was my identity yet I myself lacked an identity. Hans Berliner suffered more than I—headlines from Mexico are soon forgotten and another great issue becomes another ten-day media feast—yet he had an identity: he was a Central European Jew. I looked at the photographs of President Cárdenas: he was a man of another lineage; he did not appear in the repertory of glossy, seductive images of the saleable North American world. He was a *mestizo*, Spanish and Indian, with a faraway, green and liquid look in his eyes, as if he were trying to remember a mute and ancient past. Was that past mine as well? Could I dream the dreams of the country suddenly revealed in a political act as something more than a demarcation of frontiers on a map or a hillock of statistics in a year-book? I believe I then had the intuition that I would not rest until I came to grips myself with that common destiny which depended upon still another community: the community of time. The United States had made me believe that we live only for the future; Mexico, Cárdenas, the events of 1938, made me understand that only in an act of the present can we make present the past as well as the future: to be Mexican was to identify a hunger for being, a desire for dignity rooted in many forgotten centuries and in many centuries yet to come, but rooted here, now, in the instant, in the vigilant time of Mexico that I later learned to understand in the stone serpents of Teotihuacán and in 'the polychrome angels of Oaxaca.

In 1939, my father took me to see a film at the old RKO-Keith in Washington. It was called *Man of Conquest* and it starred Richard Dix as Sam Houston. When Dix/Houston proclaimed the secession of the Republic of Texas from Mexico, I jumped on the theatre seat and proclaimed on my own and from the full height of my nationalist ten years, '*Viva México! Death to the gringos!*' My embarrassed father hauled me out of the theatre, but his pride in me could not resist leaking my first rebellious act to the *Washington Star*.

I n the wake of my father's diplomatic career, I travelled to Chile and entered the universe of the Spanish language, of Latin American politics and its adversities. President Roosevelt had resisted enormous pressures to apply sanctions and even invade Mexico to punish my country for recovering its own wealth. Likewise, he did not try to destabilize the Chilean radicals, communists and socialists democratically elected to power under the banners of the Popular Front. In the early forties, the vigour of Chile's political life was contagious: active unions, active parties, electoral campaigns all spoke of the political health of this, the most democratic of Latin American nations. Chile was a politically verbalized country. It was no coincidence that it was also the country of the great Spanish-American poets Gabriela Mistral, Vicente Huidobro, Pablo Neruda.

· I only came to know Neruda and became his friend many years later. This King Midas of poetry would write, in a literary testament rescued from a gutted house and a nameless tomb, a beautiful song to the Spanish language. The Conquistadores, he said, took our gold, but they left us their gold: they left us our words. Neruda's gold, I learned in Chile, was the property of all. One afternoon on the beach at Lota in southern Chile, I saw the miners as they came out, mole-like, from their hard work many feet under the sea, extracting the coal of the Pacific Ocean. They sat around a bonfire and sang, to guitar music, a poem from Neruda's *Canto General*. I told them that the author would be thrilled to know that his poem had been set to music. What author? they asked me in surprise. For them, Neruda's poetry had no author: it came from afar and had always been sung, like Homer's. I learned in Chile that Spanish could be the language of free men. I was also to learn in my lifetime, in Chile in 1973, the fragility of both our language and our freedom when Richard Nixon, unable to destroy American democracy, merrily helped to destroy Chilean democracy: the same thing Leonid Brezhnev had done in Czechoslovakia. An anonymous language, a language that belongs to us all, as Neruda's poem belonged to those miners on the beach, yet a language that can be kidnapped, impoverished, sometimes jailed, sometimes murdered.

Let me summarize: Chile offered me and the other writers of my generation in Santiago both a fragile, cornered language, Spanish, and one that preserved the Latin of our times, the lingua franca of the modern world, English. At the Grange School, a mini-Britannia under the awesome beauty of the Andes, José Donoso and Jorge Edwards, Roberto Torretti, the late Luis Alberto Heyremans and myself, by then all budding amateurs, wrote our first exercises in literature. We all ran strenuous cross-country races, got caned from time to time and recuperated while reading Swinburne; we were subjected to huge doses of rugby, Ruskin, porridge for breakfast and a stiff upper lip in military defeats. When Montgomery broke through at El Alamein, the assembled school tossed caps in the air and hip-hip-hoorayed to death. In South America, clubs were named after George Canning and football teams after Lord Cochrane; no matter that English help in winning independence led to English economic imperialism, from oil in Mexico to railways in Argentina. There was a secret thrill in our hearts: our Spanish conquerors had been beaten by the English; the defeat of Philip II's invincible Armada compensated for the crimes of Cortés, Pizarro and Valdivia. If Britain was an empire, at least she was a democratic one.

And here lay, for my generation, the central contradiction of our relationship with the English-speaking world: you have made universal the values of modernity, freedom, economic development and political democracy; but when we develop these values in Latin America in our own way within our culture your governments brand us Marxist-Leninist tools, side with the military protectors of a *status quo* dating back to the Spanish conquest, attribute the dynamics of our change to a Soviet conspiracy and finally corrupt the movement towards modernity that you yourselves have fostered.

Nevertheless, my passage from English to Spanish determined the concrete expression of what in Washington had been the revelation of an identity. I wanted to write and I wanted to write in order to show myself that my identity and my country were real: now in Chile as I started to scribble my first stories, even publishing them in school magazines, I learned that I must in fact write in Spanish.

In Chile I came to know the possibilities of our language for giving wing to freedom and poetry. The impression was enduring; it links me forever to that sad and wonderful land. It lives within me, and it transformed me into a man who knows how to dream, love, insult and write only in Spanish. It also left me wide open to an incessant interrogation: what happened to this universal language, Spanish, which after the seventeenth century ceased to be a language of life, creation, dissatisfaction and personal power, and became far too often a language of mourning, sterility, rhetorical applause and abstract power? Where were the threads of my tradition, where could I, writing in mid-twentieth century Latin America, find the direct link to the great living presences I was then starting to read, my lost Cervantes, my old Quevedo, dead because he could not tolerate one more winter, my Góngora, abandoned in a gulf of loneliness?

After Santiago, I spent six wonderful months in Argentina. They were, in spite of their brevity, so important in this reading and writing of myself. Buenos Aires was then, as always, the most beautiful, sophisticated and civilized city in Latin America, but in the summer of 1944, as street pavements melted in the heat and the city smelled of cheap wartime gasoline, rawhide from the port and chocolate éclairs from the *confiterías*, Argentina had experienced a succession of military *coups*: General Rawson had overthrown President Castillo of the cattle oligarchy, but General Ramírez had then overthrown Rawson, and now General Farrell had overthrown Ramírez. A young colonel called Juan Domingo Perón was General Farrell's up-and-coming Minister of Labour, and I heard an actress by the name of Eva Duarte play the 'great women of history' on Radio Belgrano. A stultifying hack novelist who went by the pen name Hugo Wast was assigned to the Ministry of Education under his real name, Martínez Zuviría, and brought all his anti-Semitic, undemocratic, pro-fascist phobias to the Buenos Aires high school system, which I had suddenly been plunked into. Coming from the America of the New Deal, the ideals of revolutionary Mexico, and the politics of the Popular Front in Chile, I could not stomach this, rebelled and was granted a full summer of wandering around Buenos Aires, free for the first time in my life, following my preferred tango orchestras as they played all summer long in the Renoir-like shade and light of the rivers and pavilions of El Tigre and Maldonado.

Two very important things happened.

First, I lost my virginity. We lived in an apartment building on the leafy corner of Callao and Quintana, and after ten a.m. nobody was there except myself, an old and deaf Polish door-keeper and a beautiful Czech woman, aged thirty. I went up to ask her for her *Sintonía*, which was the radio guide of the forties, because I wanted to know when Evita was doing Joan of Arc. She said that I had missed it, but the next programme was Madame Du Barry. I wondered if Madame Du Barry's life was as interesting as Joan of Arc's. She said it was certainly less saintly, and, besides, it could be emulated. How? I said innocently. And thereby my beautiful apprenticeship. We made each other very happy. And also very sad. This was not the liberty of love, but rather its libertine variety: we loved in hiding. I was too young to be a real sadist. So it had to end.

Second, I started reading Argentine literature, from the gaucho poems to Sarmiento's *Memories of Provincial Life* to Cané's *Juvenilia* to *Don Segundo Sombra* to . . . to . . . to—and this was as good as discovering that Joan of Arc was also sexy—to Borges. Borges belongs to that summer in Buenos Aires. He belongs to my personal discovery of Latin American literature.

I read Borges's *Ficciones* as I flew north on a flying boat courtesy of Pan American Airways. It was wartime; we had to have priority. All cameras were banned, and glazed plastic screens were put on our windows several minutes before we landed. Since I was not an Axis spy, I read Borges as we splashed into Santos, saying that the best proof that the Koran is an Arab book is that not a single camel is mentioned in its pages. As we glided into an invisible Rio de Janeiro, I started thinking that the best proof that Borges is an Argentinian is in everything he has to evoke because it isn't there. And as we flew out of Bahia, I thought that Borges invents a world because he needs it. I need, therefore I imagine.

By the time we landed in Trinidad, 'Funes the Memorious' and 'Pierre Ménard, Author of Don Quixote' had introduced me, without my being aware, to the genealogy of the serene madmen, the children of Erasmus. I did not know then that this was the most illustrious family of modern fiction, since it went, backwards, from Pierre Ménard to Don Quixote himself. During two short lulls in Santo Domingo (then, horrifyingly, called Ciudad Trujillo) and Port-au-Prince, I had been prepared by Borges to encounter my wonderful friends: Toby Shandy, who reconstructs in his miniature cabbage patch the battlefields of Flanders he was not able to experience historically; Jane Austen's Catherine Moreland and Gustave Flaubert's Madame Bovary, who like Don Quixote believe in what they read; Dickens's Mr Micawber, who takes his hopes to be realities; Dostoevsky's Myshkin, an idiot because he gives the benefit of the doubt to the good possibility of mankind; Pérez Galdós's Nazarín, who is mad because he believes that each human being can daily be Christ, and who is truly St Paul's madman: 'Let him who seems wise among you become mad, so that he might truly become wise.'

As we landed at Miami airport, the glazed windows disappeared once and for all and I knew that, like Pierre Ménard, a writer must always face the mysterious duty of literally reconstructing a spontaneous work. And so I met my tradition: *Don Quixote* was a book waiting to be written. The history of Latin America was a history waiting to be lived.

When I finally arrived in Mexico, I discovered that my father's imaginary country was real, but more fantastic than any imaginary land. It was as real as its physical and spiritual borders. Mexico: the only frontier between the industrialized and the developing worlds, between my country and the United States, between all of Latin America and the United States, and between the Catholic Mediterranean and the Protestant Anglo-Saxon strains of the New World.

I approached the gold and mud of Mexico, the imaginary, imagined country, finally real but only real if I saw it from a distance that would assure me, because of the very fact of separation, that my desire for reunion with it would be forever urgent, and only real if I wrote it.

My first contact with literature and its language had been sitting on the knees of Alfonso Reyes. When the Mexican writer was ambassador to Brazil in the earlier thirties, Reyes had brought the Spanish classics back to life for us; he had written superb books on Greece; he was the most lucid of literary theoreticians; in fact, he had translated all of Western culture into Latin American terms. In the late forties, he was living in a little house the colour of the *mamey* fruit, in Cuernavaca. He would invite me to spend weekends with him, and since I was eighteen and a night prowler, I kept him company from eleven in the morning, when Don Alfonso would sit in a café and toss verbal bouquets at the girls strolling around the plaza that was then a garden of laurels and not, as it has become, of cement. I do not know if the square, ruddy man seated at the next table was a British consul crushed by the nearness of the volcano; but if Reyes, enjoying the spectacle of the world, quoted Lope de Vega and Garcilaso, our neighbour, the *mescal* drinker, would answer, without looking at us, with the more sombre stanzas of Marlowe and John Donne. Then we would go to the movies in order, Reyes said, to bathe in contemporary epic, and it was only at night that he would start scolding me: You have not read Stendhal yet? The world didn't start five minutes ago, you know.

He could irritate me. I read, against his classical tastes, the most modern, the most strident books, without understanding that I was learning his lesson: there is no creation without tradition; the 'new' is an inflection on a preceding form; novelty is always a variation on the past. Borges said that Reyes wrote the best Spanish prose of our times. He taught me that culture had a smile, that the intellectual tradition of the whole world was ours by birthright, and that Mexican literature was important because it was literature, not because it was Mexican.

One day I got up very early (or maybe I came in very late from a binge) and saw him seated at five in the morning, working at his table, amid the aroma of the jacaranda and the bougainvillea. He was a diminutive Buddha, bald and pink, almost one of those elves who cobble shoes at night while the family sleeps. He liked to quote Goethe: Write at dawn, skim the cream of the day, then you can study crystals, intrigue at court and make love to your kitchen maid. Writing in silence, Reyes did not smile. His world, in a way, ended on a funereal day in February 1913 when his insurrectionist father, General Bernardo Reyes, fell riddled by machine-gun bullets in the Zócalo in Mexico City, and with him fell what was left of Mexico's *belle époque,* the long and cruel peace of Porfirio Díaz.

My father had remained in Buenos Aires as Mexican chargé d'affaires, with instructions to frown on Argentina's sympathies toward the Axis. My mother took advantage of his absence to enroll me in a Catholic school in Mexico City. The brothers who ruled this institution were preoccupied with something that had never entered my head: sin. At the start of the school year, one of the brothers would come before the class with a white lily in his hand and say: 'This is a Catholic youth before kissing a

231

girl.' Then he would throw the flower on the floor, dance a little jig on it, pick up the bedraggled object and confirm our worst suspicions: 'This is a Catholic boy after. . .'

Well, all this filled life with temptation. Retrospectively, I would agree with Luis Buñuel that sex without sin is like an egg without salt. The priests at the Colegio Francés made sex irresistible for us; they also made leftists of us by their constant denunciation of Mexican liberalism and especially of Benito Juárez. The sexual and political temptations became very great in a city where provincial mores and sharp social distinctions made it very difficult to have normal sexual relationships with young or even older women.

All this led, as I say, to a posture of rebellion that for me crystallized in the decision to be a writer. My father, by then back from Argentina, sternly said, OK, go out and be a writer, but not at my expense. I was sent, again, to visit Alfonso Reyes in his enormous library-house, where he seemed more diminutive than ever, ensconced in a tiny corner he saved for his bed among the Piranesi-like perspective of volume piled upon volume. He said to me, 'Mexico is a very formalistic country. If you don't have a title, you are nobody: *nadie, ninguno*. A title is like the handle on a cup; without it, no one will pick you up. You must become a *licenciado*, a lawyer; then you can do whatever you please, as I did.'

So I entered the School of Law at the National University, where, as I feared, learning tended to be by rote and where cynical teachers spent the whole hour of class taking attendance on the two hundred students of civil law, from Aguilar to Zapata. But there were exceptions: the true teachers—mainly exiles from defeated Republican Spain who enormously enriched Mexican universities, publishing houses, the arts and the sciences—understood that the law is inseparable from the concerns of culture, morality and justice. Don Manuel Pedroso, former dean of the University of Seville, made the study-of-law compatible with my literary inclinations. When I would bitterly complain about the dryness and boredom of learning the penal or mercantile codes by heart, he would counter: 'Forget the codes. Read Dostoevsky, read Balzac. There's all you have to know about criminal or commercial law.' He also made me see that Stendhal was right: that the best model for a well-structured novel is the Napoleonic Code of Civil Law. Anyway, I found that culture consists of connections, not of separations: to specialize is to isolate.

Mexico City was then a manageable town of one million people, beautiful in its extremes of colonial and nineteenth-century elegance and the garishness of its exuberant and dangerous nightlife. My friends and I spent the last years of our adolescence and the first of our manhood in a succession of cantinas, brothels, strip joints and silver-varnished nightclubs where the *bolero* was sung and the *mambo* danced; whores, *mariachis*, magicians were our companions as we struggled through our first readings of D.H. Lawrence and Aldous Huxley, James Joyce and André Gide, T.S. Eliot and Thomas Mann. Salvador Elizondo and I were the two would-be writers of the group, and if the realistic grain of *La Región Más Transparente (Where the Air is Clear)* was sown in this, our rather somnambulistic immersion in the spectral nightlife of Mexico City, it is also true that the cruel imagination of an instant in Elizondo's *Farabeuf* had the same background. We would go to a whorehouse oddly called *El Buen Tono*, choose a poor Mexican girl who usually said that her name was Gladys and that she came from Guadalajara, and go to our respective rooms. One time, a horrible scream was heard and Gladys from Guadalajara rushed out, crying and streaming blood. Elizondo, in the climax of love, had slashed her armpit with a razor.

In 1950 I went to Europe to do graduate work in international law at the University of Geneva. Octavio Paz had just published two books that had changed the face of Mexican literature, *Libertad Bajo Palabra* and *El Laberinto de la Soledad*. My friends and I had read these books aloud in Mexico, dazzled by a poetics that managed simultaneously to renew our language from within and to connect it to the language of the world.

At thirty-six, Octavio Paz was not very different from what he is today. Writers born in 1914, like Paz and Julio Cortázar, surely signed a Faustian pact at the very mouth of hell's trenches; so many poets died in that war that someone had to take their place. I remember Paz in the so-called existentialist nightclubs of the time in Paris, in discussion with the very animated and handsome Albert Camus, who alternated philosophy and the boogie-woogie in La

Rose Rouge. I remember Paz in front of the large windows of a gallery on the Place Vendôme, reflecting Max Ernst's great postwar painting *Europe after the Rain*, and the painter's profile as an ancient eagle; and I tell myself that the poetics of Paz is an art of civilizations, a movement of encounters. Paz the poet meets Paz the thinker, because his poetry is a form of thought and his thought is a form of poetry; and as a result of this meeting, an encounter of civilizations takes place. Paz introduces civilizations to one another, makes them presentable before it is too late, because behind the wonderful smile of Camus, fixed forever in the absurdity of death, behind the bright erosion of painting by Max Ernst and the crystals of the Place Vendôme, Octavio and I, when we met, could hear the voice of *el poeta Libra,* Ezra, lamenting the death of the best, 'for an old bitch gone in the teeth, for a botched civilization.'

Octavio Paz has offered civilizations the mirror of their mortality, as Paul Valéry did, but also the reflection of their survival in an epidemic of meetings and erotic risks. In the generous friendship of Octavio Paz, I learned that there were no privileged centres of culture, race or politics; that nothing should be left out of literature, because our time is a time of deadly reduction.

For my generation in Mexico, the problem did not consist in discovering our modernity but in discovering our tradition. The latter was brutally denied by the comatose, petrified teaching of the classics in Mexican secondary schools: one had to bring Cervantes back to life in spite of a school system fatally oriented towards the ideal of universities as sausage factories—in spite of the more grotesque forms of Mexican nationalism of the time. A Marxist teacher once told me it was un-Mexican to read Kafka; a fascist critic said the same thing (this has been Kafka's Kafkian destiny everywhere), and a rather sterile Mexican author gave a pompous lecture at the Bellas Artes warning that readers who read Proust would proustitute themselves.

To be a writer in Mexico in the fifites, you had to join Alfonso Reyes and Octavio Paz in the assertion that Mexico was not an isolated, virginal province but very much part of the human race and its cultural tradition; we were all, for good or evil, contemporary with all men and women.

In Geneva, I rented a garret overlooking the beautiful old square of the Bourg-du-Four, established by Julius Caesar as the Forum Boarium two millennia ago. The square was filled with coffee-houses and old bookstores. The girls came from all over the world; they were beautiful, and they were independent. When they were kissed, one did not become a sullied lily. We had salt on our lips. We loved each other, and I also loved going to the little island where the lake meets the river to spend long hours reading. Since it was called Jean-Jacques Rousseau Island, I took along my volume of the *Confessions*. Many things came together then. A novel was the transformation of experience into history. The modern epic had been the epic of the first-person singular, of the I, from St Augustine to Abélard to Dante to Rousseau to Stendhal to Proust. When Odysseus says that he is non-existent, we know and he knows that he is disguised; when Beckett's characters proclaim their non-being, we know that 'the fact is notorious': they are no longer disguised.

I did not yet know this as I spent many reading hours on the little island of Rousseau at the intersection of Lake Geneva and the Rhône River back in 1951. But I vaguely felt that there was something beyond the exploration of the self.

Could I, a Mexican who had not yet written his first book, sitting on a bench on an early spring day as the *bise* from the Jura Mountains quieted down, have the courage to explore for myself, with my language, with my tradition, with my friends and influences, that region to which the literary figure bids us? Cervantes did it: he brought into existence the modern world by having Don Quixote leave his secure village (a village whose name has been, let us remember, forgotten) and take to the open roads, the roads of the unsheltered, the unknown and the different, there to lose what he read and to gain what we, the readers, read in him.

The novel is forever travelling Don Quixote's road, from the security of the analogous to the adventure of the different and even the unknown. In my way, this is the road I wanted to travel. I read Rousseau, or the adventures of the I; Joyce and Faulkner, or the adventures of the We; Cervantes, or the adventures of the You he calls the Idle, the Amiable Reader: you. And I read, in a shower of fire and in the lightning of enthusiasm, Rimbaud. His mother asked him what a particular poem was about. And he answered: 'I have wanted to say what it says there, literally and in all other senses.' This statement of Rimbaud's has been an inflexible rule for me and for what we are all writing today; and the present-day vigour of the literature of the Hispanic world, to which I belong, is not alien to this Rimbaudian approach to writing: say what you mean, literally and in all other senses.

I think I imagined in Switzerland what I would try to write some day, but first I would have to do my apprenticeship. Only after many years would I be able to write what I then imagined; only years later, when I not only knew that I had the tools with which to do it, but also, and equally important, when I knew that if I did not write, death would not do it for me. You start by writing to live. You end by writing so as not to die.

In the summer of 1950, on a hot, calm evening on Lake Zurich, some wealthy Mexican friends had invited me to dinner at the elegant Baur-au-Lac Hotel. The restaurant was a floating terrace on the lake. You reached it by a gangplank, and it was lighted by paper lanterns and flickering candles. As I unfolded my white napkin amid the soothing tinkle of silver and glass, I raised my eyes and saw the group dining at the next table.

Three ladies sat there with a man in his seventies. This man was stiff and elegantly dressed in double-breasted white serge and immaculate shirt and tie. His long, delicate fingers sliced a cold pheasant, almost with daintiness. Yet even in eating he seemed to me unbending, with a ramrod-back, military bearing. His aged face showed 'a growing fatigue', but the pride with which his lips and jaws were set sought desperately to hide the fact, while the eyes twinkled with 'the fiery play of fancy'.

As the carnival lights of that summer's night in Zurich played with a fire of their own on the features I now recognized, Thomas Mann's face was a theatre of implicit, quiet emotions. He ate and let the ladies do the talking; he was, in my fascinated eyes, a meeting place where solitude gives birth to beauty unfamiliar and perilous, but also to the perverse and the illicit. Thomas Mann had managed, out of this solitude, to find the affinity 'between the personal destiny of [the] author and that of his contemporaries in general.' Through him, I had imagined that the products of this solitude and of this affinity were named art (created by one) and civilization (created by all). He spoke so surely, in *Death in Venice,* of the 'tasks imposed upon him by his own ego and the European soul' that as I, paralyzed with admiration, saw him there that night I dared not conceive of such an affinity in our own Latin American culture, where the extreme demands of a ravaged, voiceless continent often killed the voice of the self and made a hollow political monster of the voice of the society, or killed it, giving birth to a pitiful, sentimental dwarf.

Yet, as I recalled my passionate reading of everything he wrote, from *Blood of the Walsungs* to *Dr Faustus,* I could not help but feel that, in spite of the vast differences between his culture and ours, literature in the end asserted itself through a relationship between the visible and the invisible worlds of narration. A novel should 'gather up the threads of many human destinies in the warp of a single idea'; the I, the You and the We were only separate and dried up because of a lack of imagination. Unbeknownst to him, I left Thomas Mann sipping his demitasse as midnight approached and the floating restaurant bobbed slightly and the Chinese lanterns quietly flickered out. I shall always thank him for silently teaching me that, in literature, you know only what you imagine.

I went back to Mexico, but knew that I would forever be a wanderer in search of perspective: this was my real baptism, not the religious or civil ceremonies I have mentioned. But no matter where I went, Spanish would be the language of my writing and Latin America the culture of my language.

Neruda, Reyes, Paz; Washington, Santiago de Chile, Buenos Aires, Mexico City, Paris, Geneva; Cervantes, Balzac, Rimbaud, Thomas Mann: only with all the shared languages, those of my places and friends and masters, was I able to approach the fire of literature and ask it for a few sparks.

At the very end we came upon him—others had seen him from time to time, and reported that he was still out there —and he was bigger even than we had expected. We knew him to be great, but we found him to be gargantuan. The eyes were tiny hidden holes pressed apart in that massive fleshy head. A wide wrinkled brow lifted to our gaze, from which the glistening spray fled in sheets. The white stage-skin (of fifty suits he had outgrown all but two) encrusted with jewels like barnacles, trailing seaweedy tassels and fronds, humped and bellied out with blubber. The audience rose and fell back in coruscating waves all around, we descried him wallowing and blowing in front of us in the dazzling light, and we had never seen anything so immense and monstrous. We had not journeyed all this way to see a mere person, certainly, but it was a shock, nevertheless, to know that finally we were in the presence of a great white whale, that it was indeed Moby Dick.

Everyone had their ideas of what he meant—to them and to us all. For some he had been the Devil: his rhythms, his hell-raising rebellion, but mostly the sex, simple Sex! in those gyrating hips— not only un- but anti-Christian. For others he was a god who took away their doubts, who watched over them above the bedhead, who required (so they felt) the supplications of hysteria or of quiet private devotion: a fair, innocuous god, then, who left his followers to make the demands. Moby Dick was something for everyone, all things to everyone, democratically capacious. He let us choose, as everything about him, when we considered where he had started out, said 'I chose'. He was as big as all of us put together, swallowing us all: America. Immortal, in any light; something that was always going to be there. Everyone we met on the chase agreed about that.

But above all, a whale. He had lived down in darkness, his windows covered with tin-foil, rarely came up into daylight. The air-conditioning, turned to full, purled ceaselessly: it was always cold down there. Not a land animal at all—he weltered in bed all day and oozed along on an electric cart. More than 5,000 pills in the last seven months alone—uppers, downers, sleeping-pills, waking-up pills, slimming pills, pain-killing pills, every new brand: he sucked them in like plankton. Even that was not enough, for in the final stages Moby Dick let them go after him with the harpoon. He was thrashing and plunging when he needed to be calm—the syringe in the hide brought him down; he was slumbering away from it all when he was supposed to be up—another dart roused and revved him.

The more we thought about it, the more whale-like this Whale was. When he did surface from the deeps, he spouted—a fountain-shower, spraying everyone, friends, employees, chance acquaintances—deluged them all with Cadillacs, Lincolns, jewellery, airplanes, houses even. The foaming geyser never ran dry, and as many as could clustered underneath it—well, but he *invited* them to! and how could you say no? He didn't just spend money like water, he lived in an ocean of it, bottomless and horizonless: anything he wanted, it gave; however much you drained it, the waters closed inexorably over the gulf. He was a whale because he knew that whereas a person can live anyhow, Moby Dick could live only in an ocean. When by the end he had, inconceivably, precious near emptied it (three airliners in one night) and although an ocean was always flowing in more than an ocean was pouring out, he could only think of replenishing it.

This was when we started to have *the unearthly conceit that Moby Dick was ubiquitous.* He was sighted everywhere, during those last few years, all over America, every night or even twice nightly, twelve places in as many days, then a week off, then twelve more. The more he had to be seen, the more people must have thought he was appearing for them, when in fact he was only being more of a whale than ever, and looking to his ocean.

How, most simply, could we tell at once it was him, and not just any whale? Ask anyone: in the final years he would even jerk his lip up with a wryly self-mocking finger. Moby Dick was *the great white whale with the crooked jaw.*

Now the study of a Whale is as big as a whale itself. There is a lot of fat in a whale; so is there in our bulky versions of him. Our vast Cetology became our industry—became bigger than the Whale! We knew him in every extremity; we knew him *inside.* The Teeth of the Whale, then, if you please: we recorded that on the very last day but one his dentist filled an upper right first bicuspid and an upper left molar—porcelain fillings. The Stomach of the Whale: we noted the swollen and twisted colon, the liver three times normal size . . . Venturing further in, we discovered the enlarged heart, the blood clots in the legs, the hypoglycaemia, the furred arteries, the lupus erythematosis. On top of all this—below, we should say—a painful ingrowing toe-nail. And what went into that stomach? Cheeseburgers. Peanut butter and jelly sandwiches. Ice cream. If there were none nearby he would charter a plane. In what quantities? One needs to know. Ten at a time; six trays-full; by the quart.

For this is the study of a leviathan: start out on it and soon you will not be sure if, rather, it started you. You must be *omnisciently exhaustive in the enterprise; not overlooking the minutest seminal germs of his blood, and spinning him out to the uttermost coil of his bowels. Having already described him in most of his present habitatory and anatomical peculiarities, it now remains to magnify him in an archaeological, fossiliferous and antediluvian point of view.*

So to account for the Whale we looked back, the further the better. It was his wife leaving him, we saw: all stemmed from that. Back: it was his mother, in fact—responsible for everything, the making and the unmaking. Back: it was his only brother whom he never knew, above all—that was where it started, whatever it was. By now we were stranded in petrified pre-history! Whales go back a long way.

The fossilized traces of the Whale: we found every example— every carol for Christmas, every mumble in the studio: the imprint was unmistakable. Catalogued and collected them all in albums, repackaged them so we could collect them again. It augmented, inflated our knowledge because it was more, more. This is the science of studying whales.

But ours was a singular Whale. What was it about *him*? What made Moby Dick so ineffably appalling?

It was the whiteness, the whiteness of the Whale that was the horror. This was not the whiteness of love and perfection people had seen in him at other times. Now it was another whiteness: the pallor of a face after days in darkened rooms; the whiteness of a drugged sleep; the starched whitebread whiteness of a cheeseburger bun. This was what it was: a mind that had lately taken to slurring 'My Way'; that whited out on lyrics in the middle of a song; that said

Yes, gave No, and couldn't tell the difference. A featureless whiteness, a passive whiteness, *an unbounded prairie of driven snow*—but snow that was warm, slushy, melting as you regarded it. This was the whiteness of the Whale.

And yet we bequeath our Cetological System to posterity *unfinished, even as the great Cathedral of Cologne was left, with the crane still standing upon the top of the uncompleted tower.* Indeed, barely started, now we look at it again, for the lone cope-stone we lack is as big as the Whale himself: of all things, WE DON'T KNOW WHY HE DIED. The doctors said so; the PR men diagnosed 'respiratory failure'—he had, as we all do when we die, stopped breathing. Everyone was certain that no one had any idea.

But later we wondered if, in the final tumult, he had simply escaped us. Thousands continued their pilgrimages; there were séances; the records came out faster than ever. Something had ended, anyway—that was all, lamely, we could say. Whatever we had been chasing had gone.

There had been one moment, just before the end, when we had havered: when one of those on the chase had up and spoken.

See! quoth he, *Moby Dick seeks thee not. It is thou, thou, that madly seekest him!*

Madness indeed, after all this way, to be hunting only ourselves! To feel we had made the Whale by treating him as such!

But now, at last, we were in sight of him. And when the Whale cast his eyes up in placid reproach to murmur, Don't be cruel . . . the sentiment was intolerable to us. The chase had to go on.

If there was any madness at the end, though, surely it was in Moby Dick—let us use the proper word, however. There was certainly something inhuman about him, unearthly if you like. We are talking about a Whale, not a person. We know because we were there, we saw him at the last—he was even singing about whales, the one about *a tidal wave*, and going *Way dow-ow-own, dow-ow-own, Way, way on down* . . .

Photo: Rex Features

NOTES FROM ABROAD

Madrid
Tony Lyons

I got home at half past four for lunch. Tuesday is a short day. The women were out, the house was empty. Silence is never just a lack of noise. In the kitchen I lit the gas under the pot on the stove and turned on some classical music.

There was a note on the table: Phone Rafa, 983754.

There were different Rafas known to me in Madrid, and at the moment I was in touch with none of them. I was perplexed. I changed my clothes in the bedroom but the person of Rafa refused to come back to me.

I had lunch and rested for half an hour in the armchair by the window. There would be time tomorrow to phone Rafa.

There were other things to do: Rosi died two weeks ago, and Manolo had come back from America for a few days to see her buried. They were brother and sister. A requiem mass would be said for her tonight at seven o'clock. So I had to be out by six to cross Madrid.

It was the worst time for traffic, and I got lost in the brick ravines of flats and shops and bars. Then I couldn't find a space to park the car. Nor could I find the church. The mass was half over when I arrived.

It was the same church where the requiem for Manolo's mother had been held fifteen years before. It had been the same sort of evening. The sun had set early. The streets were wet from recent rain. But the people and the atmosphere were different. Fifteen years before there had been Franco, the fear of the ruthless grey police, the open repression of workers and intellectuals. In this church of Saint Joseph the Worker, the worker priest had let the Workers' Commissions hold their meetings till the night the grey police had broken down the street door. The leaders were beaten up, thrown out and then carried off. Then they were beaten up again in the police station.

This time everything was lit up. In the streets, there was a bar for every dozen inhabitants, the shops were full and resplendent, young people dominated the pavements.

The priest was different too, relaxed, though the church itself was the same—poor and cheap, with the same open windows through which, fifteen years ago, workers had scrambled and escaped.

After the requiem there were relatives and friends to kiss and console and of course Rosi's husband, Paco, and the two children.

'Wait for me,' Paco said, 'do not go, we can have a drink together.'

We saw the children home and then we went for a drink, and he let me have everything that was in his head, gave me verbatim the history of his thought and action since the day he was born.

There was nothing I could say because I was of no interest to him. His obsession was his own dilemma, as it had always been, even when his wife was alive. It was he, Paco, who would carry on doing all the shopping and the cooking, and who would look after the two children, work his eight hours as an electrician, and read Freud and Jung, contemplate the mystery of the cross imprinted on the upper palate of his mouth—to show how cold and collected and objective he was, and God knows what else, and on and on through unknown paths of a psyche that Jung himself would have delighted in studying. Then we went on to another bar for another drink. He drank only a drop of beer drowned in lemonade and gave me a little book which he said he always carried, *The Imitation of Christ* by Saint Thomas à Kempis, and he borrowed a pen from the barman to write a dedication. Off we went again along the brick and cement gulch with its torrent of people and traffic and lights. I thought that this time we would reach my car, but he said, 'Wait a minute,' and rushed once more into a bar. He came out five minutes later with a bottle of wine which he gave me so that I could drink and remember him and his two children and his dead wife. He said, 'But do not pray for me. Pray for them but do not pray for me.'

We arrived at my car.

'I am sorry, Paco, but I have to go now. I have to get over to the other side of Madrid.'

We embraced.

It was then that he burst into tears.

*I*n the car afterwards I was in a turmoil. The book and the bottle lay on the seat next to me. The streets were chaotic and unknown. At last I reached a part of the city that was more familiar. It was possible to relax.

My thoughts stayed with tragedy, the tragedy of the living. Manolo had flown over from America the day after his sister's death, and I had picked him up at the airport, just as I had when his mother died fifteen years before. We stayed together all day and wherever we went I lived again the death of the mother, as well as the deaths one by one of those who had lived a moment of great hope under the new Republic in the thirties; they had fought and suffered the brunt of the Civil War, and then had been crushed by Franco back into the black paintings of Goya, deceived into the tinfoil and shiny chrome of the Coca-Cola culture.

Manolo and I spent the day together and I missed my classes but I could not miss them the following day because there were exams and two dozen people waiting for me. So I missed his sister's funeral which followed the same path the mother had taken through the cypresses and among the muddy spaces between the graves under the damp sky.

The day after the funeral, Manolo and I had bought some food, and driven off to a cabin I have in the mountains. The cabin was anchored high in the rock and surrounded by ancient rock walls. It offered us a short rest, a two-day escape from death's bureaucratic decrees.

'What are you going to do, Manolo? Do you want to do some writing?' I asked him.

He said nothing.

The morning was warm and sunny and there was work to be done, water to be brought up to the tank, rocks to be carried in to repair one of the terraces, a seed-bed to be prepared.

Eventually he came out of the cabin where, in fact, he had been writing for some hours, tense, concentrated, not moving even when I entered from time to time. He came out into the sun and stood there with his hands thrust down into his pockets and his head hanging down.

I could hear his sobs from down below, where I was hoeing weeds.

He was standing on one of the terraces of stony earth that stepped down the side of the mountain. There were still a few tomatoes and peppers that had survived the months of blasting heat and drought. Further down, the mountain levelled out into the flat valley that ran among the austere ilex trees for two or three kilometres down to the road from Madrid. In the distance was the lake that collected the water from the streams created by the rain and snow, and on the horizon were tiny rectangular dots, blocks of flats on the outskirts of Madrid itself. He stood there without moving. The world was at his feet. He sobbed and sobbed.

I said, 'Hey, Manolo. Come on, boy, that is enough now. Why don't we go off for a walk down in the valley before lunch?'

His head came up a little, and, as though in response to the pressing of a button, his feet moved slowly and he came down the stone steps.

We went out through an old heavy door in the wall and down the side of the mountain. Then we moved on into the valley across the dry bed of the stream and in and out of the shadows of the ilex trees that remind me always of Antonio Machado, those trees that passively resist the first freezing months of the year and then the long heat and drought of summer like the austere Castilian people themselves; perhaps even like me. 'My heart is waiting,' Machado wrote, 'for the Spaniard with rough hands who will know how to carve from the ilex of Castile the austere God of that brown earth.'

Manolo had already carved his own austere God from the few books that were left in the few remaining libraries in Madrid after Franco swept away the Spanish Republic. His home was on the third floor of a block of poor flats built around a small patio. There was a small room for him and his family to live and dine in, an alcove on the left and another on the right. There were no windows except for one in the door of the living room that opened on to a balcony. There was no bathroom. The toilet at the end of the balcony served all the families on that floor. When he came home from delivering the groceries in a rich part of the town he sat under a lamp in the street to read and study. He was in contact with the ageing Republican Quixotes who were being released one by one from the Franco gaols and his austere God was Marx. He was in Chile with Allende, then back in Spain to fight Franco, never knowing when he would be confronted by a grey uniform with a drawn pistol. Multinational pharmaceutical firms provided him with the pills to help him sleep, the pills to wake him up, the pills to help him digest the pills to help him shit, and the pills to stop him shitting. Life was serious, grey, deadly.

He said to me once, 'Statistics give us a maximum of three years before Franco gets us and I am already in my fourth.'

Communists were caught and tortured. Some fell or jumped or were pushed through the window on the fourth floor of the police headquarters. They were all prepared for the final *coup de grâce*.

Thus his own mother had died. It was the most cruel of blows. He could not accept it. Years later he was to flee in terror from his father's last agony. Now it was his beloved sister and again he was swamped in death. It is something he cannot accept because of its implication of total and definite defeat. Now Manolo has no family left, no roots, no connection with the past, and he himself is the next on the list to fall into the hole that has no bottom. So he is driven like a madman to prove his own existence, to justify his own life before he too steps into space, into nothing.

This is what he wrote at the table in my stone cabin about his sister: 'Tomorrow when you are reunited in the tomb with our mother and father you will be able to pick up again that dialogue so full of humour and confidences that you maintained in life.'

A neighbour told Manolo that two days before her death Rosi had dreamt that she was with her mother and father and brother. The four of them were singing and laughing.

At about the same time Manolo had dreamt of his father who had asked him why he did not write about what was REALLY happening.

Here are the next sentences that Manolo wrote in my cabin: 'Is it that they were waiting for you to join them? Is it that they knew of the imminence of your going and that Father wanted to let me know? Could you perhaps be reunited with Mother and Father, you who so dearly belonged to them? I wish with all my heart that right now you are all together again, happy in the long awaited meeting.'

Not long before he died, the last mayor of Madrid, a professed Marxist, said, 'God never abandons a good Marxist.'

The rain began to patter against my windscreen. Ahead of me there was a straight run up to San Anselmo's and the traffic was sparse. I parked the car in front of a block of flats, and Pedro came out to see me.

'Have you heard the news?' he said.

I knew something had happened.

'Natcho is dead.' Last Friday night Marijose was driving him down to Seville where he was going to give some lectures to the Workers' Commissions. A forty-ton lorry went right over them. They could scarcely get their bodies out of the car.

'Oh, my dear God!'

'We thought of phoning you on Saturday morning so that you could come to the funeral but we knew you would be in the mountains.'

Pedro led me into the group meeting. We received the Eucharist, remembering Natcho in our prayers. There was no more talk of him. The talk was done with. I was the last person to find out. I felt the unshed tears within me.

It was after one in the morning when I got home. I took off my shoes and emptied my pockets on to the kitchen table. The note was still there. Phone Rafa, 983754. Of course. Now I knew who Rafa was. He and Natcho had fought and prayed together for many years. They had lived side by side in hovels in different parts of Madrid, working in the Communist Workers' Commissions and Catholic groups, saying mass where it had never been said before.

It must be this Rafa. Yet it was some years since we had met. Where had he got my phone number from? My name was not in the book. Natcho had always been easy to get into contact with but not Rafa. Someone had told me that he was no longer a Jesuit, that he had left the order and got married.

The following day my classes started early. It was not till I finished the last class at five in the evening that there was time to pick up the phone. I did not know the woman who answered. She seemed to know me.

'Hang on a second. I think it is Rafa opening the front door right now.'

Then Rafa spoke, 'Hello? Hello, how are you?'

I was not sure of the voice. I said, 'Hello, Rafa? Which Rafa are you?'

He did not understand that I was in doubt about his identity. It was as if the secrecy of the Franco days were still upon us. There was a moment of confusion because I did not want to mention any surname. Then he said something about Natcho.

'Have you heard the news?'

'About Natcho?'

'Look, we must get together and do some talking. When have you got a free night?'

'A free night is something that never comes my way, Rafa, so if it is possible for you let's make it tonight.'

He agreed and said he would pick me up as I came out of the metro at eight.

I was outside the metro in a distant Madrid suburb at two minutes to eight. I stood there at the top of the steps, my hands thrust down into my raincoat pockets, and it would have been easy for me to sob as Manolo had done only two weeks before. The few people around were packing up for the night and those that came up out of the metro made off straight towards the high-rise blocks of flats. The night was humid and the trees reflected light on their wet leaves. The young women going home from their work in the city centre seemed out of place in their decorative tight trousers. They should have been wearing white blouses and long grey skirts, but then Franco was no longer around.

Then I saw him. We embraced with Castilian austerity, and then I, being much older, kissed him on both cheeks.

We walked a few steps into the light of a streetlamp and I took him by the arm.

'Let me see your face, Rafa.'

It was fuller and fatter and the wrinkles were much less pronounced than before. His eyes were cleansed of that tired red that they used to have—blood-shot from never getting enough sleep. There was no cigarette between his lips, and his clothes were new and expensive.

'It has been a long time, Rafa.'

'That is true, Tony.'

'They tell me that you left the priesthood and got married.'

'Yes, that is true, too. I reached the point where I just couldn't do any more, no matter how hard I tried. Then I met Ines. And that was that.'

Rafa took me to his flat, and Ines opened the door. She was just like Rafa, identical: two aristocrats, priest and nun, who had spent years and years fighting for justice.

We sat at the table and talked. We talked about Natcho, trying to get used to the idea that he was dead.

'Did you know,' Rafa said, 'that it was Natcho who organized the first workers' strike under Franco?'

I remembered; he told me.

When it was all over the Chief of Police, the Governor General of the Province and the Mayor of the town accompanied him personally to the railway station and saw him aboard the first train back to Madrid. They did not know what else to do with him because his brother was Franco's right-hand man. Those were important days: it seemed like the first time in Europe that the Christians and the communists were able to work together.

Then we got talking about Nicaragua because Natcho had been there as well.

Rosi will be with her God.

Natcho with his.

It was already late when I started on the long metro journey back to the other end of Madrid, with so many memories flickering through my mind that it was like watching a silent film. Manolo and Natcho and Rafa and Ines: we had been through a lot.

Back home there was the warm, peaceful silence of sleeping women's bodies, the mother and her daughters. I emptied my pockets on to the table in the kitchen and on top of some papers and letters next to my chair there was still the note saying, 'Phone Rafa 983754.'

Notes on Contributors

Doris Lessing's new book, *Prisons We Choose to Live Inside*, is a series of five lectures that she gave for the Canadian Broadcasting Corporation. *The Wind Blows away our Words*, her book on Afghanistan, was published at the beginning of this year. The first two parts of her autobiography appeared in *Granta* 14 and 17. **Hanif Kureishi** wrote the script for *My Beautiful Laundrette*. His new film, *Sammy and Rosie Get Laid*, opens in London on 15 January. The script and film diary will be published by Faber & Faber on 25 January 1988 at £3.95. His pieces on Pakistan and Bradford appeared in *Granta* 17 and 20. **Wycliffe Kato** is Uganda's Director of Civil Aviation. He lived in exile in Kenya until Amin was overthrown in 1979. He is currently attending a re-education camp in the Ugandan bush. 'An Escape from Kampala' is his first published work. **James Fenton** is the *Independent*'s correspondent in Manila. 'The Fall of Saigon' and 'The Snap Revolution', James Fenton's account of the fall of Marcos, were published in *Granta* 15 and 18. His writings on Asia will be included in *All the Wrong Places*, to be published by Viking Penguin next autumn. Details about purchasing advance copies of his forthcoming book will appear in the next issue of *Granta*. **Leslie Cockburn** is a producer with CBS television news. She spent three years investigating covert US government operations in Central America; 'America's Secret War' will be included in her book *Out of Control*, to be published by Bloomsbury in January. **Adam Mars-Jones**'s 'Remission' will be included in a new edition of *The Darker Proof*, a collection of stories on AIDS. The edition will be published by Faber & Faber in January. **Nadine Gordimer**'s latest novel is *A Sport of Nature*. **Maurizio Chierici** is a special correspondent for the Milan newspaper *Corriere della Sera*. He is currently on assignment in China. **Carlos Fuentes** is the author of many novels including *Terra Nostra* and *The Old Gringo*. He now teaches at Harvard University. **Graham Coster** was, until June 1987, the Assistant Editor of *Granta*. He now teaches at the Universities of Cambridge and London. 'How Great Thou Art' is his first published work. **Tony Lyons** has lived since 1955 in Spain, where he now teaches English. 'Madrid' is his first published work.

Details of ordering back issues of *Granta* are published on page 256.

B⌐CK ISSUE⊃

Please send me the following back issues of Granta. (Only £3.50 each when 4 or more copies ordered.)

Name_____

Address_____

_____

_____

☐ I enclose payment of _____ by cheque (pay Granta)
☐ Visa/Mastercard/American Express

Card number_____

Put this completed form in an envelope (do not affix a stamp if you live in the UK) and send it to Granta, FREEPOST, Cambridge CB1 1BR.